Canadian
Mosaic

Canadian Mosaic

6 Plays

edited by

Aviva Ravel

Simon & Pierre
Toronto, Ontario

Editor: Jean Paton
Designer: Andy Tong
Printed and bound in Canada by Best Book Manufacturers

The publication of this book was made possible by support from several sources. We would like to acknowledge the generous assistance and ongoing support of **The Canada Council, The Book Publishing Industry Development Program** of the **Department of Canadian Heritage,** and the **Ontario Arts Council.**

Kirk Howard, President

1 2 3 4 5 • 0 9 8 7 6

Canadian Cataloguing in Publication Data
Main entry under title:
    Canadian mosaic

    Plays
    ISBN 0-88924-264-X

    1. Canadian drama (English) - 20th century. *
    2. Canadian drama (English) - Minority authors. *
    3. College and school drama, Canadian (English).*
    I. Ravel, Aviva.

    PS8315.C35 1995   C812'.5408   C95-930801-6
    PR9196.6.C3 1995

Order from Simon & Pierre Publishing Co. Ltd., care of

Dundurn Press Limited	**Dundurn Distribution**	**Dundurn Press Limited**
2181 Queen Street East	73 Lime Walk	1823 Maryland Avenue
Suite 301	Headington, Oxford	P.O. Box 1000
Toronto, Canada	England	Niagara Falls, N.Y.
M4E 1E5	0X3 7AD	U.S.A. 14302-1000

In one of my Canadian Drama classes at McGill, students observed that there were few current play anthologies that reflect minority communities, the mosaic of many and diverse cultures making up this country. In an attempt to address this lack, this volume presents six Canadian playwrights whose writing is predominantly shaped by the culture of their particular heritage. The playwrights, who understand intimately the specific social and individual concerns of their member communities, interpret, illumine and clarify these issues for us through the medium of theatre.

The dramas intend to inspire a response to ideas, problems and concepts arising out of cultural communities with which the reader or actor may not be familiar. The issue of identity permeates all of the plays: should immigrants or members of minority groups abandon the culture of their origins in order to integrate into mainstream Canada, or is it possible to preserve their culture and be no less Canadian?

Shirley in *Path With No Moccasins* is sustained by her culture during periods of profound duress. Tillie *(Dance Like a Butterfly)* finds fulfillment in her role as worker and homemaker within a supportive community. While Shirley is at the beginning of her life and Tillie is in her final years, their individual strengths are derived from a strong sense of identity with their respective cultures.

Although Aiko *(The Tale of a Mask)* and Jeena *(No Man's Land)* know precisely who they are, they are unable to survive in the larger community from which they are alienated, a society within which they suffer discrimination or exploitation. Lettie in *Going Down the River* occupies a responsible position; aware that her ancestors suffered intolerance and prejudice, she transcends societal and social barriers, managing to retain her integrity and simultaneously fighting for justice. The children of immigrants in *Just a Kommedia* come to terms with belonging to two worlds and learn to appreciate the value of their own rich cultural community.

The plays run the gamut from tragedy to light-hearted comedy; from monologues to pieces that require large casts. The conflicts presented are varied and multi-faceted: between self and family, self and the social and economic structure, self and immediate community; self and society at large. The plays explore diverse universal issues: child abuse, racial prejudice, aging, family relations, and generational differences.

Foreign terms and expressions enrich the plays and reflect the personalities and origins of the characters; they are listed in a glossary following each play, along with pronunciation guides to assist actors, directors and teachers.

Theatre is an excellent medium to portray the lives of members of our various and varied communities. The plays in this volume have all been produced and proven to be stageworthy. While a number of the plays were originally written and performed with specific communities in mind, they have subsequently all appealed to wider audiences.

This volume, which contains six plays, does not begin to reflect all the cultures that comprise the Canadian mosaic, and I expect that further volumes will broaden the scope of this one. I hope this volume will reach high school and university students as part of their literature and drama courses, and readers who will find the plays informative and entertaining. Most of all, I hope the plays will be performed for wide audiences so we may all gain a better understanding of each other.

I would like to thank my husband, Nahum, for his continued support and encouragement, Jean Paton for her patience and editorial assistance, and Simon & Pierre Publishing Company for believing in this project. Finally, I would like to thank Shirley Cheechoo, Kevin Longfield, Nika Rylski, Rahul Varma and Terry Watada, who provided glossaries and study questions, and contributed their fine plays to this volume.

CONTENTS

Path With No Moccasins

by SHIRLEY CHEECHOO

Actress, musician, playwright, composer, scriptwriter, singer, director, author of children's stories, artist, model: Shirley Cheechoo is a multi-talented artist.

A member of the Cree tribe, her childhood memories are of growing up within a warm extended family along the northern trap lines. She now lives on Manitoulin Island, where she founded and was writer in residence of the De-ba-jeh-mu-jig Theatre Group.

Shirley Cheechoo's acting credits are many, most recently Sophie in *Magnificent Voyage of Emily Carr*, Linda *in Tangled Sheets,* and Annie Cook and Marie-Adele in different productions of *The Rez Sisters.* She was host and writer for *Full Circle: Native Way* for TVOntario, acted the part of Judy in CBC's *Where the Heart Is,* and has had several dramatic parts on CBC Radio.

After a remarkable start as singer at the Northern Lights Festival in Sudbury, Ontario, she performed in several music festivals in Canada and the US, and has opened concerts for Blue Rodeo and Buffy Sainte Marie.

Shirley Cheechoo is also a talented artist; one of her paintings was selected for a 1992 UNICEF Christmas Card.

As well as *Path With No Moccasins,* Shirley Cheechoo is the author of the plays *Tangled Sheets, Shadow People, Nothing Personal* (co-writer) and *Nanabush of the 80's* (co-writer).

ORIGINAL PRODUCTION

Path With No Moccasins premiered at Lakeview Public School, West Bay First Nation, Manitoulin Island, October 25, 1991, produced by PAS Cultural Exchange Arts in association with The Association for Native Development in the Performing and Visual Arts. Shirley Cheechoo was the writer, producer and featured performer, and also composed words and music for the songs. The play was later performed for CBC Morningside Drama.

ORIGINAL CAST AND PRODUCTION TEAM

Producer	Shirley Cheechoo
Shirley	Shirley Cheechoo
Director	Richard Greenblatt
Set Design	Jim Plaxton
Costume Design	Blake Debassige
Lighting	Patsy Lang
Sound Effects	Evan Turner
Stage Manager	Jeffery Trudeau
Dramaturges	Allan MacInnis, Richard Greenblatt
Publicity	Pat Seymour
Production Manager	Aidan Cosgrove
Carpenters	Will Sutton, Jeremy Hill
Props	Stephanie Tjelios
Scenic Arts	Ed Fielding
Moccasins	Lillian Cheechoo
Starblanket	Elva Lloyd
Fundraiser	Jane Woodbury
Seamstress	Deborah Pitawanakwat

REVIEWS

"Introspective, haunting and appalling in its blunt blast of reality to anybody who claims to know what life was like in Indian residential schools." (Regina *Leader-Post*)

"The imagery is exceptionally vivid and the work is sensitively and intelligently crafted." *(Globe and Mail)*

"*Path With No Moccasins* confronts painful memories in a gentle style full of good humour and sharp observation and rich in remembered detail." *(NOW)*

"[It] blends big, dramatic moments and wonderful wry humour with touching moments of pathos and insight." *(Vancouver Sun)*

NOTE ON THE PLAY

The play you are about to read is a reflection of the struggle that many native people face today. In reading it, we begin the process of healing for ourselves, for the people we love and to the community of lives that carry native traditions and languages to the coming generation of little ones.

Many of our people never recover from this struggle for identity and confidence. It's the tragedy of our times, that our brothers and sisters become trapped in a life of abuse and can find no solutions to rid themselves of this maze of institutionalization and hopelessness.

We only pray that the message of hope this play offers reaches those who need it most. To struggle is to succeed. The time has come to rise up together in peace.

For indigenous people to express themselves in words on paper is testament to our growth as a people. The ability to bare one's life in written word is how far we will go to help each other. In that spirit of sharing, I offer my thanks to the writer for her humble effort that all may see.

Gary Farmer, Los Happios, 1993

PERFORMANCE PERMISSION

For permission to perform *Path With No Moccasins*, please contact **THE TALENT GROUP,** 387 Bloor Street East, 3rd Floor, Toronto, Ontario M4W 1H7, (416) 961-3304.

DEDICATION

This play is dedicated to the memory of my father
George Wm. Cheechoo who died on November 11, 1980.

I would like to thank my son Nano, my husband Blake, my mother Lillian Cheechoo, my brothers Ben, Roger and Billy, my sisters Linda, Una and Greta, Jackie Burnell, Richard Greenblatt, Allan MacInnis, JoAnn McIntyre, Marion Seabrook for their support as I transformed my life into a 90 minute play, not knowing that it would be seen by so many people.

The play opens with a nine year old **Shirley** *locked in a room at the residential school. She walks back and forth, fiddle music playing in the background. There is only a small window and a potty in the room. She lies down, pulling at her lower lip. The moon can be seen through the window.*

TO US: If my brother Ben was here, he wouldn't let them lock me up like this. But he's in another residential school. I don't even know where.

Pause

TO MOON: The moon, the moon, I wish you'd come into this room. I want to know how Eleanor is doing. Is she dead? Everyone says she won't make it.

TO US: They all said it was my fault. But it wasn't my idea to run away.

The sound of a far off train whistle.

TO US: That train. Always taking me away, making me let go of my father's hand, to show him that I have to be brave, to go learn to be a white man.

When the moon comes into my room, it's a ball of smoke surrounding me. It's me inside that ball of smoke. It protects me. Inside it is cold, but I don't care. I can find my feather blanket that my grandmother gave me. It comes with the moon. I'm glad I can find it: my Kookum Sarah would ask me where it was. She always did.

TO MOON: They put you on a calendar and say when you're gonna be full. But they're not always right. You are not full. There's a lot of space in there.

TO US: My Kookum Sarah was always picking up sticks, hardly ever smiles. You know what I think? I think because she married the wrong man. Back in those days you didn't get to pick who you were gonna marry. That's what my mom told me. It's not like Elvis Presley and Ann-Margret in the movies. Yup! I think that's why my Kookum hardly ever smiles. Ever awful, eh?

RELIVING: And there she is, picking up sticks and putting them on her back. She's smaller than me. I'll run in front of her and beat her at her game. I'll get the sticks and run and put them on her back. This is a stupid game, but it's like these sticks keep her alive. And when we get home I'll look back at the clear path we made. Jei pit hen pay yuk. She said, "You missed one."

TO MOON: The moon, the moon, come into this room. Hold me. I only wanted a small cut on the finger like I saw in the movie last Saturday.

TO US: It was her idea to cut on the wrists. She said the more blood we shared the stronger we'd be.

TO MOON: The moon, the moon, come into this room, and take me to Eleanor so I can see if she's alive.

TO US: I wish summer was here, travelling across Moose River on a boat, water splashing my face.

RELIVING: Smoked fish all hanging in rows, the water singing as it hits the shore. The loon's calls out in the middle of the lake. The shadows of my parents paddling, checking the nets, floating in the water as the sun tries to come through the mist. I walk along the shore. I gather flat stones and try to skip them on the water. How many skips is how many fish you catch. *(she laughs)* Two. One. Here comes Roger. Maybe he'll have more skips.

A banging in the radiators is heard.

TO US: My cousin farted in class yesterday. We laughed. She was so cute going *(she demonstrates)* until she saw Miss Stapleton walking over. The teacher grabbed her by the hair and pulled her to the front of the class. "What do you say?" Silence. Jessie was searching for an answer from us. We didn't know what she was supposed to say. Teacher kept yelling, "What do you say, you useless dirty girl? What do you say, you stupid Indian girl?" Jessie's eyes lit up. Ours did too. She found what to say. She looked so brave. She stood up straight and said "Oops."

Miss Stapleton, who is she to do that? She has bad breath that stinks worse than the dogs on the reserve. She spits in our faces, even when she just talks. She chews cigarettes, you know. Her teeth are all brown and crooked and they stick out from everywhere. Reminds me of a dog's mouth, the mouths that almost killed me once, those husky dogs that ripped at my clothes trying to eat my blood. They wanted something inside me. I think she's one of them dogs. She punished Jessie for her smell, but who's gonna punish that teacher for her smell? It won't be the principal. She has something over him, I think.

TO MOON: The moon, the moon. Is my grandmother there with you? Does she still fart? No, I guess she doesn't fart, cause I got it now. Hey, can I use my fart smell like a skunk does to get rid of his enemies?

TO US: I don't want to smell like Miss Stapleton, though!

She tries to fart.

TO US: Anybody hungry? I am. I didn't get any supper. Hey, anybody got a cookie? I don't want dog biscuits, though. Too many bones in them. Yup, we found bones in our cookies.

RELIVING: They gave us cotton candy in Niagara Falls. It was like it just melted in my mouth. I didn't have to chew it.

There's a big clock on the earth over there in Niagara Falls. There's flowers growing in it. I don't know their names. They're not like the wild roses growing back home. They're strange to me. Yet it seems like I know them. Were they put there? Aren't flowers supposed to grow where they want? They must have moved them. Put there without their choice. Are you sad like me, lost like me, taking a place in a clock? But you're pretty. Those flowers in Niagara Falls don't talk to me.

She smells. She looks at the audience.

TO US: Okay, okay, who brought the beaver tails and bannock? It's okay, it fills me up when I just smell it, anyway. At night I smell things from back home. Rabbit stew and dumplings. And the tea that boils and boils.

That's probably why my sister Linda wouldn't eat her ice cream. That supervisor kept shoving her face in it. This was about the second or third time we had ice cream. Like, usually if we don't like something we pass it to another girl. But I guess the supervisor was watching her so she made sure Linda didn't pass it. It was white ice cream. I wouldn't a-mind eating it for her. Linda just knocked it on the floor. And they got out their best tennis racket and just let her have it. There were two that had to whip her cause Linda is known as one of the toughest girls in the school. Even though she was crying, she yelled, "It didn't hurt. You didn't hurt me!" They'll never get her to eat ice cream. I know her.

She looks at the moon.

Like a ball of smoke, the moon comes into my room. I can hear my mother speaking Cree to my Aunt Clara in the kitchen. It sounds so good.

TO MOON: The moon, the moon, come into this room. I want to know what my mother is doing. Is she having another baby that's gonna end up like me? Did she get that letter I told them to mail to her?

SHE RECITES: Dear Mrs. Lillian Cheechoo, In the Bush, Ontario. I am writing this letter to prove that I can write now. You can come and get me now, mom. I can even speak English like the older kids. I really miss you and I miss helping you get water and chop wood. I'm really big and I can watch Una when you're working hard. So are you gonna come? Your friend, Shirley Cheechoo.

TO MOON: I guess she never got it. She's not here yet ... but the bush is a big place, you know.

TO US: I guess they'll let me out of here when it's time to pick apples again. That's what we were doing when Eleanor decided she was gonna run away. Well, I was picking apples; Eleanor was picking her nose. She kept looking off where the railroad tracks were. I got mad cause I didn't want to pick any more stupid apples for her. Stupid apples with worms in them. I guess worms is flavour to white people.

RELIVING: "What are you looking at, Eleanor? What about the railroad tracks? How can you just get on the train? I'm not gonna walk. I OH! I OH! Okay, okay, I can walk. But what about what they said? Our parents will die if we run away! I care! I don't know, the principal probably calls the Indian agent and they probably go and shoot them or something. And if you make me run away with you, you're killing my mom and dad. You'll be a murderer! Your mom and dad are dead? Oh, so you ran away before!"

TO US: I made Eleanor promise that my parents would only get a little bit sick, like with a cold or something, and two extra people from her family has to die instead.

TO MOON: The moon, the moon, did I kill my parents?

TO US: Linda ran away. I saw her cross the first line of fence. She went down the lane, crossed the second line, the devil's line, the curse on the other side. She touched it. All the girls were hanging out the windows yelling, "Go, Linda, go!" Pushing her. She moved slowly, that curse hanging over her head. She turned around. Everyone yelled "Chicken!" She just kept coming back. And when she got to the yard she yelled, "I don't want my parents to die." I thought she crossed the line. Our parents will die anyways. So maybe if I chopped off her feet that touched the line, our parents would live. I decided to wait a couple of days just to see, then I would chop off her feet.

TO MOON: The moon, the moon, come into this room.

Nothing happens. The train whistle blows.

Eleanor? Eleanor. Are you dead? Answer me.

TO US: Eleanor is always bossing us around, making us do things that would get us in trouble. Like jumping from one bunk to another. Jump! Jump! Jump! That's how I lost my hair, Well, I didn't lose it, it got chopped off by the supervisor. Chop! Chop! Chop! Just a bunch standing on top of my head straight up. The supervisor put a chair in the middle of the dorm and told me to sit in it. Everyone giggled. I felt sick to my stomach and the pain kept shooting up and down my back, sitting there with my brush cut hair. I should have screamed but I didn't. The supervisor said, "Shirley #37 has a new name. She will now be called Woody Woodpecker. Everyone say Woody Woodpecker. All together now, Woody Woodpecker. And no one is to call her Shirley from now on." That's when I jumped up and ran across the beds as fast as I could go until I fell down. She came over to me and said, "That won't work, Woody Woodpecker. I know what you're doing. I'm not cutting the rest of your hair off."

She pees her pants.

RELIVES: I didn't know how to say nei-wentou-sei-chein, I have to
pee in English. All the other kids are staring straight ahead.
They've all been here before.

She clutches at her tunic.

Mr. .... throws me across the desk and pulls down my wet panties.
No, not my panties!

*She bends over suddenly. We hear the sound of a leather strap coming down
on bare flesh. Ten times. Suddenly she screams. A loud, shattering howl
from the soul.*

TO US: Wha. I'm just like a Pas kei sei gun.... I'm not useless. I'm
not dirty. I'm brown, and wet, with a very sore bum.

TO MOON: You're not gonna come into this room, are you? It's
okay, I can wait.

She picks up her pillow.

TO MOON: Every day at school I wait. And every night I wish for
summer. Pulling the fish out of the fish nets, one slips through my
fingers. He is free, I say to myself. I can slip away too. I'm as
slippery as this fish, as you.

TO US: Is the moon slippery? It slips in and out of the clouds. I
guess it's slippery. Wah, I shouldn't talk about the moon like that.

TO MOON: I can't let you slip away from me now.... Mr. ... made
me stay after class again, to wipe ...

RELIVING: Eleanor? Eleanor! Look, whoever falls off the rail first
has to do everything the other one says. Okay? You agree? Okay!

Do you have any more family in Paint Hills? Well, you know the
Indian agent will go and shoot all the family you got, that's how it
works. I OH! I OH! Okay, okay. I just thought you should know
what happens. Don't call me that, my hair's longer now.

TO US: Oh! Tonight is movie night and I'm gonna miss it. Unless
they let me out of here. Nah! I don't mind missing the cartoon.
(she imitates Woody Woodpecker) Every time it's a Woody Woodpecker
cartoon. The first time they did it I wanted to leave. Then the
movie started. It was Elvis Presley singing, and when I looked up,

there with him was the movie star they all told me I looked like, Ann-Margret. They were right. In the dark, I looked just like her. I pretended my hair was long like hers, long red hair I could toss over my shoulder. Beautiful, thick, red hair just like ... Woody Woodpecker. Oh, Elvis would never sing to Woody Woodpecker. I've got to grow my hair fast. Ann-Margret will be too old soon and Elvis will have to have someone to sing to. It's got to be me. Hudson's Bay Presents: "Singing on the Beaches of Moose Factory," starring Elvis Presley and ... Cactus Rose. That's me.

I'm gonna be a movie star. I already look like Ann-Margret, and I can shake and rock like Elvis. The girls make me sing to them like Elvis, and they all scream like they do in the movies. I guess I'm pretty good. I make sure I do him exactly because my mother told me if you make fun of someone, cheh kummit teck ta goon. Oh, I'm not supposed to speak Cree.

She lies down.

TO MOON: The moon, the moon, when you come into my room like a ball of smoke surrounding me, it's me inside that ball of smoke, and my Kookum picking up sticks.

TO US: The man, the man in the moon is Elvis singing to Cactus Rose ... and there are a lot of children in there playing, playing "You can't touch me."

She sings a lullaby in Cree.
>Mei mei gee gee mei mei,
>gee gee mei mei,
>mei mei gee gee mei mei,
>ay koo tei gee gee mei mei.
>Mei mei gee gee mei mei
>gee gee mei mei,
>ay koo tei gee gee mei mei.

Ah Ah Ah Ah .... Sash nuh-bou.

RELIVING: Eleanor! Eleanor! Jump off the tracks, the train is coming. Ah! You fell off the rail first. I'm boss now. You have to do everything I say. And I say we're going back to the school. No, it's not too late. I OH! I OH! But I'm boss. Okay, okay, let's go.

TO US: I'm not a very good boss. I'm gonna have to get her to teach me.

RELIVES: We started walking down the tracks and Eleanor she got real tired. I don't know why she was tired. I wasn't. So I said, "Let's be blood sisters, like in the movie, so we'll be stronger." It was her idea to cut on the wrist. I only wanted to cut the finger. She said it wouldn't hurt and that there'd only be a little blood. She lied. I scratched mine, but Eleanor, she had enough blood there to be blood sisters with the whole bloody school. I wrapped my apron around her wrist and I helped her down the tracks. As I dragged Eleanor down the tracks I started to think about home. Maybe if we get there faster, nothing will happen.

REMEMBERS: Scrape the hides and pull as hard as you can. The smell of smoke tanning the moosehides, my mother's rough chapped hands work day and night. Her face never changes. She's not an angry woman. I wonder if she knows what I go through at school. *(she step dances)* The sound of the fiddle into the night, looking at my feet going fast as everyone cheers for me to win the step dance. There's only two of us left, me and my mom. Everyone started bidding and my mom says, "What's in it for us?" They put all the money into the pot and there's four hundred and eighty dollars. I lost that dance. How does my mother stay up on her feet so long? She says, "You didn't lose, you just don't have the experience," and she gives me fifty dollars.

TO US: I bought clothes with that fifty dollars and I wanted to wear them at school but they took them away. And they gave me this stupid tunic, again. So I ripped it. See?

She shows a ripped tunic. Train whistle.

RELIVES: Come on, Eleanor.

REMEMBERS: The days of summer must never end, but they always do. The lines of boats docking in Moosonee. With all the children sad and mothers crying, wailing over the sound of the train whistle. My father holds my hand and I pretend to be strong so he'll be proud of me. He gives me twenty dollars and puts me on the train. He smiles and kisses me but his eyes tell me he's sad. I run to get a window seat so I could wave good-bye as the train slowly pulls away.

Little Donna says, "Holy Cow!" What kinda animals are those?

TO US: They were cows. Then she said, "Well, how was I supposed to know, there's no cows in Moose Factory."

REMEMBERS: It's time to speak English again. Wah! I've forgotten so much. And those yardsticks on my knuckles. And the way Mr. ... makes me use my hands. I guess my hands will get old first before the rest of me.

TO US: I'm going home. I'm going home with my friend Eleanor. I'm boss now. I have a choice. I don't have to do this train ride any more.

RELIVES: Eleanor, hurry up. Eleanor, come on. We have to hurry. If we're gonna do this, let's do it. We got no choice now. Eleanor, you got lots of blood. Make it stop. I'm boss and I said that's enough! You're cold. We have to keep moving. Come, I'll carry you. I can't carry you. They said our parents would die if we ran away, not you. Maybe if I cut my tongue, I can give you more blood. No. We have to go back. Eleanor, don't die on me, or I'll leave you right here, I mean it. The rest of the girls would probably pay me if I left you here. But you're my blood sister and I can't leave you here alone and you can't leave me here alone. You okay? Come on, Eleanor? Answer me. We're almost there. We shouldn't have tried to run away. See. Look. The pointed chapel.

SHE SINGS:

> Jesus loves me this I know
> For the bible tells me so
> Yes Jesus loves me
> Yes Jesus loves me
> Jesus loves me this I know

Train whistle

> Jesus loves me this I know
> For the bible tells me so
> Yes Jesus loves me
> Yes Jesus loves me
> Jesus loves me this I know

TO US: God helped us get back. They told us if we're good we'll go to heaven. I think I'm ready now to find out what heaven is like. It's gotta be better than here. So I'll sing all those hymns and kneel on my knees and pray that I'll be good until I die, so I can go to heaven and be with god.

TO HERSELF: The day never comes when you wait for it. The sun only shines when it wants to. When I wait for tomorrow to come, I don't know where I am. I don't know where my blood runs through. I don't know whether my toes touch the ground and my fingers feel like they're tied to the ceiling. And every time I wait to be freed more strings go up to freeze me. Like the way Virgin Mary is, but without a smile. I am waiting for the next day so I can be free from today. But the more I wait for tomorrow, the longer I wait, the more in jailed I feel.

TO US: I don't want to be me.

SHE SINGS:

Well, since my baby left me ...

She sings a verse of two of "Heartbreak Hotel."

We hear Elvis Presley singing "Heartbreak Hotel" as she does the scene change.

PART TWO

She is twenty-one and under an empty house, a crawl space that she can't quite stand up in. She has a razor blade and a bottle of C.C. that's half full. We hear a transport truck go by. She laughs.

TO HERSELF: Yeah, as if. As if. How? They probably put it in my hand, that two-by-four with the nail sticking out.

She crawls to the edge of the house and shouts.

So what if I hit him? He deserved it!

Another transport truck goes by, sounding its horn.

TO US: Y'know, I couldn't wait until I was old enough to drink, and now that I'm twenty-one they lower the drinking age. Boy, that pisses me off. I grabbed the supervisor's strap one time at the residential school in Brantford, and I started hitting her back until I got her on the floor, cement floor. I jumped on top of her and started banging her head until another supervisor pulled me off. They made her into a white Indian and I made her bleed. I fought back. I always fight back. *(drinks from the bottle)*

TO US: That's when they hosed me in the showers. Along with four other girls. They knew those girls would come after me later. I got angry. I thought, I'm gonna fix her, I'm gonna kill myself. *(she laughs)* I tied my sheets together and tied one end to the top bunk and the other end around my neck and I jumped off my bunk. I landed on my bum. So next I made it shorter. I stood on my bunk and I jumped. I landed on my feet. I was so mad. I thought, in the movie she put her bed sheets out the window, so I looked for a place to tie it. My friend woke up and said "What y'doing, anyways?" I told her I was hanging my sheets out the window, but they were still tied around my neck. She asked, "Did you pee the bed?" I thought, good idea. "Hm mm." "Oh," she said, and went back to sleep.

TO BOTTLE: My true friend. You who takes away the sins of the world. Drink thee and thou shall not remind us of our sins. *(she kisses the bottle)* Nee! When was the first time I found you? All of a sudden you were just there. Good friend. *(drinks)* And you taste damn good, too.

She goes for her lighter in her pocket and pulls out a razor blade.

TO HERSELF: I OH! Damn razor blade. *(she looks for her cigarette.)* My last cigarette. *(she finds it behind her ear.)*

TO US: If I'm supposed to be Robin Hood's wife, I guess I wouldn't have a cigarette. *(she shrugs her shoulders and lights the cigarette.)*

I was really good with the bow and arrow, like it's been in my blood for centuries. I won trophies shooting arrows. I know what you're all thinking. She's good cause she's Indian. That's what they said in high school, that's why I quit. How did they figure that out? I thought I was good cause I was a Japanese princess, or Robin Hood's wife.

Puts the cigarette out, saving it.

I hated school, y'know, cause I couldn't read like everybody else. I still can't. I can read upside down, thank god I'm not color blind anyway, probably would have got runned over by now. Yeah, I'm dialesick ... dialetick, ahh! Boy, I had a hard time with long words, especially when they were teaching us how to pronounce. I couldn't see what they were talking about. How come when you ask how to spell a word, they always tell you to go look it up in the dictionary? How can you find it if you don't know how to spell it? And they'd always say, "Pronounce it." I'd go, "Phone: F.O.I.N." And Webster didn't even know how to spell it.

SHE SINGS: She loves you yeah, yeah, yeah, she loves you yeah, yeah, yeah. With a love like that ...

REMEMBERS: Hey, my sister Linda's beautiful, eh, especially her hair. It shines like wet charcoal in the rain. That charcoal makes your teeth white, you know. When I was twelve my sister dressed me up to look sixteen, so we could go to the over-sixteen dances. She put a cigarette in my hand, and make-up on my eyes, and we tried on all our clothes, all four sets. She's a good dancer, isn't she? Doesn't she look like Annette – you know, Frankie and Annette? With her full skirt and her fair skin. She doesn't even look Indian. All the boys want to be her friend. They can stay away from me.

TO BOTTLE: My bottle is my friend, you protect me like I'm your baby. You're always here when I need you. They said that guy was beating her up. That's why I went after him with a two-by-four. I don't like it when my dad does it. If my brother Roger was there, he would have taken care of me. I shouldn't have gotten mad at Roger. *(drinks)*

Another transport truck goes by on the highway.

TO US: Those damn transport trucks. *(lights the cigarette.)*

One time I tried to stop my dad from going to town to drink. I cut the heels of his socks and cut one leg of his dress pants and laid them on the bed like the way my mother had them. He washed his face, shaved and washed his hair. Then he went into his room and said, "Wha, what happened here?" He came out with one leg of his pants cut off. He wanted to know who did it. I didn't answer. My mother gave him another pair of pants. Then he put on his socks and he started laughing and wouldn't stop. So I ran to this room to laugh too, thinking he liked what I did. He stopped laughing, he knew who did it. He tricked me. He went to town anyways. *(puts cigarette out)* I thought, next time, I'm gonna hide the damn town and he won't find it, and he'll have to stay home.

TO BOTTLE: He won't find you, either. *(drinks)* You weren't always here. I can remember a time when you weren't here. But you're everywhere now. Boy, you sure make your rounds.

REMEMBERING: He'd come home late at night from checking his traps. My mother always knew when he was close. She'd get up, make the fire and cook him something to eat. We'd hear him banging his snowshoes together and standing them up. He'd come in the flap, put down his gun, and toss his packsack on the ground. And he'd walk over to the stove to warm his butt.

TO US: One time we almost starved. I think it had to do with me feeling sorry for a small beaver. My mother told us, "We're not supposed to feel sorry for animals we kill for food, because if we did, they'd stop coming." But this beaver was so cute. She was right. They didn't come. But my father also got sick, so it was harder for us to get food to eat. He had this growth on the back of his neck. He was in so much pain. We waited for the plane to come but it didn't come. My mother told us she was going to cut it out. And she said we had to be very still, and I was responsible for keeping Una quiet.

REMEMBERS: My mother boiled the water and burned the needles and sat my father down on a stump. She took out her scissors and cut him open.

TO HERSELF: My father sat there with no expression on his face, just silent tears running down. She took out this thing that looked like a big spider, the size of a man's hand, or at least my father's hand. She put it in a jar and sewed his neck and she put oatmeal on it to heal the wound. When she was finished he passed out for about four days.

TO US: While he was out, I put his hockey game on the radio or his favourite country station, hoping he'd wake up. We'd check the traps and snares and always came up with nothing. Bannock is all we ate. Till we ran out of flour.

Transport truck goes by.

TO BOTTLE: You play tricks on us, I know you do. Remember the time we wanted to ditch the car we stoled and you made us drive it over the cliff and into the lake. It was a good idea, only we forgot to get out. Were you mad cause we were on drugs too? It was such a nice feeling flying in the air for awhile. Till we hit the water and we all panicked. You didn't let us die cause you weren't empty. A true friend never leaves. *(She drinks and picks up the lighter.)*

TO US: This is my dad's, I stole it. They said that guy was beating her up. That's why I tried to kill him. I don't remember. I don't remember no two-by-four. I always get drunk and don't remember.

It wasn't always like this. I can remember a time when nobody drank. I can remember the fiddles playing and people dancing till five in the morning and Uncle James playing. *(she imitates the sound of the fiddle)* I used to live with Auntie Flo and Uncle Mark then. They were rich. She had a jewelry chest, just costume jewelry, but she always said she'd give it to me. My uncle worked at the Hudson's Bay store. He was one of the best-paid people on the reserve. My auntie permed ladies' hair. She burnt mine but I was still proud of it. They used to bring home goodies and give me good clothes to wear. They were always joking around with each other, always laughing. I went away on the trapline with my parents and when we came back that spring, first thing I did was go move in with Auntie Flo and Uncle Mark. I was shocked to see that Auntie Flo didn't have any teeth. She said they fell out. Me and Auntie Flo were waiting for Uncle Mark to come home for supper. He came home drunk and they got into an argument and he started beating on her. I ran home and walked into the surprise of my life. There sat my dad, also drunk.

TO BOTTLE: C.C. bottle. How come everybody started drinking, like at the same time? Why were they beating on each other? Was it my fault?

TO US: I heard a noise in the kitchen one night. Sounding like someone crawling around, being real sneaky. I took my flashlight and went into the kitchen. I shined the light on the floor. There was my uncle and my aunt, fighting, wrestling, cursing very quietly! Trying not to wake anybody up. "Ssh! Ssh!" she said. "Ssh! Ssh!" she said.

My girlfriend died from drinking. I wasn't there. I knew something was going to happen. My whole body told me so. I thought something's going to happen to my mom or dad. So I went home to Hearst. They said she drank a whole bottle of lemon gin by herself. She died while everybody partied around her.

A gas station letting out pressure is heard.

TO BOTTLE: Holeh! *(drinks)* My friend, I can find you no matter where I go. Remember laughing at David at the railroad tracks, when he told us that Mrs. King was forcing him to do things in bed with her. We didn't believe him. He killed himself, that David. We all decided if David can do it, we can do it. So, so let's all do it together, you included. Remember laying down on the tracks with us. We knew that train would be coming in tonight, always comes roaring in. It haunts us. *(she laughs)* Remember the railroad tracks shaking under us and Mary screaming. *(she screams)* You and me jumped up first as the train rumbled by us on the other track. Maybe next time we'll be flat pennies.

TO US: At the residential school, I made a voodoo doll once that looked like Mr. ...; it had his buttons, his gloves, his hair.

RELIVES: What do I do with it? I can't burn it like the girl in the movie. It might burn the school down and my brother Roger might not get out. I could chop the doll's legs off. Nah! He might still come after me. I don't want to kill him, I just want to hurt him, like he hurt me.

TO US: I threw that doll out the window and a week later that teacher fell down the stairs and broke his back. Wha, was it my fault?

I know why I didn't believe David. I said to myself, if Mrs. King really made him do those things he wouldn't tell anyone. Because they always told you not to tell or they'd do something to you. Even with a gun.

REMEMBERS: Mr. ... made me stay after class again, to wipe ... to wipe the blackboards. It made my hands real dirty. So dirty I wanted to chop them off with a meat cutter because they were his hands now. He loved them.

TO US: I should have cut them off and put them on his plate for everyone to see. But that cook in the kitchen stopped me before I could slide my hands through the blade.

I'll never tell. Who'd believe me? Even the ones that you're made to believe will protect you do the same damn thing.

RELIVES: Hey Claude! I saw the cops at your house. They were looking for you. They questioned me and searched me, and handcuffed me and then they.... After they were finished they said, "I've never had an Indian before." So Claude, you better watch out, eh! *(she lights the cigarette.)*

TO US: My mother worked late at the hospital and one of us always had to take her to work. I don't know why. When it was my turn, I took the bike so I could bike home. I was twelve. There was a row of boys holding hands across the road stopping me.

They pulled me off the bike, dragged me into the ditch. They took my clothes off. They didn't rip at them. I didn't fight back. I recognized all their fuckin' faces.

It seems like no matter how old I am, someone always wants to do this to me. I don't want to be beautiful like Ann-Margret any more. It's my fault for asking to be a movie star. Boy, they want movie stars.

Puts out the cigarette, picks up the razor blade.

TO HERSELF: I shoulda been a horse. Horses are free, strong, and so in control. It was Zorro who introduced us to a horse. I could destroy the whole world and put my mark on it: "S." Nee. They're still my favourite. Horses. It would be nice if Zorro could save me now. Ohh! I wouldn't want him to come here, though. Too embarrassing. My house is full of boxes, no dressers. We don't even have a freeze box or a toilet, but we do take a shit sometimes, in the outhouse.

SHE SINGS:
As I sit here tonight
The jukebox praying
The song about my wild side of life
As I listen to the words I am saying
It brings memories when I was a trusting ...

TO US: You guys still here? I guess my farts don't work any more. Hey, anybody want to fart out there? Do it now. Nee.

I was told I almost killed a guy last night with a two-by-four, a nail sticking out, a four inch nail. That guy coulda been my dad. What kind of a person am I? Who am I?

Picks up the razor blade and goes for her wrist.

See this razor blade? I'd use it, except I'm dying for a shit.

TO BOTTLE: This is another one of your tricks, isn't it? I must have done what they said. I can't remember. I drink you to forget but you won't let me. You keep punching me with memories, so I drink more and more until I don't remember anything at all. *(she drinks)*

Damn C.C. you.... There's a message in that C.C.... See. See. See what you've done.

Transport truck goes by.

Hey, maybe I could hitch a ride into town. Hey! Hey! Hey!

She does the scene change as we hear her song play; she sings along: "Whiskey Drinking Woman"

> I'm a whiskey drinking woman
> I've drank C.C. all my days
> Hung around in smoky bar rooms
> Looking for a whisker to take home

> I got worn-out cowboy boots
> And holes in my jeans
> Listening to live country music
> And learning a few dance steps too

CHORUS: No one with a sense of humor
> No one's a happy too
> Just a crying with the tunes
> No one knows how to get home too

> I find myself a walking
> It's way past morning time
> Just some down lonely dirt road
> Far away from my hometown

CHORUS: No one with the sense of humor
      No one's a happy too
      Just a crying with the tunes
      No one knows how to get home too
      No one knows how to get home too

PART THREE

All throughout this act we hear the water splashing against the rocks. She is twenty-eight years old. She puts down tobacco.

TO WATER SPIRITS: Water Spirits of the Black Rocks, I've come again. Show me a sign that you're listening.

Water Spirits, so full of love, eh? I trusted you. I quit drinking to find out who I am. I cried out my fears to you. I told you everything, suddenly I feel ashamed. You was always listening quietly and sometimes quickly. First you protect me and then you hate me. Why? What did I do? I'd never do anything to hurt you. You allowed me to be introduced to you. Blake took me to you. I married him, you know. He loves me. He taught me how to paint. I know how to write in pictures, writing them upside down on a canvas. He wouldn't let me down. He'd never take my family away from me. Why did you do it? Will he leave me too? He means so much to me; deeper than words.

RELIVES: Why did you leave me? You were always there when I was drinking. You're my best girlfriend. I love you. Is it because of Blake? Am I moving too fast? Your hands were always soft, now they feel so cold. Why? Why are you mad at me? What did I do?

We hear a helicopter fly by.

TO WATER SPIRITS: Water Spirits, you replaced all my friends. You know when I entered the Native Princess Pageant? One of my girlfriends told me, "You'll never win, you don't know anything about being Indian. That's what they'll ask you at the contest. You'll never win." I know how to survive in the bush, don't I?

RELIVES: I'll just put some javex on this cloth and wash my skin with it. It should turn my skin real white, like my underwear does when I wash them in javex. Ouch! Boy, that burns my skin. I'm all covered in a rash. I sure am a red Indian now.

Me? Thank you. Megwetch. This is a dream come true. I never thought I'd actually win. Canadian Native Princess, that's me. I have a chance to be Indian again. I'm going to need help.

She tries to beat her drum to the sound of the water beating on the rocks. She lays down tobacco.

TO WATER SPIRITS: Water Spirits, I've come again. Bet you thought I wouldn't just because I took a couple of drinks after five years to ease the pain. But I've been there before, it doesn't work. My heart is still aching and endless tears run down inside me. Where do I turn? I need to hold my brother Billy. Where does he turn. He feels empty inside. Did my father feel the same way? Why did you help him break his promise? Why did you break your promise? When I stopped drinking you promised to be my friend. Why? I didn't have nowhere to go. I'm an alcoholic.

TO US: When I told my girlfriend, "Doo, I'm gonna quit drinking," she said, "Ah, you'll fall off the wagon." Well, I told her, "I'm not gonna get on." She laughed at me and said, "Are you gonna join A.A.?" I said, "It's nobody's business but mine and I don't want anybody to know who I am."

I didn't know the other A stood for anonymous. I don't want to be stupid any more. I don't want to forget about trapping and hunting, too, but why don't I remember my education at school? All I remember is the full days and cold nights on the trapline. My father, he loved it there. He always smiled and laughed and he never hit my mom, there.

TO VOICES: What? Who said that? Ohh! Water Spirits, are you finally talking to me? What? You're not the Water Spirits. Who are you? No, I'm not afraid.

TO US: Did one of you ask me that? Holeh! I'm starting to hear voices, I think I'm going crazy. I sometimes see things and my dreams scare the shit out of me.

TO HERSELF: There's a wall, a wall of stone with high peaks, smooth, can't climb it, my family's on either side. I'm the wall. I don't want to be. There isn't a crack in me for them to peek through at each other. Is it my fault?

We hear a helicopter flying by.

RELIVES: Once on the trapline, when the ice was thin, they brought us food and they parachuted the food down to us. My father was trying to tell them where to put down the food. They didn't listen. Most of the food spoiled; it crashed through the ice.

TO WATER SPIRITS: Water Spirits, I'm doing my part, aren't I? Why won't you show me a sign?

RELIVES: No. I didn't do anything. I didn't tell them to take the car. If you shoot me, my son will be alone. Please don't shoot my head off, no one will recognize me. Shoot me here.

We hear a gun go off.

TO WATER SPIRITS: Water Spirits. I thought it was me you were gonna take, not my father. Why did you show me how I was going to die? Why? I sit here hoping for a vision. Aren't Indians supposed to have visions?

TO VOICES: That was a vision? Me seeing myself getting my head shot off? I don't want those kind of visions. You're crazy too. You want to dance with me? How are we supposed to do that? You're not the Water Spirits. Go away.

TO US: I really am going crazy. Indian children are never alone, I was told. They have grandparents and uncles, all kinds of relatives to hold them. Where are mine? Am I just too old? Am I alone on this rock? I think I've lost me.

She picks up her drum and chants a song in Cree.
    Kei pei tah tin a tah po shen numshoom
    Kei pei tah tin a tah po shen nookoom
    Astum bey jeh wee chah heen
    Astum bey jeh wee chah heen

    Nootahwe ke nic a tok numshoom
    Nootahwe ke nic a tok nookoom
    Astum bey jeh wee chah heen
    Astum bey jeh wee chah heen.

She lays down her tobacco.

TO WATER SPIRITS: Water Spirits of the Black Rocks, I've come again. Show me a sign that you are listening. You, you cleansed my body, my mind, and you broke my silence as I allowed you to dance with my spirit. Now, I'm aching, tired and I don't want to be a wandering spirit walking with holes in my moccasins with no place to go and mend them.

TO US: In a dream I was having an operation, and I wasn't quite asleep. I was trying to tell the doctors but they can't seem to hear me. The doctor said, "First the clitoris." He pulled it and stretched it to the ceiling and hooked it on a hook. I screamed from pain, but they can't seem to hear me. Then, "The tubes," he said. He grabbed one and stretched it and hooked it on the ceiling, then the other. I was in so much pain, I thought my head was gonna burst. "There it is," he said. I felt a sharp pain and out came this glass ball from my womb. It was foggy inside. "Okay, we got it," the doctor said. They unhooked my tubes and they came springing back inside and I awoke. I was told by my mother that dreams always have a meaning. I'm gonna have to ask her about this one.

She scratches her name on the rock.

REMEMBERS: When my grandmother died, Indian Affairs wouldn't let me go to her funeral. They said she wasn't a close family. She was my, my grandma. She was the one I slept with, the one who gathered up the sticks. She made a feather blanket for me and showed me how to make bannock. How could they say she was not my Kookum? I wasn't there when they laid her down. I quit school after that. I hated everyone.

TO VOICES: Yeah. Who are you? Answer me! Damn you! What's not my fault? Ca-ga-doo. Awus!

We hear a helicopter fly by.

REMEMBERS: They flew my father's body in his coffin across Moose River attached to a helicopter. I kept thinking he's going to fall and we'd never find him, flying in mid-air just like us.

TO WATER SPIRITS: Water Spirits, where are you? Come on, I've come to confront you. Damn you! I trusted you! Show me a sign. Why did you take my father away? Talk to me! And don't say you screwed up, either! Greta always says that. He knew how to cross the ice. You tricked him, didn't you? All I can think of is him trying to get out of the water and nothing could help him. Why didn't you help him? Is it my fault? Did I do something to you? He's coughing, he's coughing and he can't control it. And you kept hanging on to his ankles, didn't you? You were cold and freezing and you wouldn't let go of him. Why? He was going to teach our son how to be a hunter, he was going to take him to the bush and teach him how to survive, like him. How can you give me something as beautiful as this and take it away. And you took all that away from a child. Water Spirits. Yeah, right. It was safer when I was drunk. Sleeping it off, at least I didn't care if you betrayed me. Liar! You promised you'd always be here, just like my father promised. You made him break his promise. You. You. You who taught me how to find my heart beat.

She hits the drum hard.

REMEMBERS: One time there was a big drunken family fight and everybody was beating up on my father. I kicked everybody out of the house and when I came back in, there stood my dad with a knife in his hand. He'd drawn a big circle on the floor. He was gonna kill himself. He said, "No one is to come into this circle." I said, "I'm gonna kill myself after you." He told me it's not right to take your own life. "Why are you doing it then?" He started to cry. I never saw my father cry like that, ever. I told him I can't live without him. So I told him he has to promise me that he won't die before me. We made a promise. He chipped away an opening to the circle and he said, "You can come in now."

RELIVES: Every morning I splash my face, to wipe away my sorrow. I brush my hair, hoping I've grown wiser. I gargle my mouth to wash away all the dirty language I use to beat myself. It's nine o'clock, ten o'clock it's coffee time, ten thirty, twelve o'clock it's lunch time, twelve thirty, three o'clock it's coffee time, three thirty, five o'clock it's quitting time. Holeh, what have I done all day?

This road I'm on doesn't seem to have no end. As I travel up and down these hills wondering what's on the other side. Here comes a field of water, rolling in, trying to grab me. Getting closer and closer, I know you want me too. Do I have the guts to walk on top of it like Jesus?

She steps into the water and we hear her thoughts.

I can't breathe. The fish is swimming by me, smiling, poking at my nose. There's bubbles rolling up. I'm running out of air. There's a bright blue light. I can do this. What? Stop it! Stop pushing at my feet. I want to go to paradise, you know, heaven. You wanted me. Take me too. You took my father. Why won't you take me? I want to die! I feel heavy, it must be time. It's getting dark. Listen. Shit, I don't want to go up. What's pushing my feet? Water Spirits, stop it. No.

She gets thrown out of the water and lands on the rocks.

TO US: I dreamt that small layers of steel were growing all over my body. There were two steel blades growing out of my mouth, pushing my mouth apart. I was able to pull them out and when I did this the rest of the blades disappeared. I thought no one will believe me. I got up, went outside and my husband Blake says, "I'll back you up." Our son Nano was playing with another boy. He put his hand into his pocket and showed me a steel blade, just like the ones that were growing in my body. This made me feel good and it felt like our son would be okay. I got into my car, drove down the street turning all the traffic lights from red to green as I drove into the night. Hmm, the sun warms my soul.

We hear a chant as she changes the set.

CHANT: Way ha ha ha way ha ha ha way ha ha ha way ha ha oy
    Way ha ha ha way ha ha ha way ha ha ha way ha ha oy

PART FOUR

Dreamer's Rock on Manitoulin Island. August 17, 1987. It is before dawn; the wind is blowing. We can hear the trees whispering. She lays out her star blanket, moccasins, sage and a feather wing and a clay bowl. She is thirty-five years old.

TO US: I'm waiting for the sun to rise. You too? I'm here to let go of my old self. I don't know how, but I figure I'll find out here. You're supposed to have visions here on Dreamer's Rock.

TO HER FATHER: Baba, I miss calling you. I miss saying, baba do you want some tea? You would drink it even if it was cold, as long as I put sugar in it. You never complained. I'd just look into your eyes and they would tell me what you were thinking. They were made of black marble, they were honest. I didn't want to believe it when Una told me, because when I asked how you died nobody would tell me the truth. But you waited until I had a baby before you left me. You were smart. When the moment came of going over the edge, Nano would cry. No words can describe the feeling of I had to be there. He makes it so clear.

TO US: I wanted my baby to be born at home because I knew beautiful souls hung around our house and the soul that would take the first breath of our child would be someone Blake and I knew. He was five weeks early, we thought he may need oxygen so we went to the hospital. The doctor pulled him out with forceps and broke his nose. I didn't trust or take the risk for my mother to deliver him and she delivered many babies before. I felt guilty about this at first, but there was so much love when I fed from my breasts, nothing mattered. Our son's name is Nanoshkasheese. It means hummingbird, the symbol of joy. We built an art gallery and called it Kasheese Studios.

RELIVES: Yeah? Yeah, Shirley's Cree from James Bay. No, they're all Crees up there. No, they're different from Ojibways. They can relate, but they are different. No, I don't think the artist will come down in price. Well, because you're speaking to the artist. Yeah, it's the sky. Just take a train to Moosonee and you'll see a sky like that.

TO US: Hey, anybody out there know what muted means?

RELIVES: Your sofa? I want the little girl in my painting to have a red coat because there's a meaning behind the color. Beige? Beige is the color of nature, like moosehide, like my painting already has nature in it. But red, this little girl is covered in this red because she needs to deal with her female power. Red is a healing color. It heals ... uh ... uh....

TO US: I didn't know how to say it.

RELIVES: Uh ... your crotch ... goodbye.... Paint your fucking sofa.

TO US: Why do some white women hang star blankets on their walls? Those colors, the colors of the rainbow, of red, orange, yellow, green, blue, purple, why would you hang it on your wall when you could sleep under the biggest star with all those healing colors that heal different parts of your body?

TO HERSELF: Wha! Who am I fooling? Do I have a star blanket hanging on my wall? I hope not.

TO US: I have no right to judge. I used to talk to the moon. I used to talk to the bottle. I used to talk to the Water Spirits at the Black Rocks till they took my father away, so who could I trust? The loneliness that shoots up and down my spine, and me searching out there for someone to answer me.

TO HER FATHER: Baba, I use a glass shield to protect myself now. I'm getting pretty good at it. No one can come in. I feel safe in my ball of glass, but I can't hear anything when I am surrounded by it. It's not like the moon. I am alone in it. Not even you can come in.

Silence as she takes a deep breath. The wind whistles.

TO US: Today's supposed to be a powerful day for making connections. Today the planets align.

They weren't all the same, those supervisors at the residential school. They didn't all think they were superior to us. But living it at the time, I felt tricked. I didn't trust any of them. We were so unsure of that one lady who smiled and took us to wiener roasts, and helped us with our chores and she even talked to us. The boys said her boyfriend was just as nice. No wonder they connected.

TO HER FATHER: Baba, do I put up my shield because I'm afraid that nobody will like me or approve? Baba, am I killing you over and over again? Will you not find your way if I don't accept your death?

TO US: Death is something I fear, and when it happens to me, will I find my way? I wonder how many times I died. How old I really am? Wha, maybe I'm an alien. Maybe we're all aliens.

RELIVES: One time I was getting into my car to go home to Manitoulin. I went to turn the key but it wouldn't turn. I wiggled the steering wheel, still I couldn't turn the key to start my car.

Okay, I guess it's not time to leave. I'll try later. One hour later the car started no problem. As I was driving on 401, I started to lose control of the car. I thought, I'm going to cause an accident. Okay, take me if you want. My car is coming alive. Okay. Okay, it's all yours. Someone is in my body. It's driving me home. I feel so rested. I feel at peace.

TO HER FATHER: Baba, is that you? You won't let me die, eh?

TO US: It took five hours to get home, 350 miles and I only burned a half a tank of gas. Nanabush!

In Calgary I was walking to work and I ran into an Indian guy. He asked me for some money and I said, "I don't have any. I'm doing what you're doing." He said, "Oh. Well, why don't we sell your suede coat, we'll get enough money there for the both of us." When I got to the theatre I told the girls and they said, ah, Nanabush. Nanabush, to me, is the trickster in everybody. He's half-spirit and half-human. *(pause)* And we are half-human and half-spirit. Ohh!

I got a job one time as a clown at a theatre in Toronto. And the director told me to act Indian. I went blank. So I did what they do in the movies. *(she demonstrates)* How! Me big chief. Ooooooooooo.... I didn't know then that Indian clowns did everything backwards. A straighten-outener, you know, honest two face, heyoka. *(she takes a deep breath)*

TO HERSELF: Those sleeping Indian children taking their path with no moccasins slowly awake. I am one of them.

TO HER FATHER: Baba, those voices are my power, aren't they? It's Nanabush, my instincts. Wha. I don't need a shield. But baba, I'm still afraid to cry because my body hurts so much I might never stop. All the tears I have to share would flood this whole world.

The sun rises. The wind whistles and the trees whisper and a hole appears in the sky. A perfect circle forms around the rock. The sky looks like waves of water.

TO HERSELF: I have seven friends, seven women sitting in a circle. All different in color. The beauties of the sister moon. My sisters from a different time protecting me so I can walk into the light and tell my story with no fear, with no sadness, no judgement, leaving behind my old self, self-betrayer that has trapped me in silence, in a box of cockroaches crawling all over me, sexually abusing me against my will, telling me they loved me. I felt the fear making my crotch ache. I could not say No! No! No! I want to talk to me now. Down to where my gut is aching, aching to answer me. I must take my position in the sisterhood because I am a woman. One sister must not let down another.

She gathers her bowl and lights the sage.

TO US: I sometimes don't understand what I'm going through. So, I might as well stay on this path until I do.

She smudges herself and prays.

Oh, Great Spirit, Help me to understand. I want to go forward. Every time I let go of something in my past, things seem clearer.

SHE CONNECTS: This is my body. No one is allowed to touch it unless I allow it. I have the choice to dance, to dance the dance of life. I hate those men for not dancing with me.

SHE CONNECTS: The eyes of others are my mirrors. What I put out will come back to teach me. Is that why everybody was so angry around me, because I was?

SHE CONNECTS: Those sleeping children taking a path with no moccasins awake. I am one of them.

RELIVES: I see them. They are real. I see the spirits. I feel them. I'll never dismiss them. I won't file them away under UFO.

I know who you are. You were in my car. You're here now. First there's complete darkness and then a flash of light. I see myself being born. I'm on my mother's breast. Then all of a sudden I'm sitting at the residential school, peeling potatoes and wondering why I'm peeling them when there's a potato peeling machine. I climb into the machine. It starts spinning and it throws me out there like a bubble gum. I'm sliding into the water. I can't breathe. A shark is coming after me. I swim to the top. I take a big breath. I'm driving a car and I'm so drunk. I crash the car in the ditch and the steering wheel comes off into my hands. I'm running from bees, they're pulling at my hair, I scream. I'm singing on stage with a famous person and I can't find my words. I'm playing Cinderella and a prince is dancing with me. It's an Indian Warrior. A pack of wolves are tearing my clothes and these wolves turn into men on top of me. I kick, I bite, I'm climbing a ladder. I start to fly. I'm flying on top of the clouds. I've never seen these colors on clouds and the sky is a new blue to me. It's so perfect. In the distance I see a pyramid. It's stone. I'm flying real fast. I want to stop but I can't. I'm going to crash into that mountain. I'm going to die. I stare at the pyramid as it comes closer and closer. I fly right into the pyramid. There are people inside. They are trying to grab me. They're moving in slow motion, as if someone's controlling them. Some almost reach me. They want help from me but I don't know how to help them. I fly right through the pyramid and I land on my bed.

She jumps up screaming.

TO HERSELF: It's true you can have visions here on Dreamer's Rock.

TO US: You know what I think? I think we should all make the biggest star blanket. Me, you, no matter what color you are. We'll put our marks on it. A star blanket full of healing colors made by us with no judgement of the past. And we'll cover our world with it, with us underneath to be healed as one. I wonder if we can do that?

She puts on her moccasins and folds up her star blanket.

TO US: I have seen the seven sister moons. They were all lined up in different sizes across the sky. I only met the biggest one. I'll take you to meet the others when I know how to see them again. Let's say it's a date. Even if you're in Japan or anywhere in the world, you can say, "I have a date in Canada with one of my sisters to see the seven moons. But the date isn't set yet. I just know it's coming." You can say, "I shall wait. For my sister spent a long time waiting, so she can love herself, so she can be free, like a horse gliding over the grassfields. So she could become whole, instead of torn apart by those who want her power." You can say, "I'm all right, that date will come."

TO HER FATHER: Baba, I'm letting you go now, you can go now. *(in Cree)* Mahjhee.

We hear the sound of rain falling like droplets on leaves and on the rock. The wind whistles and trees whisper.

TO US: It's raining.

She covers herself with the star blanket and she turns to the four directions.

I'm going to be able to move towards my healing without fear and into the new light, with no future, no past, just a beginning. Heaven is a choice, to choose my own path. Wha, it's all up to me.

The sleeping Indian children taking a path with no moccasins awake. I am one of them.

She turns and spreads out the star blanket to the audience as the lights fade.

kookum	grandmother
pas kei sei gun	shot gun
cheh kummit teck ta goon	you will be cursed
sash nuh-bou	she's sleeping now
ca-ga-doo	shut your mouth
awus	get away!
baba	father, daddy
mahjhee	you can leave now

Lullaby:
Mei mei gee gee mei mei,
gee gee mei mei,
mei mei gee gee mei mei,
ay koo tei gee gee mei mei.
Mei mei gee gee mei mei
gee gee mei mei,
ay koo tei gee gee mei mei.

Sleep baby sleep ...
that's the way

Chant:
Kei pei tah tin a tah po shen numshoom
Kei pei tah tin a tah po shen nookoom
Astum bey jeh wee chah heen
Astum bey jheh wee chah heen

Nootahwe ke nic a tok numshoom
Nootahwe ke nic a tok nookoom
Astum bey jeh wee chah heen
Astum bey jeh wee chah heen.

I hear you calling me, grandfather
I hear you calling me, grandmother
Come and help me
Come and help me.
My father left me, Grandfather
My father left me, Grandmother
Come and help me
Come and help me.

The Tale of a Mask

by TERRY WATADA

Terry Watada writes a popular monthly column in the *Nikkei Voice,* a national Japanese Canadian community journal. With its 50,000 readership, the newspaper offers readers a keen insight into the issues and concerns facing the Japanese Canadian today.

His first play, *Dear Wes/Love Muriel* premiered at the 1991 Earth Spirit Festival at Harbourfront; his second and third *(Tale of a Mask* and *Vincent)* were commissioned by Workman Theatre Projects. *Vincent* was presented at the 7th annual Forensic Conference (1993), a research conference of professionals working in the forensic mental health system and criminal justice field.

Terry Watada's fiction and poetry have been published by literary journals such as *Canadian Literature, Grain, The Antigonish Review, The Dalhousie Review* and *The Greensboro Review.* His first book of poetry, *A Thousand Homes,* was published in the spring of 1995.

He edited the anthology *Asian Voices: Stories from Canada, Korea, China, Vietnam and Japan,* and *Collected Voices: An Anthology of Asian North American Periodical Articles.*

As a musician and composer, he has seven albums to his credit. *Runaway Horses, Living in Paradise* and *The Art of Protest* are his best known.

In 1991, he received the City of Toronto's William Hubbard Race Relations Award, and in 1993, the Ministry of Multiculturalism and Citizenship's Citation for Citizenship for his extensive community work.

ORIGINAL PRODUCTION

The Tale of a Mask was developed by Workman Theatre Projects and produced for the company by Lisa Brown, with Lloy Coutts as dramaturge. Presented by Workman Theatre Projects, the play premiered on December 1st, 1993 at the Workman Auditorium, Queen St. Mental Health Centre, 1001 Queen St. West, Toronto, Ontario.

Original Cast and Production Team

Aiko	Dawn Obokata
Masato	Peter Kosaka
Sumiko/Setsuko Harrison	Brenda Kamino
The Detective	Tom Free
Melanie Henry	Jody Braybrook

Director Lloy Coutts; Stage Manager Cheryl Mills; Set Designer Bev Horii; Costume Designer Robyn Kelly; Music Composer Boko Suzuki; Choreographer Denise Fujiwara; Production Manager David Hoekstra; Lighting Designer Glenn Davidson; Sound Designer Claude Allard.

Reviews

"A striking play.... In a multi-textural, layered and stylized production addressing the theme of madness brought about by alienation and isolation, Watada effectively uses the personae of the mask to relate his story ... [there is] the mask of the story itself, the mask that needs another mask to unmask itself, and the mask worn by each of the protagonists in the play, for the mask ... is the presentation of the self in everyday life...."   *(Nikkei Voice)*

"The interweaving of the story and the folktale creates an eerie mystic tone to the play, and the two elements come together at its tragic conclusion." *(The New Canadian)*

"Terry Watada is an assured and committed playwright." *(Nikkei Voice)*

"If there's one purpose that runs through all [Watada's] work, it's the expression of a Japanese Canadian culture." *(Toronto Star)*

Note about the Theme of the Play

"We are from societies where 'men and dogs roam, while women and cats remain at home.' Unable to communicate fluently, the woman's apartment soon becomes her prison." *(Immigrant Women's Group of Prince Edward Island)*

Performance Permission

For permission to perform *The Tale of a Mask*, please contact **TERRY WATADA**, 99 Ivy Avenue, Toronto, Ontario M4L 2H8, (416) 465-7688.

CHARACTERS

Aiko Shinde: A first generation immigrant woman, post war, age 32 at time of incident. She is thin, with shoulder length black hair.

Masato Shinde: A first generation immigrant man, post war, 35 at time of incident. Average build and height.

Detective: Middle-aged white male in a rumpled suit. There is a hint of seediness that surrounds him.

Setsuko Harrison: Middle-aged Japanese woman. Energetic woman with a commanding presence.

Melanie Henry: Young white female of average looks and build. There is an earnest sincerity to her character. She means well, but is not enlightened.

Sumiko: Neighbour in Japan. Much younger than Aiko and about to be married. A good friend and confidante for Aiko.

Harumi: Doubled by Aiko Shinde

Samurai: Doubled by Masato Shinde

Immigration Officer: Officious. Monotone voice and bored.

Time and Place: Scenes in Japan: January 1988 to April 1992. Scenes in Canada: May 1992 to May 1993

Set: Essentially, the stage is based on a Noh *design. There is a bridge that runs the length of the stage and then turns on a 90 degree angle and runs to the front. In the elbow of the bridge, a rake at a 12 degree incline extends to the front of the stage. At the head of the rake is a* noren *on a door frame that acts as an entrance way. Across the top of the* noren *is a rope.*

Sound of gagaku *music blended with a Japanese pop tune.* Taiko *music emerges.*

Soft, dim light comes up. Two figures are seen. A woman in yukata *sits with head down. Sword remains at her side. A masked man stands before her with sword raised. The mask is a devil's mask. When* taiko *crescendos, woman rushes forward and fatally wounds man. As man falls, lights go to black.*

SCENE ONE

Light comes up on **Detective** *stage right.*

Detective *(on telephone)*: Captain, we got a bad one this time. A family, all three dead. Really sad. I've been in Chinatown for ten years, but I never seen nothing like this before. *(flips through notepad)* The parents were Mass and A-ko Shin-die. Their son, Ken, was ten years old. Recent immigrants. Japanese. They lived in a first floor flat in a semi-detached house on Cecil Street. The husband, Mass, was stabbed 33 times. A real mess. The kid was strangled and the wife was found hanging from the shower rod in the bathroom. Must've happened last night. A real tragedy. They come all the way from Japan just to end up ... end up murdered.

Lights come up on stage. Stage has bare minimum of furniture. **Masato** *enters in his morning garb. He stretches before taking off his* yukata *to put on a shirt and pants.* **Aiko** *enters opposite. She is dressed in casual western clothing. She is obviously happy.*

Aiko *(no accent): Akemashite omedeto gozaimasu! (Rushes over and kisses him on cheek)*

Masato *(surprised but happy)*: *A-re!* Okay. Okay. Happy New Year!

Aiko: Oh Masato, it's such a wonderful time of year! All the businesses are closed. We're together at home. I feel like a newlywed!

Masato *(chuckles)*: Newlywed! We have a five year old child!

Aiko: I know, but we never get to spend time together. We're too busy with our jobs. But not today. No morning rush hour. Listen, it's so quiet out there.

Masato: Well, this is a tall building.

Aiko: No, everyone's home getting ready to celebrate *Oshogatsu*. I still have to make the *inari sushi* for your parents' place. I can't wait to buy a house. Then everyone can come over to our place.

Masato: All in due time.

Aiko *(coyly)*: Maybe when we have a second boy?

Masato *(smiles and puts his arms around his wife)*: Well, I suppose *Oshogatsu* is one of the few times I get to be with you and Kentaro all day.

Aiko: Sit down. I made some *ozoni*.

Masato: Really? Great. *(chortles)* Ah, I hate that stuff. It tastes like paste.

Aiko: You have to eat it. If you don't, we'll have bad luck all year round.

Masato: Well of course I'll eat it! *(Tries to eat* ozoni. *The consistency is too pasty for his taste. Chokes a bit. With difficulty, he speaks.)* Where's Ken-*chan*?

Aiko: Hiding.

Masato: Hiding? Why?

Aiko: He saw me making the *ozoni*.

Masato *(laughs)*: What a kid! Like father, like son.

Aiko: Wouldn't it be nice to have a second one?

Masato *(stares at her but says nothing)*: Hey, I taped Kohaku last night. *(stands and goes to the television set and turns it and the VCR on)* Sawada, Kenji! Wow, he's still singing? He's so great! *(Begins singing along to "I Can't Get No Satisfaction" by the Rolling Stones.)*

Aiko *(as if smiling to herself)*: You and your singing. Now where is that boy? Ken-*chan!* Ken-*chan!* Your *ozoni* is ready!

(music and lights fade)

SCENE TWO

Light on **Detective**.

Detective (*still on telephone*): It's not clear what the motivation was. Nothing was taken. I found a hundred dollars in a bedroom drawer. There's no obvious signs of break-in. A window was open, but no broken glass, all doors locked. (*pauses, listens*) Yeah, I'm checking into their background. So far, I learned they come from Tokyo. That's all. 'Bout a year ago spring time. During this month in fact. Yeah, the landlord told me. Okay, okay, I'm on my way in. I'll fill you in more when I get there.

(*Lighting change*)

Voice over: *Ca-na-da ni iki taku nai!* (*Phrase repeated several times and overlapped in several different ways.*)

Aiko: *Ca-na-da ni iki taku nai!* But I don't want to go to Canada!

Masato: Shhh! You'll wake Ken-*chan*. Now don't be ridiculous. You'll like it there. We'll have the good life. A big house. Ken-*chan* can have his own T.V. in his room. And we can buy a car. A luxury Toyota! Trips! We'll go on trips and see all the things we've read about! Banff Springs. Disneyland in California. Dollywood!

Aiko: We can save money to do all those things here. We both have good jobs. We saved for this house. We can save for the good life.

Masato: But in Canada, we'll have the good life now, not in thirty years! You won't have to work. With my English, I'll make enough for us to live on. Ken-*chan* won't be a latchkey kid any more. I've never felt good about that. He's only eight years old. He should come home to a clean house and his waiting mother.

Aiko: That's not what you said when we married. You didn't want a wife just sitting here waiting for you to return. Too much pressure on you to do well, you said. You encouraged me to keep my computer programmer job even after we bought this place. "Make use of your college education. Be a *ka-ri-a wo-man.*" I didn't want to keep working, but I listened to you and did as you said.

Masato: That was before. Don't you see, going to Canada fulfills all our dreams. We'll have a big house, a nice car and make long trips. Ken-*chan*'ll have a good education with all opportunities open for him. He won't have to go to school six days a week and then Cram school at night and weekends. His fate won't be sealed at eighteen when he fails the entrance exams and has to go to an inferior college. He won't have to work 9 to 5 every day and then work overtime until 10 o'clock for some miserable little trading company that doesn't care about its employees. He won't end up not knowing his family. Better still, he won't die of *karoshi* at the age of forty-two.

Aiko: Are you sure you're not thinking about something else?

(**Masato** *looks at her, puzzled.*)

Aiko: Of yourself, maybe?

Masato: You mean my *karaoke?*

Aiko: You and your *karaoke.* You think you can be Neil Diamond in America.

Masato: And why not? America is the land of the free. All restrictions are off. Madonna! Star Trek! American Express! If I want to be the world's best *karaoke* singer, I can go for it!

Aiko: There are no famous *karaoke* singers from America.

Masato: How do you know? Maybe they're famous there.

Aiko: *Otoosan*, are you listening to yourself?

Masato: Okay, Okay. I know you're afraid to go. Me too! But I'm thirty-three years old. I got to try to make something of myself. Maybe not a *karaoke* singer, but I can be a someone. I can't do it here. In Canada, I know I've got a chance.

Aiko (*sighs*): You keep dreaming, *otoosan*. Keep on dreaming.

Song "I Am I Said" comes up. **Masato** *sings to the music. Music subsides and lights go to black.*

SCENE THREE

Single light on **Aiko,** *who is alone on stage.*

Aiko: Ken-*chan!* Ken-*chan!* Where is that boy? Oh there you are, you *yancha bozu. (laughs)* Come now. Sit and eat your *gohan. Otoosan* won't be home till late. Eat quickly, you know you have to study before you go to bed. Exams are less than a month away. Now no arguing. There's no time tomorrow with church and everything. Good thing you have Cram school during the week. *Naniyo?* What's all this fuss? Look, you're going to make me proud. You're not like your father. Oh, he works hard but his heart's not in it. He has ambition too, but not the right kind. He can never be what he wants in his head. *(shakes head)* Pie-in-the-sky wishes. You, you're such a smart boy, you're going to the University of Tokyo and then work for Mitsui Corporation. You'll work your way to a respected position some day. I don't expect you to understand, but remember, you are not like your father.

(**Sumiko**'s *voice is heard off stage*)

Sumiko: Aiko-*san!* Aiko-*san!*

Aiko: *Hai!* I'm here. Ken-*chan,* eat your dinner.

Sumiko *(enters with magazine in hand):* Oh! I didn't mean to disturb your eating.

Aiko: That's okay. *(turns to* **Ken-*chan*)** Take your food and go watch television. *(turns back to* **Sumiko)** Now, what's got you so excited?

Sumiko: Oh yes, I've got the latest *Bride Magazine.* Look, look! I found the exact dress I want! *(The two sit down as* **Sumiko** *points out the dress.)* Isn't it gorgeous?

Aiko: Sumiko, you can't wear this. The hemline's too short and the neckline's much too low.

Sumiko: Oh, you sound like my mother. She didn't like it either. We argued for days! I thought you'd be on my side. Give it another chance. Look at it. Just imagine me in it!

Aiko: You'll look like a stuffed turkey. Let's see what else is in this magazine. *(scans pages)* Ah, how about this one? A nice simple princess gown.

Sumiko *(looks before commenting)*: How many years ago were you married?

Aiko: Ten.

Sumiko: That dress is something my mother would pick out.

Aiko: Well, maybe she knows best. *(Put off, she turns away from the magazine.)*

Sumiko: Oh come on, don't be angry. I just want to look my absolute best. It's my one big chance to be beautiful.

Aiko *(ignores her)*: Yes, yes. So you don't like the princess gown?

Sumiko: Speaking of princess, look who's in this magazine.

Aiko: *A-ra!* Masako-*san*. She's so beautiful. She's going to be such a wonderful Princess.

Sumiko: She hasn't accepted the proposal yet.

Aiko: Who could turn down the Crown Prince?

Sumiko: She has for the past five years!

Aiko: It's only a matter of time. She's waiting for a good deal. On her terms.

Sumiko: She wears short skirts. Why can't I?

Aiko *(ignores her)*: A commoner. Harvard and Oxford educated. She really has a mind of her own.

Sumiko: I think she should stay single and commit to her career!

Aiko: Sumiko, why? I thought you were going to quit.

Sumiko *(thumbs through magazine as she speaks)*: Kohe thinks I should. Wouldn't be right, I should be at home with the kids. I think he might be embarrassed bossing around his wife at the Rental Agency. But I look at you. You're still working and you're happy.

Aiko: Well sure, but I thought life would be different. I'd like to stay home with Ken-*chan* and maybe have another baby. I'd like a bigger house with fine furniture. Someday, I'll have it my way.

Sumiko *(not listening)*: You know, I think Empress Michiko will take to her daughter-in-law right from the start.

Aiko: Why?

Sumiko: Remember, she was a commoner too. When she married Akihito, her mother-in-law looked down on her, always reminding her that she really didn't belong in the Imperial Court.

Aiko *(gossipy tone)*: Did you know that when Empress Michiko was single she thought about marriage with Yukio Mishima?

Sumiko: The writer? The one that ...

Aiko: That committed *hara-kiri*. The same one. She even went through an *omiai* with him.

Sumiko: He wanted an arranged marriage? I couldn't imagine marrying such a man. Too creepy. Good thing he didn't interview me for marriage! I would've said a few things to him!

Aiko: You would've been one year old, Sumiko!

Sumiko: Well, you know what I mean! He must have been out of his mind to kill himself. Especially like that!

Aiko: Oh, I don't know. Not that I approve, but Mishima-*san* saw himself as a *samurai* with an intense duty to the Emperor. For him, his path was clear once his duty was complete. Suicide was the only true choice.

Sumiko: Aiko-*san*, how can you say such things! Nothing he did was important to Japan. Only a few fanatics admired what he did. Anyway, why are we talking about such things? How's Masato doing? Is he still talking about moving to Canada?

Aiko: Of course. He even had me sign some papers about immigration or something.

Sumiko: What? You're going to miss my wedding!

Aiko: Sumiko, no no. It's just talk. We're not going.

Sumiko: But you signed papers!

Aiko: Over six months ago. Nothing's happened yet.

Sumiko: Geez! I was counting on you to be there for me! I can't talk to my mother. We argue all the time. I want the wedding to be red and white. She wants purple. I don't want a kimono. She does. I want a Christian ceremony. She says Shinto is the best.

Aiko: Wait a minute, Shinto is the best. We're all born Shinto, marry Christian and die Buddhist! How can you go against tradition!

Sumiko: See, I need you to tell me things like that! How am I going to get along with you in Canada?

Aiko: I'm staying, for crying out loud.

Sumiko: How about after I'm married? Who's going to give me advice about kids, about house finances, about controlling my husband?

Aiko: I am! Masato says and does a lot of silly things but he never means anything by them. He says he wants to be a professional *karaoke* singer in America. You think I take that seriously? I just humour him until he settles down and forgets. You'll see after you're married. It'll be the same.

Sumiko: Professional *karaoke* singer? In America with all those big, rude red meat eaters? Never heard of such a thing. *Karaoke* is Japanese. Masato and you are Japanese. This is Japan! Canada is not Japan.

Aiko: Sumiko, you're not listening. We are not going.

Sumiko: How can you be so sure?

Aiko: I sign the cheques.

Sumiko: Oh.

Music starts. **Aiko** *and* **Sumiko** *continue to look at the magazine and gossip. Lights go to black.*

SCENE FOUR

Lights come up on **Detective**.

Detective *(paces stage as if in Captain's office)*: I tell you, Captain, I'm really spooked about this one. When I got assigned to the Chinatown Task Force, I thought, good hours, good food. Maybe I'd come across some extortion, a few family disputes, some teenage drug busts, but nothing like this. *(pause)* Yeah well, I found a mask in the bathtub, below the body of the woman. What the hell it was doing there in the first place I don't know. It was cracked in two. *(pause)* No, no. A devil's mask. The mask of a devil.

(Lights come up on **Masato** *and* **Aiko***)*

Masato: Stupid or not, we're going to Canada. I handed in my resignation today.

Aiko *(shocked)*: What? What did your boss say?

Masato: He was surprised and told me to think about it for a couple of days. He probably thought I was *kichigai.*

Aiko: And did he say to talk to your wife?

Masato: No, why?

Aiko: So she could tell you you are crazy!

Masato *(suddenly angry)*: *Bakayaro!* Don't say such things to me. We're going to Canada!

Aiko: But I don't want to go.

Masato: So what? I'm not asking if you want to go. I'm telling you. You have no choice. You are my wife.

Aiko: But I don't want to go.

Masato *(ignores* **Aiko***'s protest)*: The papers are signed. The visas are here. I'm selling the house. We're going. *(walks away)* Taking pictures of Niagara Falls! I bet we can take the car to see Anne of Green Gables! I can even go to Las Vegas and enter the World Championship *Karaoke* Contest! Viva Las Vegas! *(sings the phrase from the song and then laughs as he exits)*

Aiko *(in a whisper)*: But I don't want to go.

*Lights dim. Single light on **Aiko**. She is crying, but she tries to hide the fact when she is disturbed by her friend **Sumiko**.*

Sumiko: Aiko-*san?* Aiko-*san,* are you ho ... Oh, I'm sorry, I ...

Aiko: No. No, Sumiko, come in. Sit down. *(pauses to compose self)* Here, let me make you some tea.

Sumiko: What's wrong? You were crying.

Aiko *(serves tea)*: No, I wasn't crying. I was ... oh, the hell with tea. You want some *sake?*

Sumiko: *Sake?* Now? *(Looks at watch.)* I just came from church.

Aiko *(gets bottle and serves a portion to **Sumiko** cold)*: Sure, why not? I hope you don't mind it cold.

Sumiko: No. I guess not. No, not so much. *(serves **Aiko**)*

Aiko *(sips slowly and sighs)*: Truth is, Masato quit his job Friday. We have to pack and get ready to move to Canada.

(The two pour for one another and continue to drink.)

Sumiko: Move to Canada? But I thought that was all talk.

Aiko: I thought so too. But the visas came through, so we can go anytime within a year.

Sumiko: I can't believe it. Does he really think he can be a *karaoke* star over there?

Aiko: I guess so.

Sumiko: Is he that good?

(Instrumental version of "Someone to Watch Over Me" is heard)

Aiko: When I first met him, he sang me a song in the college coffee house. "Someone to Watch Over Me," I think it was. You know, the way the light hit his face ... he sang just for me that night. That's what really got to me.

Sumiko *(tentative)*: Aiko-*san*, is there something wrong with Masato?

Aiko: What?

Sumiko: Such an odd thing to do. To pick up and leave just like that. Maybe he needs ... help, maybe?

Aiko *(infers meaning and becomes angry)*: Sumiko, how could you say such a thing? There's nothing wrong with Masato. Nothing a good slap in the head wouldn't cure!

Sumiko *(laughs)*: I'm sorry, but why does he want to go so badly?

Aiko *(pauses to compose self again)*: I don't know why. I don't want to go. All I know is everyone is against me. My boss was happy to let me go. He thinks I should be with my son on a full time basis! Well, I do too but not in a foreign country! Who will Kentaro play with? How will he make friends? Who will help me to raise him properly? I thought at least my mother would be on my side. She just thought it was a good idea. She said Masato lets me get away with too much. *(mimics mother)* You're not a devoted enough wife! You're not a good mother. You're just spoiled. You shouldn't work, she says. Nag, nag, nag. As if working was my idea! Do you know that she prepares ready-to-eat meals for us to freeze and eat later?

Sumiko: Well, that's nice.

Aiko: Guilt. She makes me feel guilty. She does it on purpose! Old fashioned old ... How can moving to Canada cure me of being a spoiled wife?

Sumiko: Why don't you tell Masato how you feel?

Aiko: How I feel? Why should he care about how I feel? He says, we live on his income! He makes the big decisions! *(She pauses and becomes reflective.)* I always wanted to visit America, never to live there.

(Man in devil's mask briefly appears on stage.)

SCENE FIVE

Light comes up on **Detective** *in Captain's office.*

Detective *(checks notes)*: The bodies were found by the landlord and the husband's boss, a Mrs. Harrison, owner of the Murasaki Restaurant on Avenue Road, at about 4:30 yesterday afternoon. Mass hadn't shown up for work for the 2:30 shift and no one was picking up the phone at home. Officer on the scene told me this Mrs. Harrison was pretty upset but together enough to give a preliminary statement. She seems to be a take-charge kind of person. In the first place, she rousted the landlord who lives up the street. She made him come down and open the door to the first floor flat. The landlord couldn't believe she was doing this. He thought she was imagining things. The scene was pretty grisly, but Harrison was the one to call us. When I got there, she was gone. I'm on my way to talk to her now. You have her preliminary statement.

Lights come up on **Setsuko Harrison** *working at the restaurant.* **Detective** *walks into scene.*

Detective: Excuse me. *(looks at notebook)* You Set ... Set-sue? Damn, whoever thought you could put an "s u" after a "t"? Chinese names were never this hard.

Harrison *(with accent)*: I'm not Chinese. The name is Setsuko. Se-tsu-ko. Pronounce it like it's spelled.

Detective *(begins to pull out I.D.)*: Right. I'm here ...

Harrison: You are here to ask about my employee, Masato Shinde? Such a waste. It was so horrible. I don't believe the gossip.

Detective: Excuse me?

Harrison: That it was Vietnamese gang members.

Detective *(sits down)*: Gang members? Why gang members?

Harrison: Masato was good worker. He made ready all the vegetables for the cook. He liked to do any work you ask. He learned quickly. He even bring his own knives!

Detective: Yes, but ...

Harrison: He used amphetamines.

Detective: So you think it was Vietnamese ...

Harrison: I don't think! I don't believe for a second. Everybody know restaurant worker use the drugs to keep going but not Masato. Others think so, but that's wishful thinking.

Detective: Wishful thinking?

Harrison: You don't know the Japanese, do you?

Detective: Well, no. I usually work in Chinatown ...

Harrison: What paper you work for in Chinatown?

Detective *(shows I.D.)*: I'm not a reporter. I'm a police detective with the Chinatown Task Force.

Harrison: Good. You wouldn't last too long working for the *Ming Pao Daily News!*

Detective: Why would you think I'm a reporter?

Harrison: Why do you think I'm Chinese?

Detective *(slightly indignant)*: I don't ...

Harrison *(smiles)*: Police already talked to me yesterday.

Detective: Right. So what about the Japanese?

Harrison: Japanese gossip too much. They don't want shame coming to them. So they make things up. Lie about everything. They'll say anything to avoid shame. "No Japanese would do that!" "Vietnamese gang did it when Masato couldn't find money he owed them for drug."

Detective: What're you getting at?

Harrison: No Vietnamese, Chinese or whatever did this. It was family trouble.

Detective: Why do you think that?

Harrison: Because of the wife ...

Lights dim. Off stage voices of Japanese community members:
– "No Japanese would do that."
– "He was on drugs."
– "Chinese gangs killed them."
– "Why did they have to come here and bring shame to us? Why didn't they stay in Japan?"

SCENE SIX

Light on **Detective**. *He is talking to the Captain.*

Detective: That Mrs. Harrison was sure right about one thing: the Japanese are into self-denial. Mass Shin-die was a steady worker but liked to keep to himself most of the time. Harrison never met A-ko but talked to her on the phone a few times. She feels the whole thing was due to "family trouble." But some things just don't add up. The bedroom window was wide open. A next door neighbour heard a scuffle just after midnight but didn't hear any screams or shouts for help. A circuit breaker was thrown for no apparent reason. Harrison swears Mass didn't use drugs, but drug use is common practice among restaurant workers. And there's a lot of drug activity in Chinatown these days. If this was the result of "family trouble," sure beats me how the mother was able to stab her husband 33 times so easily and then strangle her kid. Now that really gets me. I mean, how could she kill her own kid?

(lights go to black)

A journey is represented on stage. Scene opens with luggage set on stage. **Mass** *enters and picks up luggage. He is excited and anxious to get going. He gestures for* **Aiko** *to come along.* **Aiko** *enters. She is holding* **Kentaro**'s *hand. As she reluctantly follows* **Mass**, *she sadly looks at their home one last time. The couple then walk around the stage until they end in front of the official.*

Before the immigration official, **Aiko** *is fussing with* **Kentaro**, *who is playing with a Gameboy.*

Aiko: Ken-*chan!* Please put that away.

Official: Well, your immigration papers are in order. How much money are you bringing with you? Over $10,000?

Masato *(with accent)*: About $50,000. We sold house in Tokyo.

Aiko: Ken-*chan* please!

Masato: Kentaro. *Yakamashi!*

Official: Sign this declaration of goods and that'll be it. Welcome to Canada.

Masato *(in Japanese accent)*: Where we go now?

Official: Anywhere you want. The shuttle bus outside will drop you off in front of any downtown hotel. *(he points)*

Masato: Thank you. *(accent ends and turns to* **Aiko***)* Okay, we go.

Aiko: To where? Isn't anyone going to help us?

(The couple exit with child in tow.)

SCENE SEVEN

Light comes up on **Detective**.

Detective: So the Shin-die family started life in this country at the Chelsea Inn. They stayed about a week until they found the Cecil Street flat. Must have been a real head-spinning experience for them.

Lights come up on **Setsuko Harrison** *working at the restaurant. She addresses detective.*

Harrison *(with accent)*: I immigrate to Canada over twenty 'ears ago. I marry Canadian who was in Japan on a scholarship. He die about ten 'ears ago. He was a good man. That's when I opened the restaurant. Business is good. Everything not always so good. When I first came here, I was afraid of everything. I got lost in Eaton Centre the first time there. I walked and walked until I have to sit down. Imagine if you come to this *gaijin* country without good knowledge of English. I couldn't ask anybody for direction. Lucky for me Eaton Centre only goes one way! Up and down! I was lucky, my husband was a Canadian. I had a place to stay and I didn't need a job. But English is so hard to learn. Rules don't make sense. Once I talk to Canadian friend. I was angry about my husband not come home. My friend say, "Why are you so mad?" Mad? Mad? I am not mad. How could she say such a thing to me? I don't know mad mean angry too. Masato and Aiko, they come from Tokyo middle class. The immigration department feel they don't need help. When they came to Toronto, there were no services for them to turn to. No temporary house. No English lesson. No information about health and placement services.

(**Detective** *leaves stage. Image of woman in* yukata *with head bowed and on her knees. Sword is by her side on ground.*)

It is really terrible. Just a little help could have prevented so much tragedy.

(*Lights open as* **Masato** *enters stage.* **Harrison** *begins cutting vegetables at the restaurant.*)

Masato: Excuse me please.

Harrison (*gruff – with no accent*): Yes?

Masato: I ... I am sorry to bother ...

Harrison: How many times are you going to apologize to me? You Japanese, you're so Japanese!

Masato: I'm sorry.

Harrison: A-a-aw! (*frustrated and then calms herself*) You're here about the kitchen helper's job in the *Nikkei Voice* newspaper.

Masato: Yes, I am. Is it that obvious?

Harrison: You've got "newcomer" written all over you. Besides, customers don't come in through the kitchen.

Masato: My name is Shinde Masato. I just came here with my wife and son last week.

Harrison: Yes, yes. Do you have any restaurant experience?

Masato: No, but I have my own knives. I heard cooks bring their own knives ...

Harrison: Well you've got initiative. I like that. You start tomorrow. 2:30 to 11:30 at night, five nights a week. Every Wednesday and Sunday off. Your wife going to mind?

Masato: No, no. What's the pay?

Harrison: Good. You learn fast. You're acting like a Canadian. You don't share in the tips, but you'll make enough to live on. Don't look so disappointed. You don't intend to be a kitchen helper the rest of your life, do you?

Masato: No. I want to be a *karaoke* singer!

Harrison: *Karaoke* singer? *(laughs)* Are you serious? *(sees he is)* Well, Shinjuku Karaoke Bar is right around the corner. Maybe you'll be discovered there as the next Barry Manilow!

Masato: Barry Manilow!!!?

Harrison: Enough. Enough. I have too much work to do. I'll see you tomorrow. (**Masato** *leaves.* **Harrison** *chuckles to herself.*) *Karaoke* singer!

SCENE EIGHT

Lights change to emphasize **Detective** *talking to Captain.*

Detective: Eventually, the Shin-dies moved into the Cecil Street apartment. Money didn't seem to be a problem. Besides the job at Murasaki Restaurant, Mass had plenty of money in the bank. You know, Captain, I'm starting to feel sorry for that wife. With the husband either working or sleeping, he spent little time with her and his own kid. A-ko must have gone a little stir crazy, not knowing English and having no friends. No chance for a job. I doubt I woulda gone out myself in that situation.

Light comes up on couple. **Aiko** *sits centre stage.* **Masato** *is busy running around her gathering his work materials.*

Aiko: *Otoosan,* do you have to go to work today?

Masato: That's a stupid question. Of course I've got to go to work today. What're you thinking? Hey, where are my knives? Do you know where I put them?

Aiko: We've been here about three months and I never get to spend time with you. I'm kind of lonely.

Masato: Lonely? There's Kentaro.

Aiko: But he's in school most of the time. Maybe we can take him out. It is summer vacation!

Masato: You know Kentaro needs to learn English. Be ready for public school in the fall. Come on, have you seen my knives? You never complained about being lonely in Japan.

Aiko: In Japan, I had lots of friends. Sumiko was always dropping by to see how I was. I went out with girlfriends from work. Here, there's no one. The neighbours are all *gaijin*. They don't understand me. They don't speak Japanese.

Masato: Well then, learn English like me!

Aiko: Learn English? That's not the point. I don't belong here. Can't you see that? Everything is so ... so different. I went to Eaton Department store last week. The clerks were so unfriendly. No one would offer to help me. They just shouted at me and shoved a bottle of *kusai* perfume under my nose. In Japanese department stores, the clerks smile at you. They say, *"Hai! Irasshai-mase. Welcome to Seibu Department Store. Ladies' fashion is on the second floor. The latest from Kenzo and Yamato are featured."* And the buses and subways! They are the worst! At home, the stops are announced. Here, I have to guess where I am. I get lost all the time. No one says anything. When I came home from Eaton, the bus was packed with foreigners. Chinese, Indian ... a negro sat beside me! Canada is full of dirty immigrants.

Masato: This is just nonsense. Ah, there they are! *(points behind screen)* Look, I've got to go now. We'll talk about this later.

Aiko: I'm afraid.

Masato: Afraid? Afraid of what?

Aiko: I'm afraid to be here alone at night.

Masato: That's nothing to be afraid of.

Aiko: Someone might break in here.

Masato: What?

Aiko: It's easy, you know. The windows are easy to break and the door is weak.

Masato: You're just paranoid. Look, I'll be late from work tonight. There's a *karaoke* contest at Shinjuku's after the restaurant closes.

Aiko: Could I come?

Masato: You? Oh no, you'd be bored. And it's so late.

Aiko: But I'd like to see you win. You're forever bragging how you win these things.

Masato: No. You stay at home where you belong. You're forgetting Ken-*chan. (motions to leave)*

Aiko: Are they pretty?

Masato *(stops):* Who?

Aiko: The Working Holiday girls.

Masato *(pauses):* What do you mean?

Aiko: I figured they must be there for you to go so much.

Masato *(angry): Bakayaro! (turns back)*

Aiko *(in a timid voice):* It's just that ... it's just that we never ... you don't ...

Masato: Stop! Put those stupid thoughts out of your head. I go to Shinjuku to sing. That's all. I'm going now. Don't wait up for me. *(exits)*

Aiko: *Otoosan,* don't leave. I didn't mean it. I just want you to stay home. Please don't leave. *(pause, and then turns to audience – lights narrow to a spot on her – she hangs her head)*

SCENE NINE

Aiko *is seen writing a letter. When she completes it, she reads it to audience.*

Aiko: Dear Sumiko, Canada is full of *gaijin.* I hate them, I hate them all. I stay at home most of the time. It wouldn't be so bad if I had someone to care for. Another baby ... but Masato wouldn't hear of it. He won't even discuss the possibility. I tried to go to the Buddhist Church the other day. I thought I could talk to someone.

I miss the sound of Japanese! Gossiping with you. Laughing at work with my co-workers. Even arguing at my mother's place about the meals she made for us. It's so hard to meet anyone at that church. The *nikkei* are so unfriendly. They're not real Japanese anyway. They're like white ghosts. I don't speak English and they don't know Japanese. I've been having a recurring dream lately. A dream about the *onibaba*. You remember the children's story. Scared me half to death! I know mother did it to keep me under the covers at night. Aiko-*chan*, she would say, it was the time of the feudal wars. *(stands to tell story)*

Aiko *(as mother)*: *Samurai* generals fought *samurai* generals. Kyoto was in flames and the emperor fled to Mount Yoshino. There were no sides. Just gangs of mercenaries roaming the country until they ran into others to do battle. In the high grass plains about 50 miles from Kyoto, there lived a woman named Harumi. A great general came and took away her husband and son. "Please don't go!" she pleaded with her husband. "How can I survive? How can you leave? Glory? Riches? What good are glory and riches to a dead wife?" But they left, drawn into battle by golden promises. Harumi's fate was not to die, however. With war comes opportunities.

Aiko: Sumiko, I don't know why I'm dreaming about *onibaba* now, but I am. *(sits down, exasperated)* I can't sleep because of it. I haven't had a good night's sleep in weeks. Masato is ... Masato ...

Crumples paper and throws it away. Lights go to black.

Man with devil's mask appears briefly.

SCENE TEN

Light comes up on **Detective** *and* **Ms. Henry**.

Detective: Hello, you the Vice Principal here?

Ms. Henry: Yes, I'm Melanie Henry.

Detective *(shows I.D.)*: I'm from the Chinatown Task Force.

Ms. Henry: Oh yes, you called earlier.

Detective: Yeah, I'm here to ask you about *(refers to notepad)* Mass and A-ko Shin-die.

Ms. Henry: The Shinde family? Yes, a very sad case.

Detective: How'd you say that last name again?

Ms. Henry: Shin-de.

Detective: Shinde. Okay, thanks. What's your connection with them?

Ms. Henry: Their son, Ken, was causing a lot of trouble here at Cecil Street Public School. I suppose it's understandable.

Detective: What do you mean?

Ms. Henry: Well, Ken came to us last September with only a basic command of English. He had some ESL under his belt through some summer courses but not enough to be accepted by the other students.

Detective: But you got mostly Oriental kids here. They're all in the same boat, so to speak.

Ms. Henry: Children can be so cruel. *(said pointedly)* His classmates quickly picked on Ken because he was Japanese. The only one in the school. He wasn't one of them and he couldn't even communicate in English. So he started to get into fights and disrupting classes. He was a real discipline problem.

Detective: What did you do about it?

Ms. Henry: What we normally do, I called the parents.

Detective: And what did you find?

Ms. Henry: Mrs. Shinde came here and I talked to her, or rather I talked at her. She never looked up at me. I couldn't get more than two words out of her, even when I brought in a translator.

Detective: What happened in the end?

Ms. Henry: Well, I got tacit agreement that she would do something. More like a nod of the head. Then she did something strange. She went into the lunch room with Ken.

Aiko: Ken-*chan*, you mustn't fight with others. It doesn't matter whose fault it is. Your behaviour makes your father and me look bad, and in front of Chinese! Is this the one you fought with? This one? This one? It doesn't matter, it's all so embarrassing. *(bows to student and speaks with an accent)* I sorry for Kentaro fight. Sorry. Sorry. *(breaks accent)* Stop yelling, Ken-*chan* ... please ... speak Japanese to me ... you know Japanese ... speak to me ... *(follows son off stage)*

Detective: How about the husband? Did you talk to him?

Ms. Henry: Soon after his wife. I had to call him in from the restaurant where he works.

(Light opens on **Ms. Henry** *and* **Masato.***)*

Ms. Henry: Mr. Shinde, Ken is such a discipline problem, I'm going to have to suggest something to you.

Masato *(in accent)*: Oh, you should talk to my wife about Kentaro.

Ms. Henry: That's the trouble, Mr. Shinde. I can't get through to her. She doesn't understand anything I say.

Masato: Oh? Well, she has trouble with English.

Ms. Henry: It's more than just a little "trouble with English," Mr. Shinde. Perhaps ... forgive me for saying this, but perhaps you should consider taking her to your family doctor or seek out family counselling.

Masato: What?

Ms. Henry: Given your son's attitude and your wife's odd behaviour ...

Masato *(suddenly angry)*: We don't need that kind of help. Forget about it.

Ms. Henry: But Mr. Shinde ...

Masato: Please, I don't want to talk any more!

*(***Masato*** gets up and leaves. Scene shifts back to* **Detective** *and* **Ms. Henry.***)*

Ms. Henry: I can't blame him for being angry.

Detective: Why not?

Ms. Henry: I stepped over the bounds of discretion. A complete stranger tells him there might be something wrong with his wife. I mean, I meant well but I shouldn't have ...

Detective: You think she was crazy?

Ms. Henry: Well, we'll never know now.

Detective: Do you think she was capable of murder and suicide?

Ms. Henry: Oh no. No. She may have been mentally distressed, but to the point of murder? Suicide? I doubt it. Mrs. Shinde was a frail young thing. She didn't seem strong enough. Look, even if she had the strength and wherewithal to kill her husband, how could she turn around and kill her son? What mother could do that? All that and suicide? I don't think so.

Detective: When did you see the family last?

Ms. Henry: Six months ago, before the Christmas break.

Detective: Six months? A long time to contemplate death.

Man in mask appears and walks across stage as if searching for his way. Draws his sword when he sees something in the distance.

SCENE ELEVEN

Lights come up on **Detective**. **Mrs. Harrison** *brings in tea.*

Detective: Mrs. Harrison?

Harrison *(with accent)*: Setsuko.

Detective: Right. Can I ask you a few more questions?

Harrison: You already start.

Detective *(chuckles)*: You said you talked to ... A-ko?

Harrison: Ai-ko.

Detective: You said you talked to "Aiko" a few times on the phone. What about?

Harrison: Hey, you pronounce Japanese good!

Detective: About time, eh?

Harrison: Yes. Aiko started to call here looking for Masato about three months after he start.

Detective: Why?

Harrison: Husband and wife things.

Detective: How did she sound?

Harrison: She sound like she worried. She was afraid of someone breaking into her house. Another time, she said she was unhappy at the Buddhist Church. No one would talk to her there. Reverend Shimizu, he try but he the only one. I know Buddhist people are unfriendly to "newcomers."

Detective: She told you about all that?

Harrison (*smiles*): Yes, I'm very friendly. I could get the dead to talk about themselves. (*becomes self-conscious*) Sorry, that not very nice.

Detective: You never met her?

Harrison: No, never. I once went over to her house and knocked on the door. There was no answer but I think I heard her inside.

Detective: Why'd you go over?

Harrison: I thought she could use a friend.

Detective: When was the last time you talked to her?

Harrison: The day she died.

Detective (*pauses before continuing*): There are some things I don't get. Why was Ken such a problem for Aiko?

Harrison: In Japan, mothers let their sons do anything. Sons are so precious, they get away with everything. No bedtime. No discipline. Make noise all the time. But when school start, mother make boy study, study, study. Aiko probably the same until she come to Canada.

Detective: Yeah. So?

Harrison: Kentaro learn English and forget about Japanese. She didn't learn English. Aiko no longer have control over her son. She became completely shut off from him.

Detective: So she was totally alone. Do you think she was out of her mind?

Harrison: If she was, nobody know even if they live in Japan. "Out of her mind" is a outside problem caused by devils or fate. There's no real word for it in Japanese. People just ignore it. Maybe two years, maybe twenty years.

Detective: So Masato didn't help.

Harrison: He ignored everything. The problems at home, at school. Her fear.

Detective: Her fear?

Harrison: That something was going to happen.

SCENE TWELVE

Lights come up on **Masato** *with microphone in hand. He is singing "My Way."*

Aiko: Masato! Masato, where are you? Why did you do this to me? Where's my cosy apartment in Tokyo? *(looks around)* My house, it's so beautiful. A good and quiet life with two children and friends all around. Ken-*chan,* Ken-*chan,* don't run away. Masato, you broke my heart. I feel so ... I feel so humiliated ... *(begins to cry but then composes herself)* Sumiko, I should go out. I can't go out. Not to that church. Reverend Shimizu is spreading the word about me, I know it. Telling people that I'm afraid of burglars. That I can't take care of my own son. That I'm crazy. But Reverend Shimizu, he's the one, boy. He's the one.

Masato, why are you working all the time? *(brief sound of "My Way" is heard)* The idiot. *(wraps arms around self)* I'm so alone. Sumiko, I'm still dreaming about the *onibaba.* I haven't thought about the devil woman in years. I don't know why I'm dreaming about her now.

(Lighting change.)

*(***Aiko*** puts on yukata and begins to pantomime undressing dead samurai.)*

Aiko: Harumi was alone, frightened but determined not to die. With war comes opportunities. She took to taking the armour and swords of dead *samurai* and selling them to arms merchants. In time, when hunger tore at her stomach, she began killing wounded *samurai* before stripping them of their armour. All went well until one night as she ate her millet dinner.

SCENE THIRTEEN

Aiko as Harumi *sits centre stage in a pool of light. She is eating a bowl of millet. She hears a noise. She reaches for a sword and stands.*

Harumi: Who's there? I know someone is there. Show yourself.

Samurai *enters, dressed in a* yukata *and wearing a devil's mask.* **Harumi** *steps back, so frightened she drops her sword.*

Samurai: Don't be afraid. I'm a man, not a devil. I wear the mask for my own good reasons.

Harumi: Who – who are you?

Samurai: I am a *samurai* of the second rank in the emperor's court. My men and I were separated in battle. I'm lost. I was hoping you would lead me to the road back to Kyoto.

Harumi: Go north and you'll find it.

Samurai: Show me. It's getting too dark to find my way.

Harumi: Once I take you there, you'll kill me!

Samurai: What glory is there in killing a peasant?

Harumi: You might be a devil that takes pleasure in killing.

Samurai: I've seen enough death.

Harumi: You wear the mask of a devil.

Samurai: I look strong with it on.

Harumi: There's no battle here in the middle of the night. You just look foolish. I'll wager you lost, didn't you?

Samurai: Yes, I lost the battle. This is my punishment. I'm alone, defeated and humiliated before a peasant woman.

Harumi: Let me see your face. I'll lead you to the road, but first show it to me.

Samurai: My face? I wear the mask to hide it.

Harumi: Why? Are you ashamed of it?

Samurai: No, I have the most handsome face in all of Kyoto. Such beauty should not be scarred in battle.

Harumi: The battle is over. So show it to me. As payment.

Samurai: You would faint if you saw my beautiful face.

Harumi: I've not seen anything beautiful in a long time. Perhaps not since my son was born. Show me.

Samurai: You want to see it?

Harumi: Show me.

Samurai: A face to fall in love with?

Harumi: I'm so alone here. Give me something to live for.

Samurai *(pause)*: It's not a face to show peasant women. I won't reveal it to you. Take me to the road or I will kill you. *(draws sword)*

(**Harumi** *picks up her sword as both leave stage.*)

SCENE FOURTEEN

Light on **Detective** *(he is talking to Captain).*

Detective: This case is starting to get to me. The thought of that poor woman, frightened, alone. I run into a lot of domestic cases down in Chinatown. There was a restaurant worker living in a flophouse, sleeping in a single bed during the day until he had to go to work. His wife came home from her job in a small-time garment factory and slept in the same bed until her husband came home early in the morning. Not even enough money to buy a double bed. The poverty and schedule drove him nuts. He finally exploded and accused her of cheating on him. Broke her jaw and her arm in three places. But she's still with him. What choice does she have? With no money or English, she can't even find out how to leave the guy. I never figured the Japanese could get that way too. I mean, you never hear much about them in the first place. They're so successful, you gotta figure they got no problems. The women in Japan probably think it's normal not seeing their husbands too much, but here, neglect can lead to wife abuse. Aiko was abused, no doubt in my mind, but could she have done such a thing? What did it take to push her so far? Answer me that, Captain. I wish I knew.

(**Aiko** *is flat on her back. She speaks in a very flat tone of voice. Sound of a clock ticking.*)

Aiko: Sumiko? Sumiko, are you there? I can't sleep. I'm so tired. All the time. I can't deal with Kentaro any more. He growls at me in English. So irritating. *(mimics him) Pe-la, pe-la, pe-la.* Sleep. I wish I could sleep. I don't know what's wrong with me. I'm exhausted. I feel empty. Nothing to give. I feel like I can't do anything.

SCENE FIFTEEN

*Lights come up on **Masato** at one side of the stage. He stands singing to the karaoke version of "Viva Las Vegas" by Elvis.*

(music fades)

Masato *(talks to a friend):* I love this country. You will too. Toronto is so humid in the summer and cold in the winter. Like Tokyo! It's exciting, too. The night clubs. The Blue Jays! And there's *karaoke* or *kerry-oh-key* as *gaijin* say! I am the best *karaoke* singer in this city! Maybe even in the country! Elvis. Neil Diamond. Stevie Wonder. I can be any of them. I'm very popular here at Shinjuku. I especially like meeting the young Working Holiday girls. Canada and Japan have set up a good deal for them but those girls are so stupid about American ways. So naive. They take up with any *gaijin* who knows a few phrases of Japanese. I see them on Yonge Street giggling about someone saying *"Ohayoo gozaimasu."* They end up loaning hundreds of dollars they'll never see again or they're attacked and raped. I feel sorry for them.

(He turns and speaks as if to a woman.)

You like my singing? I'm not very good at it, but thank you. How much longer are you here in Canada? Oh that long? Can I buy you a drink?

Light on **Aiko** *who sits on her legs. Sound of a clock ticking.*

Aiko: Sumiko! Stop talking about suicide! Maybe I should take Ken-*chan* and go back to Japan! But what would I do when I get there? Masato's family wouldn't have me. My family wouldn't understand. I'd be disowned. *(sighs)* I'm not strong enough to bear the shame of a failed marriage. Suicide. It seems the only thing left. The madness has to stop. It's my right. Mishima-*san* saw the path clear once he completed his task. He raised the knife toward the heavens and then plunged it into his stomach. The bright disk of the sun soared up and exploded before his eyelids. *(pause)* What about Ken-*chan*? He can't live without a mother. No. Not suicide. I'm too depressed to commit suicide.

SCENE SIXTEEN

Lights come up on **Detective**.

Detective: The first of the month, Aiko paid the rent with a cheque delivered directly to the landlord. This month she either forgot or just decided not to pay. A week later, another strange incident occurred.

Lights come up on **Aiko**. *She is sitting centre stage.* **Masato** *is off stage calling her name. Enters stage and confronts* **Aiko**.

Masato *(angry)*: What do you think you're doing?

Aiko: What?

Masato: You taped all the drawers in the house shut! *(moves to look elsewhere)* And you've taken all my kitchen knives! What do you mean by all this?

Aiko: I want you to stay home. You have to stay home.

Masato: Why? You think a little tape and some misplaced knives will keep me here? You must be crazy.

Aiko: Stay home! Be my husband. Be Kentaro's father.

Masato: I am Ken's father ...

Aiko (*explodes with anger*): Kentaro! His name is Kentaro! Not Ken. He's not a *gaijin!*

Masato: Hey, calm down. Calm down. Are you sick or something?

Aiko: Masato, please stay home tonight. I'm afraid.

Masato: Not that again.

Aiko: No, listen. I'm afraid of becoming an *onibaba*.

Masato: *Onibaba?* Don't be an idiot. Don't act crazy. I mean, you're not crazy. I didn't mean it. I said it because ... well I just said it.

Aiko: Sumiko knows how terrible you are to me.

Masato: What? What are you talking about?

Aiko: I told Sumiko everything. How you leave me all alone. How you turn my own son against me.

Masato: What? Did you call her all the way to Tokyo? That's a lot of money!

Aiko: No, I didn't call her. I talked to her yesterday. Here. Right here. She lives next door, you know.

Masato: Aiko, Sumiko is in Japan. We haven't seen her in almost a year. Look, stop all this nonsense. Maybe this Sunday we'll all go to a movie or something. (*exits*)

(**Aiko** *begins to cry as she dons a* yukata.)

Aiko: Harumi was afraid of the *samurai* as she led him towards the north road to Kyoto. However, the more she thought about her situation, the more she became angry.

(**Samurai** *in mask enters stage. They walk and then suddenly she turns on him and draws her sword.*)

Harumi (*fight ensues*): You are a devil. You lead your men to their death, and then you torment peasants like me. The dead lose everything because the dead can't come back. I have lost everything. What does that make me? Men like you took my family away with promises of gold. Men like you watched them die. Men like you have led me to insanity. It's time to end this!

Harumi *suddenly lunges and deals a death blow with her sword in hand.* **The Samurai** *falls.* **Harumi** *goes to his side.* **The Samurai** *is still. She leans forward. His hand suddenly grabs her to him.*

Samurai: Thank you. The mask will come off now. *(dies)*

(**Harumi** *recoils in horror. She slowly comes back to the body.*)

Harumi: Now let's see the face to fall in love with.

(**Harumi** *pulls mask from the dead samurai's face.*)

Harumi: Huh? It's a face of madness? A face to kick at. *(laughs)*

Stands and studies the mask. She then tries it on. To her horror, she discovers she cannot remove it. She begins to scream.

Harumi: It won't come off! Why won't it come off? Why won't it come off?

Lights go to black.

SCENE SEVENTEEN

Light on **Detective**.

Detective: Mass was pretty upset over the incident. He walked in late and in a foul mood. At first he refused to talk about it, but as the day went on, he talked a blue streak. Witnesses say he couldn't stop for most of that night's shift. It's really unusual for a Japanese man to tell everybody about his wife's crazy behaviour, so I figure he suspected something was wrong with her. Still, he didn't do nothing about it! I can't understand what people keep saying to me. What shame is there in going to a doctor about stuff like this? Mrs. Harrison said she knew something was wrong right from the moment she saw him that day.

Lights come up on **Setsuko** *at the restaurant busy cleaning and cutting vegetables.* **Masato** *enters, obviously upset.*

Harrison *(no accent)*: Masato, you're late!

Masato: I know, I'm sorry. It couldn't be helped.

Harrison: You know we have to clean up after the lunch time crowd and get ready for dinner. We're behind now.

Masato: I said I was sorry. *(Finds a knife and begins to cut up the vegetables in earnest.)*

Harrison: Where are your knives?

Masato: My what?

Harrison: Knives. You always bring your own knives.

Masato: I guess I forgot them.

Harrison: Okay, Masato, what's going on? You never forget your knives. Something happen at home?

Masato: No. Nothing's wrong. I just got behind schedule, that's all.

Harrison: Masato. You're not yourself today.

Masato: I am so! Damn! *(cuts finger)*

Harrison: Here, let's take care of that. Sit down. *(She finds a cloth and wraps it around the finger.)* Now hold your finger up in the air to let the blood drain. Good, now tell me what's going on.

(Masato *remains silent.)*

Harrison: Do I have to phone your wife?

Masato: No. *(pause)*

Harrison: Well?

Masato: I don't know what to do. My wife is doing some strange things. I can't believe she tried to stop me from coming to work today! She taped all the drawers in the house shut! She hid my knives!

Harrison: *A-ra,* that is strange.

Masato: *(Tries to lower finger.* **Harrison** *forces it back up.)* And that's not all. She keeps the house immaculately clean. Even if I smudge something, she cleans it immediately. I can't even use the washroom without her right there to clean up after me. She says I expect it!

Harrison: Masato, have you thought about spending more time with your wife?

Masato: I spend too much time with her.

Harrison: No, I mean it. You should spend more time with her, especially on your days off.

Masato *is silent.*

Harrison: You go to Shinjuku too much. I know you spend all day every Wednesday there. Look, tomorrow, on your day off, you spend at home with your wife!

Masato *(scoffs):* Ah. I need to practise my *karaoke*.

Harrison *(scoffs):* You're pretty popular there. *(said in a knowing manner)* I know you like the attention, but your family needs you.

Masato *(insists):* I need to practise my *karaoke*.

Harrison: Then you should consider getting some help for your wife.

Masato: What? Why?

Harrison: Well, she doesn't sound like a normal person. I think she needs some counselling.

Masato: She's just lonely. All she has to do is go to school. Learn some English. That's all she needs to do. She'll make friends then and get out. Enjoy life.

Harrison: She needs more than English lessons. Let me phone the Japanese Counselling Service for you. *(Goes to telephone and starts dialling.)* They don't have a lot of services, but maybe someone there can put you in touch with the right people.

Masato: "Right people"? Right people for what? Hey, put down that phone, please! I'm not talking to those kind of people.

Harrison: But your wife needs help.

Masato: You think my wife needs that kind of help? She's not going crazy.

Harrison: Who said anything about going crazy?

Masato: Look, you're my boss but I don't need you to tell me how to handle my wife. Thanks for your concern, but don't insult me and my family by bringing up these suspicions. She's not touched in the head. She's just over-reacting to being in Canada. She just needs to get out more. That's all.

(**Masato** *leaves stage angry.* **Setsuko** *remains with a worried look on her face.*)

SCENE EIGHTEEN

Aiko *enters stage agitated. Finally settles on centre stage and picks up telephone.*

Aiko: *Moshi moshi.* Murasaki Restaurant? May I speak with Shinde, Masato? He's not? Why isn't he working? He didn't say anything about a day off. No ... no message. *(hangs up)*

(Paces stage. Sits down on floor and cries out.)

Sumiko! Sumiko! Where are you? Don't you leave me too.

(Slowly crawls to telephone. Picks up receiver and dials.)

Nippon Travel? I need two tickets to Tokyo. Next week. Any day. Any day! I don't care. One for myself, Shinde, Aiko and the other is for Shinde, Kentaro. No. One way. Yes. Yes. Visa? I have a visa, I'm a landed immigrant! Oh. Visa. No, I don't have one. Payment? *(to herself)* money ... money ... *(hangs up)*

(Lighting changes. Man in mask appears.)

Shinjuku Club? I wish to speak to Shinde, Masato. He's singing *karaoke.* The handsome man who wins all the contests. Wait. Wait. I was told he was there. Please, go and look for him. Please ... *(phone cuts off; she dials again)*

Shinjuku Club. You're not telling me something. Masato is with a woman, right? A woman. A Working Holiday girl. He has a wife and child. Send him home. Don't you understand? He's married! *(hangs up and dials again)*

You people are lying about Masato. He's there at work. I know he's there. He is not at Shinjuku! I talked to them. He's not there. Why are you keeping me from talking to my husband? Why? Why? Do you hate me? You don't even know me! Let me talk to him. Please, please!

Harrison-*san*, why do you keep Masato away from me? His son needs him to be home. Send him home. Fire him! Fire him! Don't hang up. Don't ... *(she screams in anger. Throws phone to the ground. Picks it up and calls again.)*

Lights go to black.

SCENE NINETEEN

Single light on **Detective**.

Detective: Captain, as I walked into the murder scene, I could feel the fear, the madness. There was furniture broken in pieces everywhere. Blood was smeared across all the walls. The stillness got to me after a while. I couldn't stay there. If it was a murder/suicide, Aiko must have suffered a complete psychotic breakdown. My guess is she had the advantage of surprise when she stabbed her husband the first time. Still and all, that doesn't explain why he didn't yell out for help.

Harrison *enters stage.*

Harrison *(with accent)*: I tell you, detective of the Japanese man. The will will not be broken. Too unmanly to call out for help. Macho Japanese. Stupid. They make me so mad! The Japanese, I mean. I see them come here again and again and get into so much trouble. They get robbed, raped, beaten and shot. But this? This is too much. Suicide is too tragic. Very avoidable in this country, but nobody can help unless they ask for help. It is Japanese not to ask. I think Japan is a modern country but suicide is old tradition that is still there. When will the Japanese themselves become modern and help their own people?

Detective: Why did she have to kill her son?

Harrison: Oh, I don't know. She couldn't let her son go on without a mother. The shame he would have to live with. She probably felt responsible to Canada too. Kentaro would be a burden on society. She thought it was best that he die.

Detective: So she took an electrical cord, wrapped it around her sleeping son's neck and strangled him. *(lights go to black)*

SCENE TWENTY

Taiko *music comes up.*

Lights come up on **Harumi**. *She is centre stage and carries the mask beside her. She moves forward and then places mask on face. She then struggles to take it off. She moves off stage in a panic.*

Lights go to black.

SCENE TWENTY-ONE

Gagaku *music starts. Lights come up on* **Aiko** *with back to the audience. She is on the telephone.* **Masato** *(in street clothes) enters, obviously angry.*

Masato: Get off the phone! Who do you think you are, telling Harrison-*san* to fire me? You must be out of your mind.

Aiko *(turns to reveal devil's mask)*: Maybe I am out of my mind.

Masato *(surprised)*: What? Why are you wearing that mask?

Aiko: Oh don't worry, I'm human, not a devil.

Masato: Then take it off!

Aiko: I wear the mask to hide my face.

Masato: I'm the one that needs to hide.

Aiko: I have the ugliest face in the world.

Masato: Show me. I'd like to see such ugliness.

Aiko: You would faint.

Masato: What the hell are you talking about? Stop acting crazy!

Aiko *(begins to circle* **Masato**): Not until you answer for my humiliation.

Masato: Humiliation?

Aiko: I'm standing before a peasant, humiliated.

Masato *(turns away)*: Peasant! Don't call me a peasant! Come to your senses!

Aiko: You have betrayed me and led me to insanity.

Masato: Stop talking like that! Speak normally!

Aiko: It's my punishment. I'm alone and defeated.

Masato: You're crazy! Get rid of the mask!

Aiko: It was a face to fall in love with.

Masato: Take it off!

Aiko: It's the face of madness, and madness leaves only with death.

Masato: Take it off!

Aiko: It won't come off!

Masato *lunges to take the mask off.* **Aiko** *avoids him and reveals a knife. She stabs him once. He falls to his knees.* Gagaku *music blends with the* taiko. **Masato** *crawls around stage trying to escape.* **Aiko** *follows and continues to stab in a frenzy.*

Masato *dies.* **Aiko** *stands and calms herself. She then begins a stylized representation of murder. In a cold, methodical manner, she approaches her son and prepares to strangle him. His bedroom is represented by a pool of light. She ritualistically kills him.*

Aiko *then moves centre stage. As she does, she takes rope from the doorway. Centre stage, she wraps rope around her neck. She takes off the mask and pulls rope tight. Image freezes.*

Music ends.

Japanese pop song fades in. Lights go to black.

GLOSSARY OF TERMS

Akemashite omedeto gozaimasu	Happy New Year
A-re, a-ra	Masculine and feminine forms of "Oh," "Why" or "My, my"
Bakayaro (baka)	Stupid, foolish
Ca-na-da ni iki taku nai	Literally: I don't want to go to Canada
Gagaku music	Japanese Imperial Court music
Gaijin	Foreigner (considered an insult)
Gohan	Rice, dinner
Hai	Yes
Hai. Irasshai-mase.	Welcome. Come in, you are welcome.
Hara-kiri	Suicide, literally meaning "to cut the stomach"
Inari sushi	Flavoured rice balls encased by fried bean curd
Karaoke	Musical recording without voice so that participants may supply the lyrics
Ka-ri-a wo-man	Career woman
Karoshi	Death by overworking
Kichigai	Crazy
Kusai	Reeking odour
Ming Pao Daily News	Toronto Chinese community newspaper
Moshi moshi	Hello, telephone greeting
Naniyo?	What?
Nikkei	Japanese outside of Japan
Ohayoo gozaimasu	Formal greeting
Omiai	Arranged meetings with prospective husbands
Onibaba	Devil woman of folklore origins
Oshogatsu	New Years holiday
Otoosan	Father
Ozoni	Rice cake soup
Sake	Potent rice wine
Shinto	State religion of Japan; Animist based, the religion is observed during happy occasions
Sawada, Kenji	Japanese pop singer of the 1970s
Shinde	The name is a play on the Japanese term for death, "shinu"
Taiko	Japanese drums

Yakamashi	Be quiet
Yancha bozu	Mischievous boy
Yukata	An unlined cotton garment usually worn in the summer

Notes

- Cram School: Professional tutor businesses for after-hours study. Because the Japanese education system demands such high grades for life success, cram schools have flourished.

- Kohaku: Red and White team singing contest held on New Year's Day in Japan. The men are against the women.

- *Nikkei Voice*: National Japanese Canadian community newspaper.

- Noh Design: Noh staging is noted for its simplicity and its multi-levelled construction. Since very few props are used (masks primarily), the emphasis is on costuming and stylized movement. The stage must remain bare except perhaps for a small curtain (a noren) and a ceremonial rope over an entrance. The bridge is a convention used to create height and different levels of action.

- Numbers: 33 and 42 are important ages for women and men respectively. At those ages, people are to visit their temples and enjoy a raucous party with friends to ward off the spirits that bring death.

- Working Holiday Students: Japanese students given a special one year work visa in Canada to gain experience and English skills before going on with their education. Arrangements are made between the Japanese and Canadian governments.

Dance Like a Butterfly

by AVIVA RAVEL

Aviva Ravel's plays often reflect the experiences of Montreal's Jewish community where she was born and raised and continues to live. She holds a doctorate in Canadian Drama, teaches at McGill University, and directs the popular Performance Playreading Ensemble at the Cote St. Luc Library.

Ravel's stage plays include *Dispossessed* and *The Twisted Loaf,* which were both produced at the Saidye Bronfman Centre; *Moon People,* published by Playwright's Press in *Six Canadian Plays;* and *Vengeance,* published by NuAge Press in *Escape Acts. Soft Voices* and *The Twisted Loaf* were published by Simon & Pierre in *A Collection of Canadian Plays, Volume 3.* Ravel's plays have been broadcast by CBC, Israel Radio, and produced by Cameo Productions in Montreal and theatre groups across the country.

Aviva Ravel is the author of *Be My Friend,* a children's play published by Playwrights Press, and *The Sholom Aleichem Show,* published by Pioneer Drama Service; she is also co-editor of *A Point on a Sheet of Green Paper,* an anthology of Canadian poetry published with a Hebrew translation. *Separate Pieces,* a collection of monologues by Aviva Ravel, was published in Israel.

The Courting of Sally Schwartz and *My Rumanian Cousin* ran for a year at La Diligence Dinner Theatre in Montreal. Another Ravel play, *Mother Variations,* was adapted for the screen under the title *Mothers and Daughter;* it was presented at the Montreal Film Festival in 1992.

Original production

Dance Like a Butterfly was first presented in Montreal by Cameo Productions on June 1, 1993. The play had a successful cross-Canada tour in 1994.

Original cast and production team

Director	Rena Cohen
Featured performer	Miriam Samuels
Technical director	James Douglas

Original music composed and arranged by Peter Sipos

"The play's subject matter is rarely discussed in such a sensitive and humane way, or is avoided. The writing and acting are superb; an inspiring piece of theatre." (Gwen Mackay-Smith, Director, Volunteer and Recreation Services, Maimonides Hospital Geriatric Centre)

"People from young children to adults were greatly entertained by this wonderful play. The play is beautiful and appealing to all ages." (Miriam Cooper, Chief Administrative Officer, Jewish Federation of Edmonton)

"[The] play serves as an excellent teaching tool and the issues raised have led to vibrant and exciting classroom discussion." (Marilyn Bicher, Coordinator, Social and Cultural Sciences, Vanier College, Montreal)

"Tillie touches us all because she speaks the words and passions of us all — of Everyman. Thank you again, one thousand times, for an excellent play and a stirring performance. (Ruth Katz, Psychologist)

"*Dance Like a Butterfly* is not only an outstanding piece of theatre of high artistic quality, it is also an excellent educational tool for any-one dealing with the subject of gerontology." (Paula Speevak-Sladowski, Program Director, Arts Alive, Jewish Community Centre)

PLAYWRIGHT'S NOTE

Dance Like a Butterfly is a one-woman show that addresses the situation of our aging population. Set in a hospital geriatric ward where Tillie, an octogenarian, is recovering from an operation, the play is peopled with nurses, doctors, patients, a social worker, and relatives. They are involved with Tillie in the present, while her vivid memories of the past expose her life with all its joys and struggles. Tillie takes us on a journey that leads us to re-examine our conceptions of old age.

PERFORMANCE PERMISSION

For permission to perform *Dance Like a Butterfly*, and to obtain rights to the music, please contact **AVIVA RAVEL,** 5317 Lucy Place, Montreal, Quebec H3X 1L1, (514) 733-3211.

The scene is the hall of a geriatric hospital ward. **Tillie,** *age eighty-five, sits in her wheelchair and addresses the audience. She also speaks to the nurses, her companion, relatives, other members of the hospital staff and patients who never appear on stage. An oblong overbed utility table on wheels and a walker are situated on either side of her wheelchair.*

Tillie *is incapacitated by osteoporosis. However, she is still a lively and alert woman. Concerned with her appearance, she uses cream on her face, a touch of lipstick and rouge, and her hair is neat. She wears a nice dress and necklace, a pair of bulky sneakers and socks. Born in Rumania, she has had no formal schooling in Canada. Her accent is a combination of Yiddish and Eastern European.*

At times **Tillie** *rises to walk with the help of her walker or the physio-therapist. In one scene she rises and dances in her imagination as she recalls a scene from her youth.* **Tillie** *'s actions, such as knitting, drinking, eating are mimed.*

SCENE ONE

Music: opening theme

Tillie *wheels herself in. She sits in her wheelchair and knits. She smiles, nods, and reacts to the various people – doctors, nurses, visitors – who pass by in the hall. After a moment,* **Tillie** *greets her audience warmly. Music fades*

Welcome to Six North, that means the sixth floor, the north side of the hospital, famous for chronic care. It's for people that don't get better, so it's the doctors' business to see that they don't get worse. Some business. You invest a lot, but the profits amount to "bobkehs."

(motions to wheelchair) I sit here most of the time because my legs are not good no more. *(raises a leg)* Such beautiful legs they were, like Ginger Rogers,' but now, "zey toigen oif kaporehs." *(sets knitting on the table beside her)*

Not so long ago I was just like you. I could walk and run and *(gesturing)* dance like a butterfly. Now, I sit like a stone. Did I ask for it? No. It just happened, like an earthquake happens. You have no control. It's like when you play poker, you have no control over the cards you get – unless you cheat.

89

(gestures) That's my friend, Louis, over there. He has one of the ten plagues they don't mention on "Pesach." It's when some parts in the brain get used up so he forgets where he is from one minute to the next. But one thing he remembers very good – that he loves me. He sits near me and says over and over: "Tillie, I love you." Some days his head works better, so we can talk. He was a professor in a university. He tells me a story about a man that becomes a cockroach. And I tell him that people were always cockroaches and we have a good laugh. *(a beat)* The truth is I'm getting attached to him. He has nobody.

Here comes Julie the pretty nurse pushing Louis' chair. She has soft hands like a baby's face, and a smile to make you forget where it hurts. All the nurses and the doctors here are very nice, with hearts, not like you read sometimes terrible stories in the newspapers. Here they are patient, that's why they have lots of patients. *(laughs)* That's a good one, eh?

(**Tillie** *moves her chair forward)* "Julie, where are you taking Louis?"

(a beat) "Oh, for a test. Bring him back safe."

"Good luck, Louis. See you later."

(calls after him as Julie wheels him off) "I love you too!"

So here I am, eighty-five years old, in the middle of a romance with a younger man. Louis is only seventy-nine.

The nurses and the doctors like me the best, especially the male nurses. My favourite is Jacques. He's tall and handsome, a real doll. When he smiles at me, *(her hand on her heart)* my heart goes boom-boom like when I was a young girl. Watch, he'll come over and kiss me on the cheek *(Jacques does so, she relishes the kiss)* See, I told you. He makes me blush. *(Jacques' arm goes around her; she puts her arm across her chest and takes his hand)* I bet you think that older people don't feel things. They feel even more because they are so sensitive.

"What time it is, Jacques? My watch stopped."

I ask him that so he'll keep his arm around me a little bit longer, as if he doesn't know.

"Half past nine? Thank you. See you later." *(Jacques leaves)*

They treat me better than anybody else, that's why the others are so jealous. Like Mrs. Zimmler, the 'yenteh' with the swollen feet and the tangled hair. *(imitates Mrs. Zimmler)* She says: "You think you are such a queen, Mrs. Rheinblatt? You are no better than anybody else!"

But I am better, and I will tell you why. Because I know how to behave. Let me give you a couple tips just in case one day you'll be in my position, God forbid. If you want a drink of water in the middle of the night, you ring the bell. When somebody comes, even if it takes an hour, you say, "Thank you for coming. I know how busy you are. If you have nothing better to do, please bring me a glass of water." Then, when you get it, you say: "You're an angel, the best, you should have a long life." The next night you get the water in a jiffy. But if you yell: "I'm waiting an hour! You don't care nothing for your patients, you are a so and so!" – you get a bad name with the water. And they're not so anxious to please you. Sometimes I hear them talking in the hall: "Mrs. Rheinblatt is a very nice person, a pleasure to take care of."

When I was a little girl, my father teaches me: "A good name is better than the finest oil." And my father knew what he was talking about.

I'll tell you another reason why they treat me so good. Because I'm beautiful. Sure. Beauty comes in all ages. You cannot compare for instance a baby with a teen-age girl or a middle-age woman with a bride of twenty. So for my age I am very attractive.

(with appropriate gestures) When I wake up in the morning I fix my hair, put on a nice dress with a necklace to match, lipstick, perfume, so I look like a "mensch." When visitors are walking by, they look at me and smile. I make such a good impression.

You should've seen me in the old days. In the factory they called me "Miss America."

Music: brief intro: "Bei Meer Bistu Shein"

(moves her body in time to the music, then gestures as she describes herself) What a figure I have, a small waist, a bosom you could die for, long black hair I wear in a braid around my head for the working, and when I go out, it hangs down my back in waves. The men are crazy for me. Even the boss comes by my machine to pass the time and

have a good laugh. Always I find a little something extra in the pay envelope. Not that I ever give him favours, if you know what I mean. I'm a decent girl. *(a beat)* Too bad.

(**Tillie** *responds to Lucy, her companion, who calls from* **Tillie**'s *room*)
"What is it, Lucy?"
"Who's on the phone?"
"Rachel? Tell her I don't want to talk to her."
"Sure I'm sure."

(**Tillie** *brushes aside the interruption and resumes*) Anyway, I'm an excellent operator, very fast. I make the samples they show to the buyers. "Tillie the Toiler" they call me, from the funny papers. The boss knows I can get a job anywhere, so he treats me special. But it doesn't help him nothing when we go on strike. You should see me leading all the people at the head of the picket line. I'm afraid of nobody. Let the police come with their horses and sticks!

(sings with fervour)
> "You can't scare me, I'm sticking to the Union,
> I'm sticking to the Union, I'm sticking to the Union,
> You can't scare me, I'm sticking to the Union,
> Till the day I die!"

Those were good times, even with the Depression, because we know what we want and we work together. Not like today, everybody is for himself.

Even if we have nothing to eat, I send a couple dollars to my father and mother in the old country. Because there they *never* have nothing. My oldest sister saves up to bring Bessie. Bessie saves up to bring me. That's how families are in those days. *(a beat)* I also have five older brothers that spoil me something terrible. *(relishing the memory)* Boy, am I spoiled!

To this day they are all still alive for me. At night my mother says: "Tsippeleh, gedenk dee mameh hot deer zayer leeb. Zolst zein a gitteh maideleh." It helps me through the night when the bones are bad. There's also Itzik, Albert, Rubin and Doovid, the men in my life. But I will tell you about them later.

(responds to Lucy who comes out of **Tillie**'s *room*) "No, Lucy, I'm not changing my mind, I don't want to talk to Rachel, let her sweat a little."

(motions to Lucy who returns to **Tillie**'s *room)* Lucy, that's my companion, what is called a "sitter," that gives personal attention for six dollars an hour.

(sees nurse approaching) Here comes Melanie with the juice. She is also from Jamaica. *(takes juice)* She sends money to her mother. With immigrants it's the same all over.

(sips, sets drink on table and calls to Melanie who goes on to next patient) "Thank you, sweetheart."

Me, I never saw my mother and father again after I came here and moved in with Bessie, "olov ha-sholom." Bessie is an angel of a woman. She also spoils me. She calls me "princess." She never eats an orange herself. She always gives me first like I am one of her children. Rachel, the oldest, tells her friends that I am her big sister, that's how close we are. I sleep in the same bed with Rachel, I take her to the toilet at night because she is afraid of the bogeyman. Sometimes Rachel gets mad on me because she has to clean up after supper and not me. *(fondly)* She doesn't understand that I work hard all day.

Now Rachel visits me almost every day, she is so attached. I'm telling you all this so you'll understand better what happened last month when Rachel comes to visit.

She looks serious. She is always serious, but this time she talks slow and loud, like I am deaf or stupid. That's how people talk to the old. If you have trouble with your bladder, it also means that you are deaf.

She says: "Since you are in the hospital for five months already, and we don't know how long you'll be here, it's a good idea to sublet your apartment so you don't pay rent for nothing, since you're also paying here for chronic care."

My eye begins to shake. That's what happens when I'm nervous. But I talk very quiet.

"If I give up my apartment, where will I go when I leave the hospital?"

"To a nursing home," she says, "because you need somebody to look after you twenty-four hours a day."

"Why not twenty-six?" I say.

She tells me not to make jokes. I told you Rachel is the serious type.

Then she asks if it's all right to sublet the apartment. "No, it's not all right. I want my apartment."

You know what she answers me? "You can't always have what you want."

She remembers her mother spoils me. I bet she's still thinking of those oranges.

"I'm not going to no nursing home."

Now *her* eye starts to shake. I know because she's covering it with her hand.

"When I leave the hospital I am going back to my apartment!"

She says, "You can't live alone because you fell three times and that's why you had an operation. You need round-the-clock supervision."

"So I'll go to a Residence and have my own apartment like my friend, Ethel."

"They will not take you in a wheelchair," she says, "I already asked."

"What about my things, my furniture?"

She says they'll store it. "They" – that also means her sister Florence, the blonde, the pretty one.

"You will not store nothing! You will leave my apartment the way it is!"

She tells me to stop yelling.

"I will yell as much as I like. It's my apartment!"

She gets insulted and with tears in her eyes she says I can do what I like, and she goes.

I'm calling after her, "It's my apartment. I'm not giving it up!"

Melanie and Julie come running with water and a pill and they put me to bed. And all the time I can't stop screaming, "It's my apartment!!"

(a beat) So what do you think? If I give up my apartment, I'm finished, "ois balebosteh." No more kitchen, no more drapes, no more linen, no more cutlery. All your life you accumulate, in the end they tell you to get rid of everything.

You know what things are? Memories. A small ashtray, a cheap souvenir. They will throw it out. But for me it's my honeymoon with Albert in Niagara Falls. *(proudly)* I also have beautiful things. A set of dishes fifty years old, I pay a week's wages from the factory. A dining room set, chesterfield with two matching chairs. *(becomes increasingly aggravated as she lists her possessions)* A buffet, antique end tables, lamps, fancy pillows, wall-to-wall carpets, a silver tea set! Stop it already, Tillie, why are you torturing yourself?! You don't have enough pain in the legs? *(a beat)* I can't help it, it hurts so much.

Listen, if you have something you don't need, give it away now. And people will think you're doing them a favour. The truth is, you're doing yourself a favour. How much does a person need, anyway? When you figure that out, you'll see you can get rid of practically your whole house and still live comfortable.

(Julie approaches, wheeling Louis) Here comes Louis asleep in the chair.

"Put him over here by me, Julie. When he wakes up, he'll see me, so he'll feel good." (**Tillie** *moves the walker to the other side to make room for Louis.*)

"Thank you, Julie, you're an angel, the best." *(a knowing glance to audience)*

Even if I give up the apartment, I still I have money from the factory and also what the husbands left me. Let me tell you about money. It's what you need to get respect. *(a beat)* Don't look at me like that, it's true. Don't they always ask, "How much is he worth?" If you have a million dollars, they treat you like a million. If you have ten dollars, you get ten dollars' worth. That's how it is.

When you have money, even your disease is beautiful. Take the Queen, for instance. When she has the flu, she sneezes, her nose drips, she coughs. What happens? All the servants are dancing around her, they call in specialist doctors from all over the world, and the television discusses the Royal Flu. *(gesturing to herself and the audience)* But when me and you have a flu, all we have is a lousy cold and nobody wants to come near us. *(confidentially)* When you have money, nothing smells bad by you, if you know what I mean.

So I'm glad I put away a couple dollars and people have respect. Everything you have to pay for: special shampoo, presents for the nurses, a nice dress, and my Lucy.

Today she is sitting in my room and doing nothing because I feel like talking to you and not to her.

(speaks to Lucy who is behind her, in the room) "How are your children today, Lucy?"

"That's good."

She has six and I'm jealous of her. I tried four times but I always lost them. But in my place it was peace and quiet. By Bessie with her four children "kein ayneh horeh," it was always screaming, crying, jumping. Who needs that? *(a beat)* Still, if she did not have them, there would be nobody to look after me now.

It's a funny thing with children. Mrs. Zimmler, the "yenteh" with the swollen feet and the tangled hair, she has three. They come to visit once a year on Mother's Day, bring a present and "fartik." But Mrs. Kutler with the bad heart, they visit regular twice a week. *(confidentially)* Now, I heard that Mrs. Kutler was never home. She went downtown to nightclubs with red dresses, played cards and fooled around, if you know what I mean. Her children ate by the neighbours or they went hungry. "Dafkeh" *they* take care of her. But Mrs. Zimmler gave her life for the children – a good education, nice weddings – they come once a year. So go try to understand. *(a beat)* I guess I'm lucky I only have nieces, so I'm not disappointed.

(Mrs. Zimmler is passing by) "Hello, Mrs. Zimmler. How are you?"

Every day she tells me she's going home, that her children are coming for her, but it's not true, they never come. But as long as she has hope, she's happy, so I make like I believe her.

(waves) "Have a good trip, Mrs. Zimmler."

(referring to Mrs. Zimmler) Now I know why young people stay away from the old. They don't want to see how they could become. But if they don't look, it doesn't mean they won't get old. That's why everybody should live together, so we could get used to it. But nowadays they put the old separate because nobody has time or patience to look after us. And a person can live to a hundred and twenty, God forbid.

So they have a new business; it's called "geriatrics," fancy for old age. If you want to get rich, you should make canes, walkers, wheelchairs. *(a beat)* Computers, cars, clothes go out of style, but "geriatrics" – it's here to stay. There's also the denturologist, that makes false teeth. He fit me with new ones because the old ones make noise when I talk and fall out when I chew.

So you see, it's not so bad to be middle-aged with your own teeth and two legs that can walk. If you knew how I cried when I turned forty? "Half my life is gone, and what did I do with it!?" I was even young when I turned fifty, sixty, seventy. Ah, what I would not give to be a young woman of seventy again.

(Louis wakes up) "Hello, Louis, you had a good nap?"

"That's good."

"Ah Louis, if I had my legs and you had your head, we could go dancing downtown to a nightclub, with a band, and a floor show."

Music: lively theme from "Ain't Misbehavin'"

(**Tillie** *raises her arms in dancing position, she moves her body in time to the music*)

"You dance like a butterfly," my Albert says. Ah, my Albert was something special. A big talker, a big joker, a big spender, but a "klayner fardiner."

Music: fades

(she lowers footrests) If I would let him, he'd take me to go dancing every night.

(she places the walker in front of her) If I knew then what I know now, I would let him.

(she hoists herself up with the help of her walker) The most important thing is to enjoy when you have the chance. *(takes a few steps)*

I already told you I had three husbands: Albert, Rubin and Doovid. Albert I like the best because he was the first, but not as much as I like Itzik.

Music: "Margareetkelach," Brief intro

(**Tillie** *supports herself with the walker as she speaks*)

Nobody in this part of the world knows about Itzik. I'm so glad I love him, so all my life I know what real love is. The burning fire of love.

Itzik is the son of the "melamed," in the town where I live. I love him since I am thirteen. I stare at him in "shul." Sometimes he sings instead of the "chazzen" – he has a voice you could faint from. Almost like Pavarotti. We meet behind the mill where they make the flour, there is a little valley with trees all around so nobody could see us. He talks about forbidden books that he reads by Tolstoy. Ah, those nights under the stars and the moon! I tell you there are no stars and moon like there was in Rumania. *(a beat)* But my father finds out about the stars and moon and tells Itzik's father who says he can't marry me because he is promised to a cousin from Stefanest, a town not far from Botoshan where I live. And just to make sure there is no more moon and stars, he sends Itzik to the cousin's house and I never hear from him again!

(supported by the walker, she takes several emphatic steps, banging the walker in anger as she moves)

Sure I cried a lot, and since my sisters go to Canada I also want to go, but my father says no, so I say I'll kill myself, so he lets me go. You see, I had a cousin that jumped in a well for lost love. All that passion, it runs in the family. *(a beat)* Still, I have a beautiful love with Itzik. Whatever comes after it's imitation.

(she turns around and moves toward the wheelchair, pausing to dry her eyes)

(to Lucy, who has emerged from the room) "I'm not crying, Lucy, what gives you that idea?"

"All right, I'm thinking about Itzik."

"Never mind who is Itzik, just a boy I know a long time ago."

She tells me she also had an Itzik, but his name was Willy. And we have a good laugh.

(sits in her wheelchair) Sometimes I don't know how I would manage without my Lucy.

(the serving wagon approaches) Here comes Melanie with the lunch. *(looks at a tray on the wagon)*

"Louis, there's apple sauce with the 'latkehs' today. Go eat, enjoy."

(Louis is wheeled away. **Tillie** *moves the walker to the place Louis vacated, and wheels the utility table in front of her.)*

Mealtime here is a regular entertainment, three times a day. But everything tastes like mashed potatoes without salt. What can you do? This is not a resort in the Catskills.

(to Lucy, who stands over her) "You don't have to help me, Lucy, I can still cut a 'latkeh' by myself."

(eats) I used to have such a good appetite. Now I force myself to eat. I eat for my mother. She says, "Ess, Tsippeleh, mein kind, darfst zein shtark." So I eat. My advice to you is eat now what you like. A couple pounds more or less is not going to make you less beautiful.

(eats, looks down the hall at someone who approaches)

Here comes Mrs. Flomen, The Collector. *(hands food to her)*

"You can have my carrots and my bread, Mrs. Flomen. You're welcome."

(Mrs. Flomen takes the food and moves away) She says tomorrow the Nazis will come, so she stocks up. The nurses take it away later so the room doesn't stink. *(eats)*

Over there is Mrs. Rudnick, The Talker. She talks to everything – the windows, her purse, her chair. She makes up whole stories like she's in a movie with Robert Taylor. Me, I prefer Fred Astaire. *(removes particle of food caught between her teeth)*

Here comes Mrs. Syrkin, The Wanderer. I remember she has a fruit store on Main Street. Yesterday she went down the elevator and walked over to Dunkin' Donuts. Until they found her, don't ask.

"Where are you going, Mrs. Syrkin?"

"To the fruit store?!"

"Lucy, go get a nurse, she's by the elevator again!"

This is some exciting place, a real Belmont Park.

(finishes her meal, speaks to nurse who removes the tray)

"Thank you, Melanie, I finished. Everything is delicious, just like by The Brown Derby. You're an angel, the best." *(a knowing glance at the audience)*

"Lucy, please take me into my room for a nap. Then you can go home. *(moves table aside)* I have to rest up from all my hard work. Please remember to bring me the paper tomorrow."

(she starts wheeling herself upstage) A person has to know what is happening in the world. Maybe it will help me not to become a Wanderer, a Talker, a Collector. *(a beat)* Everyday I like to read the Births and the Deaths. When I don't see my name, I know I am still alive. *(moves entirely upstage, her back to the audience)*

Music: bridge to next scene

SCENE TWO

(**Tillie** *wheels herself downstage, closer to the audience*)

(sharing her dream) I had a funny dream. I am wearing the beautiful dress that I made for Rachel's wedding. Louis is walking beside me. We are just married! We are going back to my apartment. Everything is just like I left it. *(a beat)* I want to sit down, but there are no chairs. No chairs in the kitchen, no chairs in the dining-room. *(a beat)* I know what Albert would say about my dream. "Honey, it's no use, an apartment without chairs is not an apartment."

I used to tell Albert all my dreams. He understood my feelings. He always said something to make me feel good. Albert was born here, a real Canadian, not a "greener." "Honey" he always calls me, not Tillie, "honey." He had no head for business, so together we open a snack bar and I manage it. Everybody loves to eat by me because I cook with "tahm," like at home. Me and Albert live good together twenty years. Like the song:

> "We don't have plenty money,
> But life is very funny,
> We travel along, singing a song,
> Side by side."

One day there was a terrible snow storm. So I stay home. I figure there is not going to be much business on such a day. But Albert wants to drive downtown to buy supplies. I tell him not to go, but he doesn't listen. *(a beat)* At night when the police come it is still snowing and blowing. They say it was an accident with a truck. Sometimes I can still hear his voice. "Honey, it's time to close up the store."

Excuse me for a minute, Doctor Lapin is coming. She just graduated medical school, so she's still very enthusiastic.

(speaks to Doctor) "I'm fine, Doctor Lapin, how are you?"

"Sure I would appreciate a little physiotherapy this afternoon. Maybe this time Molly will make a small miracle."

(to audience) From my mouth to God's ears.

Anyway, by my dream you can see that the apartment is still on my mind, so I want to tell you what happened last week when Rachel comes to visit.

"Hello, Rachel. It's about time you come to see me."

"You came yesterday? I don't remember."

"Four times last week, is that so? You expect me to keep a record?"

"How do I feel? Lousy. How do you expect me to feel?"

"Doctor Lapin says different? A lot she knows."

Rachel gets nervous and makes a fist with her hand like when she was a little girl. I don't know why I am so nice to everybody, except to the nieces.

(charmingly) "So what's new, Rachel?"

She says they found a tenant for the apartment.

"I don't remember telling you to sublet it."

She says she's telling me just in case I changed my mind.

"I did not change my mind."

She tells me I'm paying rent for nothing.

"So I'm paying."

She says she cannot take my attitude no more.

"That's too bad, if you can't take it, you can leave it."

She blows her nose and I can see that she wishes she was somewhere else. All of a sudden Mrs. Zimmler comes over to listen to what we are talking.

"Go away, Mrs. Zimmler, this is my visitor!"

(when Mrs. Zimmler leaves, **Tillie** *turns on Rachel)*

"Poor thing, you say? It's not my fault she looks like that. You have more feelings for her than for me."

Then Rachel says very quiet if I am not happy here in the hospital maybe I want to go somewhere else.

"Go where?"

To a nice private home they found. It is on a nice street with a nice balcony and trees. I will have a nice room. She says I'm lucky to get it in my condition.

"I don't want to move. I like it here. Everyone is nice to me."

She reminds me that here I am always complaining.

"I have to think it over."

She says I have to make up my mind by tomorrow, because other people are waiting for the room. Now you know why I don't want to talk to her.

First they want me to give up my apartment. Then they want to put me somewhere else. If I could look after myself, they wouldn't treat me like baggage in the airport. "Ven dee bobeh hot reder, volt zee geven a vogen."

(a nurse approaches) "Hello, Doris."

Doris is an older nurse, very experienced. But she never smiles. She makes up my bed so perfect, she could win a Nobel prize.

"No, Doris, I don't feel like going to the entertainment today."

"If it's the same singer from last week, tell her to stay home."

"Sure I like music, but I have to think about something."

She says I can think with the music and she pushes me to the solarium.

(**Tillie** *moves her wheelchair briskly to another area on stage.*)

My Rubin would know what I should do. He never says a word without thinking it over. You know what he would say? "The nieces wouldn't put you in a bad place," he would say. "You should try it. If you don't like it, you could go somewhere else, it's not a jail."

My Rubin was a smart man, a watchmaker with a good business. He lost his family in Lodz, but he never talks about them. Fifteen years I live with Rubin, like a princess.

Music: brief intro

(during music she puts on gloves and a hat)

I'm President of my Hadassah chapter. I go to "shul" on "Shabbos" with gloves and a hat like a lady. *(a beat)* The truth is, his heart was really with the wife that he lost. But we have a comfortable home. It's what you are calling a convenient marriage.

(to nurse who stands nearby) "Yes, Doris, I like the music, it's wonderful."

(to audience) But I can sing better. I know all the popular songs.

(sings)
> "You gotta give a little
> Take a little

Let your poor heart break a little
That's the story of, that's the glory of, love."

Ah, if I was born in this country with a good education, I could be a movie star, and maybe marry a Bronfman or a Rothschild and live in a palace on top of the mountain.

(notices Louis across the room.) Oh, Louis is waking up. He doesn't look so good.

"Doris, please bring him over here by me."

(after nurse complies) "You're an angel, the best." *(a knowing glance to the audience)*

"Yes, Mrs. Zimmler, he's my boyfriend, you're jealous?"

They are making fun from me, let them make fun, what do I care.

(moves her wheelchair closer to Louis) "Louis, who am I?"

"That's right, Tillie. I have something to tell you. My nieces want I should move out from here. So what do you think?"

"Don't cry, Louis, I'm not going nowhere yet. I'm only asking your opinion. Never mind, tomorrow we'll talk some more. Give me your hand. There, that's better." *(She takes Louis' hand, looks at it, then releases it as she remembers Doovid.)*

(to audience) My Doovid had strong hands. He was a plumber. I met him at a Hadassah bazaar.

Music: "Doovid's Theme," brief intro

(during music her actions mime serving people at her booth)

He comes to my booth and buys a whole bunch of clothes for children.

"You have a lot of grandchildren?" I ask.

"No, I am never married," he says, in a Hungarian accent. "The clothes are for poor children in St. Henri."

Oh, when I hear this, I don't let him get away so easy. I recognize a tasty fish when I see one.

(coquettishly) "Excuse me, my name is Tillie Rosen, and you are ..."

He gives me his business card. Rheinblatt Plumbing. If I need to fix something, to call him day or night. One week later I find a blocked pipe in my house, so Doovid comes to fix it, I give him tea and my special mandel broit, "oon vos zol eech eich zogen," one year later we are married! He was never married before, so I am his whole life. Doovid is a funny little man, with a big round face. He has a big heart, he makes me laugh, so what do I care he wouldn't win a beauty contest. Many women look at the "kugel" on the outside and don't bother to taste, so how can they know it's good?

(a beat) Three years later he has a heart attack. So I'm alone again. *(a beat)* The truth is that mostly at night I am thinking about Itzik, the one I did not marry.

(**Tillie** *takes Louis' hand*)

"Louis, what's the matter? Why are you crying? I am not going nowhere yet."

How can I leave him? He's the only person left in the world that still needs me.

(Molly approaches her)

Here comes the therapist to torture me.

"Hello, Molly, how are you? I would love to have a little therapy. I am looking forward all afternoon."

(Molly takes both of **Tillie** *'s hands and helps her stand up. Molly steps backwards and* **Tillie**, *holding her hands tightly, takes a few steps forward. She makes an onerous effort to walk.)*

My legs feel like two heavy blocks of wood. *(turns her head about)*

"Who's clapping?"

"Ah, Louis, you like my performance?"

I am an entertainer in my old age.

"Tell me, Molly, what ship do the Jewish mothers take to go to England?"

"You give up?"

"Ess Ess, Mein Kind."

(laughs and looks at Louis)

(with Molly's help she returns to her wheelchair)

"Thank you for letting me sit down. You're an angel, the best."
(Molly leaves)

When I was a baby, I learn to walk. Now I am old, I have to learn all over again.

Look, it's getting dark outside. The music is finished. Everybody is clapping, the singer is bowing like she is Barbra Streisand, and everybody is going to his place in the hall to wait for supper. Some go in wheelchairs, some with walkers, some with canes. Some go by themselves, but they go the wrong way.

(goes into a reverie) Ah, the suppers I used to make. They are all sitting around the table – Albert, Rubin, Doovid – and I serve them. *(serves them food)* For you, Albert, the white part. For you, Rubin, "mayern tsimmes," for you Doovid I have a nice roast. It's not hard to be a good cook, if you have what to put in the "kugel." *(looking straight ahead)* Look who's here! It's Itzik! He's so young, just a boy. Make room for him, Doovid. *(hands Itzik a bowl and ladles soup and dumplings into it)* Here's some chicken soup, with "knaydel." Eat, Itzik, enjoy. *(her vision of the men slowly fades)*

If I could cook one meal again. To make a cup of coffee, to go to Steinberg *[the supermarket]*. It's not the weddings and Bar Mitzvahs that I miss, it's the little things. To call my friend, Ethel, and we go downtown by bus to a sale by Eaton's. And then we have tea in the restaurant, and I sell her a raffle for the ladies' auxiliary. And in the evening Doovid and me watch "The Golden Girls" on T.V. and we eat seedless grapes. Things like that. *(a beat)* Nobody can take me from my memories.

(a nurse approaches) "Yes, Doris, I'm going for supper. I'm sure it will be delicious, just like by Grossinger's."

*(as **Tillie** wheels herself along, she meets Annie)*

"Oh, hello Annie."

That's the social worker. She doesn't make socials and so far as I know, she doesn't work. *(a beat)* She sits in an office and talks to people that come and go all day long. Such a job I don't wish on no one. A nurse makes up your bed, a doctor gives you a pill, the therapist exercises you, but what does the social worker do? She talks. She says she would like to do more, but there's no money or it's against the rules.

"I'm fine, Annie, how are you?"

"Ah, you have a headache again, I'm sorry." *(a knowing glance to audience)*

"Yes, it's true, the nieces want I should move out from here to a private home."

"So what do you think?"

"Oh, you have a place for me in a big new nursing home? With lots of people, a 'shul,' a beauty parlour, arts with crafts, entertainment with doctors and nurses, and a social worker."

"The social worker is nice like you?"

She says nobody is nice like her and she gives me a big smile.

"So what do you think I should do, Annie?"

"It's up to me. I see." *(a beat)*

"I can't stay here in the hospital no more?"

"It's very crowded and I am recovered from the operation. I see."

"I have to think it over. I will not sleep all night thinking it over." (**Tillie** *wheels herself out*)

Music bridge to next scene

SCENE THREE

Music fades in under the dream sequence

"Mameh, ver ken meer helfen?"

Itzik can't. He's a coward. He spoiled my wedding.

Albert is lost in the storm.

Rubin has to go away to the other wife.

Doovid, give me your hand. You will stay with me forever. Doovid cannot stay.

Nothing stays the same. All my life it is changing.

I need to make some lists.

I need to visit Auntie Sophie.

I need to bring her cookies.

(Morning. **Tillie** *is now awake, but she stares into space for a moment, then shakes off her passive expression and resumes her former alertness. Looks at her watch and moves herself to her place in the hall between the table and the walker as she speaks)*

Nine o'clock already!

"Lucy, go tell Rachel to come right away. I want to talk to her."

(looks in little compact mirror which she withdraws from her pocket) Look at me! I have to fix myself up. *(proceeds to put on lipstick and rouge, tidies her hair)* There, that's better. Now I look like a "mensch."

(to Lucy who enters) "It's okay, Lucy? She's coming?"

"Good. Now I want to walk." *(she raises herself to her feet, rejects Lucy's help)*

"I want to walk by myself. Stand by close."

(she takes two steps) "My legs hurt so much, but I am not giving up."

(takes another two steps, stops and leans on Lucy)

"It's like climbing up the mountain."

(to audience) You are very lucky. Sure you have problems – you worry about the boring job, the nagging mother, the stubborn children. But if you want to leave, you can run out and slam the door. Me, I can't run nowhere or slam nothing.

"All right, Lucy, that's enough."

(Lucy helps her sit) "Vos iz geven iz geven mer nishtoo."

Music: brief intro

(**Tillie**'*s gaze is on the window. During the following she flips back the footrests, rises, and moving and dancing like a young woman, she relives in her memory those moments on the beach.*)

The sun is shining outside. That reminds me of something happy. The sun shining on the water. On the beach on St. Helen's Island. Me and Albert used to go with Alice and Jack, Faye and Henry, Ethel and Arthur. We run in the water, we swim, we splash. We play like children in the sand – running, falling, and chasing each other. And then we make – what do you call that? All the men are standing at the bottom and the girls are standing on their shoulders, one on top of the other. Me, I'm always standing on top of everybody with my arms spread out wide. We're all so young and beautiful. I have pictures.... *(a beat)* They're all gone, except Ethel. She comes to see me sometimes, an old woman with a cane. But in my memory, we are all still on the beach making pyramids. That's what you call it, pyramids!

Music resumes during following

(**Tillie** *turns around, looks at the empty wheelchair, slowly moves toward it, sits, puts footrests down*)

Music fades

(*Rachel approaches,* **Tillie** *becomes aware of her*) "Hello, Rachel, how are you?"

"I look nice this morning? Thank you. Please, sit down."

(**Tillie** *watches Rachel cross to the other side of the wheelchair and sit*)

Rachel looks just like my mother. When she talks I hear my mother's voice. And I feel like I'm a baby again, and I could start all over again. *(gestures)* But life is a circle. Every person has his own circle, and nobody knows how big it is.

"Rachel, I made some lists."

"For the apartment. You see?" *(shows a little notebook)* "On this paper are the things to give to Florence. On this paper are the things for you. This is for Ethel and the cousin that I like. This is for charity. All these things you keep for me to bring to the place where I am going. *(hands her the notebook)* And make sure you sell the wall-to-wall carpets for a good price. Doovid pays a fortune just three years ago."

"Now I will tell you what is new. Annie has a place for me in a big new nursing home. With lots of people, entertainment, arts with crafts, a shul. So what should I do? Should I go to your private home, or to Annie's place?"

"That's funny. Annie doesn't know and you don't know. So who knows?"

Rachel is looking at me like she is afraid. Maybe she is thinking one day she will be old and other people will put her here, put her there. It was better in the olden days. My grandfather lived with us. When he is old my mother takes care on him. He tells me stories and it is my job to bring the meals to his room. But the world changes. And no matter what you do you cannot stop it.

"Rachel, you remember Auntie Sophie. She used to bring you Hanuka presents when you were a little girl. A long time ago I visit her in a private home. She's a rich lady, she could afford the best. The place is very nice and comfortable. But something is wrong. All the people are just sitting and looking at the air. Everybody is quiet. Just sitting and looking at the air.

"'Hello, Auntie Sophie,' I say. 'How are you?'

"She grabs my hand. 'Tillie, take me out of here. Please take me out of here.'

"'What is the matter, Auntie Sophie? You are not feeling all right?'

"But all she says is 'take me out of here.'

"When I leave she says, 'Tell them to give me more cookies with my tea, please tell them.'"

"When I come home I phone her son. You know what he answers me? 'No matter where we put her, she complains. She's in a nice place. What more does she want? We can't make her young again.'"

"Rachel, now I know what she wants. She wants a life again. Things to do. People to talk to. I also want a life again. So go tell Annie to make all the arrangements for her place right away."

"Sure, I'm sure." *(Rachel goes off)*

(a beat) "Lucy, please push Louis over here. Thank you."

"Listen, Louis, I have to tell you something. I cannot stay here no more. They will not let me stay here no more. Don't cry, Louis. I can't help it. What can I do? I will come back to see you, I promise."

I suppose God wants for everybody to go their own way, or He would make us in pairs.

(she cannot bear to see the sorrow on Louis' face) "Lucy, take him to Julie, please."

(as Louis is taken off) "I am sorry, Louis, I am so sorry."

I am going to miss everybody. Melanie, Julie, Jacques. Especially Jacques. I will miss Mrs. Syrkin, Mrs. Flomen, even Mrs. Zimmler. Most of all I will miss Louis, my last chance for love.

(Rachel returns) "Rachel, it is all right?"

"Good."

(a beat) "Lucy, please go pack up my things."

"Rachel, don't look at me so worried. I will be all right in the new place. A person cannot be young and strong forever."

I am still a lucky woman. I have Rachel and Florence and Lucy. My head works good. And I have my memories.

"Rachel, let's go already. I have to get dressed up. What are you standing there for like a 'laymener goylem'?"

Goodbye for now, my friends. I will talk to you from the new place. I will let you know how I am doing.

In the meantime, go out and have yourselves a good time. *(a beat)* And think of me.

(wheels herself off)

Music: theme as at the beginning to end the play

GLOSSARY

Bar Mitzvah	a boy's 13th birthday confirmation ceremony
bobkehs	worthless, goat turds
chazzen	cantor
dafkeh	in spite of that
darfst zein shtark	you must be strong
dee mameh hot deer zayer leeb	mother loves you very much
ess	eat
ess ess, mein kind	eat eat, my child
fartik	finished, all done
gedenk	remember
greener	a new immigrant
Hanuka presents	presents given on the Hanuka holiday that falls in December
kein ayneh horeh	may the evil eye not injure [them]
klayner fardiner	one who doesn't earn much
knaydel	dumpling
kugel	pudding
latkeh	pancake
laymener goylem	a clay dummy
mameh	mother
mandel broit	almond crescents
mayern tsimmes	stewed sweet carrots
melamed	teacher
mensch	a human being (decent)
ois balebosteh	her housekeeping days are over
olov ha-sholom	may he rest in peace
oon vos zol eech eich zogen?	and what can I tell you?
Pesach	Passover
shul	synagogue
tahm	tasty
Tsippeleh	Tillie [diminutive, pet name]
ven dee bobeh hot reder, volt zee geven a vogen	if grandmother had wheels she'd be a wagon
ver ken meer helfen?	who can help me?
vos iz geven iz geven mer nishtoo	what was, was, and is no more
yenteh	busybody
zey toigen oif kaporehs	they are totally useless
zolst zein a gitteh maideleh	you must be a good girl

(Note: "ch" sound is gutteral)

Just a Kommedia

by NIKA RYLSKI

Nika Rylski has written extensively for television and radio, and her scripts have appeared on CBC, ITV, and TVO in Canada, as well as in England, Germany and Ireland.

Among many awards and honours for her writing were an ACTRA nomination for best TV Drama for *The Last of the Four-Letter Words* and the Eric Harvie Award for Best New Canadian Musical 1982 for *Skin Deep* (written in collaboration with composer Rosemary Radcliffe).

Strangers at the Door, written by Nika Rylski, was a Canadian Film Award finalist, and *Honor Thy Father* won Best TV Drama Award at the 1977 Yorkton International Film Festival. Her radio plays include *A Trip to the Casbah, The Tie that Binds,* and *I'm a Stranger Here Myself.* From 1989 to 1991, she worked on the book and lyrics for the annual Canadian Heritage Festival.

Rylski wrote the script for *Just a Kommedia* in 1984: "As the off-spring of Polish immigrant parents who settled in Canada after WW2, I have always felt different, divided, caught between two cultures. So when director Andrey Tarasiuk commissioned me to write a comedy revue about the trials and tribulations of growing up Ukrainian-Canadian, I thought, 'Here's an opportunity to deal with this dilemma once and for all.'"

Nika Rylski lives in Toronto and teaches screenwriting at George Brown College.

ORIGINAL PRODUCTION

Just a Kommedia was first produced as a full-length play at the St. Vladimir Institute Theatre, Toronto on May 16, 1984.

It was subsequently produced in 1985 at MTC in Winnipeg, the Globe Theatre in Regina, and the Sub Theatre in Edmonton, with the part of Boris Dutyshyn played by Larry Zacharko. In 1986, *Just a Kommedia* was produced at the Amiga Theatre, Canadian Pavilion, EXPO 86, Vancouver, following a National Tour. The part of Olech Dutyshyn was played by Peter Boretski.

This draft is based on the hour-long adaptation written for CBC radio drama's "Stereo Theatre" in 1992.

ORIGINAL CAST AND PRODUCTION TEAM

Kenny Crutchkowski	George Kelebay
Olech Dutyshyn	Len Doncheff
Anna Dutyshyn	Joan Karasevich
Boris Dutyshyn	Wally Michaels
Natalka Dutyshyn	Mimi Kuzyk
Daria Carpiak	Luba Goy
Piano/Bandura/Guitar	Walter Teres

All other characters doubled by the cast of 6

Directed by	Andrey Tarasiuk
Musical Direction	Jerry Hryhorsky
Set & Costumes	Bill Layton & Natalka Husar
Lighting Design	Donald Finlayson
Choreography	Andrey Tarasiuk & Walter Teres

REVIEWS

"The comedy is never forced; the script has a lived-in ease. And the tension between the generations, between ethnic tradition and the Canuck melting pot, is comfortably universal." *(Edmonton Journal)*

"[The play] displays an uncanny ability to cut across ethnic lines and examine all immigrants' difficulties at retaining homeland traditions while blending into Canadian society." *(Toronto Star)*

"This show is universal in its appeal and in its wisdom." *(Edmonton Sun)*

"A hilarious satire ... *Just a Kommedia* is a very funny look at a community that doesn't often ... poke fun at itself." *(Globe and Mail)*

PLAYWRIGHT'S NOTE

The phrase "chysta kommedia" is a catch-all, widely used throughout the Ukrainian-Canadian community in times of celebration or despair, to mean "that's life." Directly translated, "chysta kommedia" means "pure comedy." *Just a Kommedia* is the English play-on-words of this expression.

PERFORMANCE PERMISSION

For musical lead sheets and permission to perform *Just a Kommedia,* please contact **NIKA RYLSKI,** 155 Neville Park Boulevard, Toronto, Ontario M4E 3P7, (416) 699-4209.

CHARACTERS
(in order of appearance)

Kenny Crutchkowski: The Concert's Master of Ceremonies

Olech Dutyshyn: The Concert's Official Host

Anna Dutyshyn: His wife, the Official Hostess

Boris Dutyshyn: Their son

Natalka Dutyshyn: Their daughter

Daria Carpiak: Her best friend

War Veteran
Auxiliary Lady
Miss Odessa
Members of Church Choir
Camp Commandant
Little Daria
School Teacher
Mama Carpiak
Dylan Yaroslav
Lesya Cebulnik
Country and Western Singer
Pickets
Natalie Hays

All minor characters doubled by a cast of 6 (3m., 3 f.)

Time: Now, and in the past. The play spans a period of 25 years until the present.

Place: At a church basement concert in the North End of Winnipeg. In the original stage production, a unit set representing a church basement hall was used as the connective image for the various locations. Carry-on pieces and props were brought on by the actors to indicate specific locations, such as summer camp, the men's washroom, and the Legislative Assembly grounds.

PROGRAMME

1. **Anthem** ... With the St. Vladimir & Sophia Church Choir

2. **Official Welcome** ... With Your hosts, Olech & Anna Dutyshyn

3. **March-Past** ... Campers from Camp Smeeshu-Ha-Ha

4. **What's In A Name?** ... Recitation by Daria Carpiak

5. **Rocky-Rolly** ... The Can-Ukey Brothers

6. **Someday My Ukrainian Prince Will Come** ... The Patychok Dancers

7. **Table Manners** ... Dutyshyn Family Ensemble

8. **Boy's Night Out** ... With Country & Western Singer Jerry Bochko

9. **True Confessions** ... Natalka Dutyshyn & The Church Choir

10. **The Eleventh Commandment** ... Boris Dutyshyn, Accompanied by Himself

11. **Sponsor's Message** ... The Crutchkowski Cossack Trio

12. **Home Sweet Home** ... Greetings from the Legislative Assembly

13. **Grand Finale** ... The St. Vladimir & Sophia Church Choir

1. ANTHEM

The stage is set as for a church basement concert, with a painted rural backdrop, blue and yellow Ukrainian flags and Maple Leaf flanking the stage, a stack of wooden folding chairs off to one side, and a microphone on a stand centrestage.

Musical vamp. Cast members scuttling across the open stage as the **MC Kenny Crutchkowski** *enters to test microphone.* **War Veteran** *at curtain waiting for his cue.* **Auxiliary Lady** *coming up aisle greeting friends.*

MC: Are we ready? Everybody in? Okay, let's go!

(Curtains close. **MC** *steps through curtain to address audience.)*

MC: Most esteemed ladies and gentlemen, very reverend members of the clergy, distinguished guests, and most precious youth – welcome to our 25th Anniversary Concert in Commemoration of the Laying of the Foundation Stone of this Hall!

(flourish on piano)

Honoring us with their presence on this auspicious occasion, His Excellency, the Right Reverend and most Eminent Monsignor Hawrylo Bossy, President and Co-founder of the Association for a Good Death, who on this day 25 years ago, gave us his blessing, and upturned the first shovelful of earth.

(War Veteran *peeks out)*

And let us not forget esteemed *Pan* Professor Viktor Turetski, founding member and chairman of our Board of Directors, head of the Ukrainian Shakespeare Society, and the author of "Linguistic Aspects of the Controversy Over Shakespeare's Entrance in Slavic Literature." Soon to be published with the aid of a Canada Council Grant!

(claps, prompting false curtain)

And last but never least, let us now join in extending hearty congratulations to this year's newly crowned and splendidly regal, our very own ... Miss Odessa!

(Spotlight stage right. **Miss Odessa** *enters stage left.)*

MC: Thank you, Miss Odessa!

(Miss Odessa *is forcibly pulled back through curtain)*

MC: And for those of you who haven't been in this country long enough to learn Ukrainian, we'd like to welcome you all to the U-Know-Who Hall Silver Jubilee Concert!

(Nothing happens.)

MC *(hissing at wings)*: Slawko ...!

War Veteran *(peeks out)*: Now ...?

MC: Now.

(War Veteran *disappears. Curtain jerks open on assembled* **Choir.** **MC** *blows on pitch pipe, leads them in national anthem.)*

Choir:
> O Canada! Our home and native land
> True Patriot love, in all thy sons command.

(MC *addresses the audience as* **Choir** *softly concludes verse.)*

MC	**Choir**
We've got the St. Vladimir and Sofia Church Choir, the Crutchkowski Cossack Trio, the world's first Ukrainian-Canadian rock 'n' roll band, *and* a Ukrainian country and Western singer from the East! So sit back and enjoy the show!	With glowing hearts We see thee rise The true North strong and free From far and wide, O Canada We stand on guard for thee!

(Members of **Choir** *suddenly turn their choir books upside down.)*

Choir:
> Shche ne vmerla Ukraina, ni slava, ni vola
> Shche nam bratia molodii usmikhnetsia dola!
(books right side up)
> With glowing hearts we see thee rise,
> The true north strong and free!
(books upside down)
> Zapanuyem i my Bratia,
> U svoii storonci!
(books right side up)
> From far and wide, O Canada!
> We stand on guard for thee.
(sung to melody of Ukrainian anthem)
> God keep our land, God keep our land

That's glorious, that's glorious and free!
(sung to melody of Canadian anthem)
I pokazhem shcho my Bratia,
Z kozatskoho rodu!

(Blackout)

2. OFFICIAL WELCOME

Olech Dutyshyn *addresses the audience in the dark.*

Olech: Ladies and gentlemen. Being official host and hostess of this, the 25th Anniversary Concert, is the highest honor my wife Anna and I have ever had the pleasure of sharing.

(Lights up. He is wearing an undershirt, boxer shorts, and knee-high executive socks. His clothes hang on a bedroom valet.)

It makes my heart glad to see this positive manifestation of the still-living Ukrainian spirit among our loved ones.

(His wife Anna enters.)

Let us never forget that Ukraine is alive because we are alive! Its geography is mapped in our hearts!

Anna: Thirty-five years in this country, and you still act as if you're only here for a short visit!

Olech: How long have you been standing there!?

Anna: Thirty-five years with your bags all packed and ready.

Olech: Sure, I'm ready.

Anna: ... to what? Liberate Ukraine? It's *been* liberated!
(to audience) My parents were born here. That makes me third generation. It was a real shock to them when I married a newcomer – someone like Olech here, who came *after* the Second World War. *How could I marry a D.P!*

Olech: Where did you put my shoes?

Anna: Where they should be. *(starts to go, stops)* Have you thought about calling Boris?

Olech: No.

Anna: You're hoping he'll apologize first?

Olech: I'm not hoping for anything – least of all from my son! *(as Anna turns to go)* And don't you call him either!
(to audience) When I think of what I went through to get to this country ... **(Anna** *is handed shoes from wings)* ... and for what? So my son – a grown man – can prance around dressed up like a dill pickle!

Anna: You saw the commercial!

Olech *(a beat, then to audience)*: My son, the cucumber.
(to **Anna***)* What can I say when *Pan* Professor Turetski boasts about his son, the Dentist?

Anna: Tell him your son flew all the way out here from Toronto!
(beat) Olech, I want you to call Boris.

Olech: For what? Why? Just to get him to come to the Concert? After last night? No. Let him make the first move.

(Anna *looks at him for a moment)*

Anna: All right, that's it, I'm not going.

Olech: Not going!?

Anna: Olech, I told everyone Boris was going to be there! Now what do I say? That he wasn't in the house five minutes before you tore into him? That he spent the night at his sister's? That for all we know, Natalka's probably driving him to the airport right now! I know how much this Concert means to you, but if Boris and Natalka aren't going to be there ... *(turns away)* I'm not going to be there.

(A pause.)

Olech *(turns to audience)*: Children. Why do they have to grow up ...?

3. MARCH-PAST

Immediately an offstage whistle blows, and a **Troup of Campers** *marches onstage singing.* **Anna** *assumes the role of* **Auxiliary Lady** *addressing the audience, while* **Olech** *becomes* **Camp Commandant.**

Troup:
>Hey! Tam na hori sich ide,
>Hey! Malynóvyj stjah nese,
>Hey! Malnovyj.
>Nashe slawne tovarystvo
>Hey! Masheruje, raz, dva, try!

Auxiliary Lady *(during the above, in heavy accent)*: Dear parents! Enroll your children in Ukrainian summer camp now! Let your children experience an enjoyable and memorable summer among friends of their Ukrainian heritage!

Commandant: No Boris, you can't bring your mother! *(as **Boris** rejoins troup)* Those are the rules! No mothers! No bubble gum! No comic books! *(over loud protests)* Comic books *rot* the brain! No fighting! No smoking! And *no English!* Ukrainian will be spoken at all times! *(beat)* Any questions?

Boris: How do I get outa here ...!?

Troup:
> Hey! A po bokakh chetari,
> Hey! To storozhi vohnevi,
> Hey! To storozhi.
> Nashe slawne tovarystvo,
> Hey! Masheruje, raz, dva, try!

Boris *(during the above)*: Dear Mama and *Tat.* It's Boris. Your son? I'm supposed to write to say "I'm Okay" so ... I'M OKAY!!! Now can I please come home? I don't like the food, and we have to go to the bathroom in a hole in the ground. Love, your son Boris Dutyshyn. P.S. In case you've forgotten where I am ... I'm up here at Camp Smeeshu-Ha-Ha ...

Commandant: Dutyshyn!

(**Boris** *darts back to join the marchers as:*)

Auxiliary Lady: Parents can put their minds at ease knowing their children will be supervised at all times by experienced counsellors who speak beautiful Ukrainian.

Natalka: *Schlak trafit! Holera! Zaraza!* And double *holera!*

Daria: Natalka, what? What is it?

Natalka: They've moved the boys' camp to the other side of the lake!

Daria: Oh, no! Now we're not gonna have *any* fun!

Commandant: This isn't supposed to be fun! This is *culture!*

Natalka: Is he crazy?

Commandant: In Ukrainian! In Ukrainian!

Natalka: *Czy vy z durily?*

*(Outraged **Commandant** chases them off. **Boris** and **Kenny** stay behind.)*

Kenny: No, no, Boris. Don't suck on it. It's a cigarette, not a popsicle! Ya gotta act cool.

Boris: Gotta act cool ...

Kenny: Be casual.

Boris: Casual ...

Kenny: Like ya been doin' this all your life ...

Boris: All my life ...

Commandant *(enters):* Dutyshyn!

*(**Kenny** scoots off. **Boris** gulps.)*

Did you just swallow a cigarette? Ten times around the field! *Raz, dva! Raz, dva! Raz, dva!*

*(**Commandant** marches **Boris** off as **Natalka** and **Daria** enter.)*

Natalka: Oh, and that Kenny Crutchkowski is so cute! And now I'll only get to see him at Sunday Mass ... *(a sudden thought)* Hey! Maybe Kenny and I could sneak out at night ...!

Daria: But what if you're caught?

Natalka: I'll just say I got lost – looking for the *latrina!*

Daria: You think of everything!

Boris *(running past):* *Raz, dva! Raz, dva! Raz, dva!*

Daria: But what if – what if Kenny tries to kiss you?

Natalka *(thrilled):* Kiss me!? *(then:)* Oh, Daria – what if he doesn't ...?

(they exit as:)

Auxiliary Lady: Creativity will be encouraged in the many craft activities, such as cross-stitch embroidery, and Easter egg painting.

*(**Kenny** enters with a flashlight, emits a bird whistle.)*

And this year for the first time, there will be a workshop in Ukrainian ceramics!

(Answered by a bird whistle, from offstage.)

Kenny *(loud whisper)*: Natalka? Natalka, is that you ...?

Boris *(enters)*: Hi, Kenny!

Kenny: Oh bug off, Boris!

(**Boris** *shambles off*)

Where's Natalka? She said she'd be here ...
(beat) What'll we talk about? What'll I say to her? What if she
expects me to *kiss her?* Oh, God. Am I the only guy over twelve
who's never kissed a girl?

*(Chattering **Campers** enter for campfire, accompanied by **Daria** playing
"Lady of Spain" on the accordion as:)*

Auxiliary Lady: Skits, games, and folk-dancing are all included in
the camp curriculum. Children will also be able to utilize and
demonstrate their own talents in evening recreational programmes
round the campfire.

Boris: Hey! Wanna hear me sing another song?

All: NO!!!

Boris *(sings)*:
> I'm not Polish, I'm not Russian
> And I'm not Roumanian!
> Kiss me once, kiss me twice
> Kiss me, I'm Ukrainian!

Commandant: In Ukrainian! In Ukrainian!

Natalka: C'mon, Daria! Let's dance!

*(Boys begin a syncopated beat, then **Daria** and **Natalka** sing and dance a
rhumba.)*

Natalka/Daria:
> Tam na plaghi na Miami,
> Pershey raz zustriv yiyi!
> Tam na plaghi na Miami,
> Sertse viddala meni!
>
> Dumav yikhaty na Kuba,
> Na Miami zupynyvs,

A vynoyu bula rrrhumba
Pershey raz alyubyvs!
(big finish)
CHA CHA CHA!

(**Campers** *settling around campfire to hum "Taps" as:*)

Boris: Dear Mama and *Tat.* Forget my last letter. I still don't like the food, but now that Kenny and I are in the same cabin, we get to beat up all the little kids at night, and stuff our *kasha* down their sleeping bags! Just kidding! Just kidding! Lotsa love, you guys. Boris.

Campers:
Znamy boh ... Znamy boh ...

(Lights and their voices fading as:)

Auxiliary Lady: Parents! Don't deny your children this wonderful opportunity to discover and rejoice in their cultural heritage!

(**Natalka** *enters with flashlight, emits a bird whistle*)

Registration for camp at discounted rates can be made through the month of May ...

(answered by another bird whistle)

After June first, regular rates will apply. *Dyakuyu! (she exits)*

Natalka *(loud whisper):* Kenny? Kenny, is that you ...?

*(In the dark, the **Commandant**'s face suddenly appears, lit by a single flashlight from underneath.)*

Commandant: It's me.

(**Natalka** *screams. Pandemonium. All the **Campers** shriek, run for cover.*)

(Curtain)

4. WHAT'S IN A NAME?

Actor playing little schoolgirl enters, starts to recite poem before audience applause for previous scene has died down. If there is no applause, actor starts monologue in a tiny voice, barely above a whisper.

Little Daria: The name of my poem is "What's in a Name?" by William Shakespeare. *(little curtsey)* Thank you. "What's in a name? That which we call a ... uh ..."

(actor switches to:)

Male Teacher Voice: A rose! Speak up! Speak up, girl!

Little Daria: "What's in a name? That which we call a rose by any other name would smell ..."

Teacher: What's the matter? Don't you speak English? Speak up, speak up! Or do you think you're a little star?

Little Daria: No sir, Mr. Teacher, sir. I'm Daria.

Teacher: Diarrhea? Diarrhea? What kind of crazy name is that?

Little Daria: It's Daria, sir. Daria Carpiak.

Teacher: And are you a carpark?

Little Daria: No, sir. I'm Ukrainian.

Teacher: Well, you're in Canada now. You should have a Canadian name.

Daria *(on phone, teenage voice)*: Hi, Natalka. Guess what? I've decided to change my name. Are you ready for this? From Daria Carpiak to ... Darlene Carp! I know it's a fish – but it's better than being a carpark! Now I gotta start working on Mama. I wanna get my hair cut and permed. I mean, I must be the only girl in junior high still braiding it in a wreath around my head! And those blouses she embroiders for me? ... Yeah, I know, but I don't have the heart to tell her no one at school wears those *blusky*. Thank God *The Sound of Music* just came out. Now I can tell everyone I'm wearing my "Julie Andrews peasant-style blouse ..." *(sings without accompaniment)*
        "The hills are alive ...
(whirling round 360 degrees)
        With the sound of –"

Grownup Daria: Mama? We've decided to name the baby ... Dylan.

Mama Carpiak *(in Ukrainian if so desired)*: *Deelin!? Deelin!?* How did you dream up a name like that? Daria, have you gone crazy?

Daria: It's not crazy, Mama – it's Welsh! It means "from the sea," and it's the name of a very famous singer – Bob Dylan. One of today's biggest rock stars!

Mama: *Beat-niky! Rocky-rolly!* Those screamers with guitars and filthy hair! Phui! That's not music – that's noise! *Oy Bozhe,* why are you punishing me?

Daria: God's not punishing you, Mama –

Mama: Is he at least ours, this ... *Deelin?*

Daria: No Mama, Bob Dylan's not Ukrainian. He's Jewish.

Mama: Oh my God! Oh my God! What are people going to think? I'll be the laughing-stock of the community!

Daria: Nobody's going to laugh – besides, why should you care what other people think?

Mama: Why can't you choose a *human* name? Does your own smell? Call him Yaroslav after your father. You were his favorite child.

Daria: His favorite? Mama, I was his *only* child. And if *Tato* were alive today, you know he'd be on my side. Besides, Brian and I feel –

Mama: Brian! Always Brian! Wait, just wait. You'll be walking my road someday. For you, I'm nothing. Put me in old age home. I'll die there like a dog. This *Baba* will never know her own grandson Yaroslav –

Daria: THE BABY'S NAME IS *DYLAN,* DAMMIT!

Mama *(beat, then with feigned calm)*: Very well. You do whatever you want. Just celebrate the christening without me. Ohhh ... I feel faint. My head is spinning ... I'm fainting ... I can't breathe ... *Darochka,* some water ... Ohhh ...

(A pause)

Daria *(resigned sigh, then)*: Okay, Mama. How about ... Dylan Yaroslav? You *have* to come to the christening. *Mamochka ...?*

Little Dylan: Mummy ...? Mummy, I'm scared ...

Daria: Dylan, listen to me. You're going to be terrific. And Mummy's right here. In the wings.

Little Dylan: Okay, but Mummy, when I go out on-stage to say my poem, I don't want the man to call me Dylan. I want him to call me ... *Yaroslav!*

5. ROCKY-ROLLY

The **MC, Kenny Crutchkowski,** *bounces out onstage, clapping to encourage the audience.*

MC: Thank you! Thank you Dylan Yaroslav for that stirring recitation! As a token of our appreciation, please accept this copy of *Pan* Professor Viktor Turetski's monograph on "The Controversy over Shakespeare's Entrance in Slavic Literature." May it serve you well in all your future academic endeavors.

Little Dylan: *Dyakuyu, Pan* Kenny.

(**Little Dylan** *heads for the wings, monograph held out stiffly in front of him.*)

MC: And now a real treat, ladies and gentlemen. A trip down memory lane with the world's first Ukrainian-Canadian rock 'n' roll band! Yes, ladies and gentlemen they're back! Back after twenty-five years and reunited on our stage! The one and only ... Kenny's Can-ukes!

(Blackout. In the dark, we hear **Boris**'s *voice)*

Boris's Voice: *Kenny's* Canukes ...?

Kenny's Voice: Okay, okay, so we'll call ourselves ... the Can-ukey Brothers! *(his sexy "stage" voice)* Anda one, two, three, four ...

(Lights up on **Kenny** *and* **Boris** *who sing and play guitar, badly. Both are wearing sunglasses.)*

Kenny/Boris:
> We're rock 'n' rollers
> We raise your thermostat!
> Accordion music
> Is not where it's at!
> No more polkas, mama
> Gotta twist and shout!

Stare baraneee ...
Hey, we'll flush 'em all out!

(Sound of banging offstage, with:)

Olech's Voice *(off)*: SHADDDUP!!!

(They shut up. A beat)

Boris *(low)*: Can I help it if my old man thinks rock 'n' roll is a Commie plot?

Kenny *(equally low)*: Did'ja tell'm I got us a bookin' at the U-Know-Who Hall?

Boris: Yeah, but he says these late night rehearsals aren't doing my grades any good. Not if I wanna go to university.

Kenny: University!? That's years from now!

Boris: Says if I wanna go onstage, I should take up the *bandura*.

Kenny: The *bandura!?* Terrific. Let's get Daria in here with her accordion. What are we? Church basement Polka Dots!? This isn't just music, man. This is our life. Our future. And don't forget ... *(leans in confidentially)* ... those English chicks are real pushovers for guys like us that gotta shave three times a day ...

(Light change. They whirl round, point their guitars at the audience, give it all they've got.)

Kenny/Boris:
>Our kinda music
>Drives ya outa control!
>Canadian rock
>With real Ukey soul!
>Get us a bookin'
>At the U-Know-Who Hall –
>We'll give 'em all hell
>At the *Malanka* Ball!

Kenny: Thank you! Thank you! And now for our next number ...

Female Heckler *(off)*: That's not music! That's noise!

Boris: Sounds like Daria's Mum.

Second Heckler *(with off-stage boos)*: Out, out! Ve vant *real* music!

6. SOMEDAY MY UKRAINIAN PRINCE WILL COME

Tango music. Reflecting mirror ball to suggest church basement dance. **Boris** *and* **Kenny** *slink off as curtain opens to reveal a somnolent* **War Veteran** *and* **Wallflower Dummy** *sitting on folding chairs upstage beneath balloons and a dance banner.*

Lesya Cebulnik *enters dancing, leading* **Daria** *across the dance floor. Suddenly* **Daria** *tramples on* **Lesya***'s toes.*

Daria: Oops!

Lesya: Owww!

Daria: Sorry, Lesya ...

(They resume dancing. **Natalka** *enters.)*

Natalka: Kenny ... Kenny ... has anyone seen Kenny? *(to* **Wallflower***)* Have you seen Kenny ...?

*(***Lesya** *spins* **Daria** *around, tries a fancy dip.* **Daria** *screams.)*

Lesya: Loosen up, Darlene! Loosen up!

Daria: Daria! I've changed my name back to Daria!

Natalka: Since when?

Daria: Since I had to learn to spell Assiniboine!

(And **Lesya** *whirls her off.)*

Natalka: God. These *zabavas* take forever to get started. I mean, I wouldn't be caught dead dancing with another girl ...

*(***Daria** *re-enters. Taps* **Natalka** *on the shoulder. They dance.)*

Natalka: Where's Lash the Flash?

Daria: Campaigning for the title of Miss Odessa ...

*(***Lesya** *and* **Male Dummy** *enter dancing, and cross the stage.)*

Lesya: Oh, Professor Turetski! I just love dancing with you! You're such a good dancer ...!

Natalka: God. What a *Banyak* ... (looks around) Where is everybody? Kenny was supposed to be here an hour ago!

Daria: Is he bringing Boris?

Natalka: I mean, we are going steady. Daria, we *are* almost on the verge ...

Daria *(stops, with a squeal)*: Oh Natalka, no! *(then:)*Of what?

Natalka: Getting engaged.

Daria: How can you tell?

Natalka: We've been going steady for five years, haven't we? What else is left for us to do?

(**Lesya** *and* **Dummy** *enter dancing, and cross the stage.*)

Lesya: Oh, *Pan* Dutyshyn! You're such a good dancer! I just love dancing with you!

Daria: Did he say anything about me?

Natalka: Who? Kenny?

Daria: No, Boris.

(**Kenny** *and* **Boris** *enter "men's washroom." Plié in unison with their backs to the audience, then still in unison turn to the audience, miming a zip-up after a leak.*)

Boris: I dunno what it is about Ukrainian girls, but after two dances, I can feel their mothers breathing down my neck. Heck, they *are* their mothers!

Kenny: Never shoulda taken you to that party 'cross town –

Boris: Wanna go back ...!?

Kenny: You crazy? Natalka'd kill me!

Boris: What are you? A man – or a *nunka?*

Kenny: Hey! Watch who you call a wimp!

Boris: Well, you never wanna have fun anymore. You used to put away eight quarts a night. Hey, remember the time you got kicked outa honk school?

Kenny: I wasn't kicked out. I quit to play hockey.

Boris: Or the time you and Stefania Zaychik got caught playing doctor in the broom closet?

Kenny: Boris, that was *years* ago! Besides, I'm getting pretty busy now down at the store. My old man wants me to take over full-time.

Boris: *Kenny's* Paint and Wallpaper!? Don't look now, *boychik*, but ... you're getting *old*.

(**Daria** *and* **Natalka** *enter the "ladies washroom" for repairs.*)

Natalka: ... Lesya win the title? That committee can never agree on anything. You put three Ukrainians in a room together, you get *five* organizations!

Lesya *(enters, calling back)*: The next dance? Oh, *Pan* Carpiak! I'd just love to ...!

War Veteran *(reaching out to pinch her bottom)*: *Schtip!*

Lesya *(jumps)*: Ohhh! *(enters "washroom")* Bunch of old goats ... *(spots* **Natalka***)* Well, I see Kenny finally showed up.

Daria: What about Boris?

Lesya: Boris? Oh, we Ukrainian girls aren't good enough for him.

Natalka: C'mon, Daria. Let's get outa here.

Lesya: You know why, don't you?

Natalka: Lesya ...

Lesya: Those English girls put out, and we don't.

(**Daria** *bursts into tears.*)

Natalka: Now look what you've done! Big mouth! *(to* **Daria***)* Hey, c'mon. It's not true – and even if it is – it's just a stage Ukrainian guys have to go through ...

Lesya: Yeah. Like measles.

(*Music up with a flourish.* **War Vet** *comes to with a start. Bows to* **Wallflower Dummy**, *picks her up, whirls her across the floor.*)

Natalka *(re-entering)*: Kenny! Has anyone seen Kenny ...? It's the last dance ...

(Other couples whirl on, including **Kenny** *who grabs* **Natalka**, **Daria** *who grabs* **Boris**, *and* **Lesya** *who gallops her* **Dummy** *across the stage and into the wings.)*

Lesya: Stop! Stop, *Pan* Carpiak! You're too much for ... *(off)* STOP!!!

(Thud of a falling body, off, followed by **Lesya** *'s scream.)*

Boris: What is it? What happened?

Lesya *(runs on)*: It's Daria's Father!

Daria: *Tatush!*

Natalka: Oh my God!

Boris: Get a doctor!

Kenny: An ambulance!

War Veteran: De Priest!

(They all part rapidly in opposite directions. A beat. **Lesya** *looks right, then left, then straight out at the audience.)*

Lesya: They're not going to crown Miss Odessa ...?

(Blackout)

7. TABLE MANNERS

In the blackout we hear the opening notes of "The Wedding March," the last note of which turns slightly sour.

Lights up on **Kenny** *pulling* **Natalka** *onto his lap.*

Kenny: One little kiss ...

Natalka: Kenny, no! My parents are out there!

Kenny: We're engaged now, remember? *Vse* okay.

Natalka: Not here. Not in my Mother's kitchen –

Kenny: C'mere, you ...

Natalka: I want everything to be perfect tonight ... for them. For your parents. I don't want –

*(He cuts her off with a kiss. She responds. **Daria** bursts in.)*

Daria: Oh, it's awful – it's just too awful! Why did I come? What am I doing here!? *(as they break apart)* Why did you invite me in the first place!?

Natalka: Daria! What is it? What's the matter?

Daria: Boris brought a girl!

Natalka: You're kidding!

Kenny: Is she cute?

Daria: She's from *Ottawa!*

Kenny: *This* I gotta see!

Natalka *(running out after him)*: Kenny, wait ...!

Daria: I never shoulda come. I hate engagement dinners ... especially when they're not my own. At parties I'm a total nerd. I always spill things, or have one drink too many, and end up singing "Tam Na Plaghi Na Miami" just before I throw up ... Oh, why was I born ...!?

Anna *(enters, calling back)*: ... no, no problem! I'll just set another place at the table ... where am I going to find another Chicken Kiev at this hour!? *(notices **Daria**)* Daria! What's the matter?

Olech *(follows **Anna** in)*: Wendy? Wendy Wagon-heimer? What kind of name is that? Is she a Ukrainian girl?

Anna: Daria, speak to me!

Olech: What could Boris be thinking of? Bringing a strange girl home from the university. She doesn't *look* Ukrainian ...

Anna: As long as she doesn't *eat* like a Ukrainian.

Olech: Send Boris to the F.B.I.

Anna: *I.G.A.*, Olech – and it's closed.

Daria: Ohhhhhh ...

Olech: What's the matter with her?

Anna: She's not well, Olech. Can't you see that? Is it your stomach, dear? Is that what it is? Here, let me feel your head. Have you got a headache? Do you want an aspirin?

Daria: I WANT BORIS!

Natalka *(running on)*: Mama! *Tato!* Kenny's parents are here!

Anna: So soon? Oh my God! My hair's a mess! Natalka, get Daria something for her headache – *(as* **Natalka** *exits)* And while you're up there, spray the bathroom with a little air freshener! Olech, fix them something to drink while I make myself presentable ...

Olech: Where are you going!?

Anna: Out the back. I can't face the Crutchkowskis looking like this! I've got to fix my hair. *(exits)*

Olech: All this fuss and bother for the owner of a paint and wallpaper store ...

Anna *(pops back in)*: And keep an eye on the mushroom sauce! Don't let it burn! *(disappears)*

Olech: Here. This will make you feel better.

Daria: What is it?

Olech: *Vishniak.* Better than aspirin. My own personal recipe.

Daria *(takes a sip)*: It's ... strong.

Olech: Best thing for an upset heart ...

(A beat. **Boris** *runs in.)*

Boris: Mineral water! Wendy wants some mineral water –

Olech: Boris, why couldn't you bring a nice Ukrainian girl?

Boris: 'Cause all the nice Ukrainian girls I meet wanna get married.

Daria: What's wrong with that?

Boris: I don't wanna get married.

(A beat. **Daria** *knocks back the* vishniak.)

Daria: This *vishniak* tastes better every minute ...

Kenny *(pokes head in)*: Boris, no ice for my *Tat*. It freezes his dentures.

Olech: Tell your father I'm coming ...! *(follows **Kenny** out jovially with:)* Well, here we are, *Pan* Crutchkowski! Here we are at last ...!

(**Daria** *pours herself another drink.* **Boris** *continues searching.*)

Daria: Wanna sip?

Boris: No way. Wendy says most of the food we put in our mouths is poison. Don't we have *any* mineral water in this house?

Daria: Try soda water. *(under)* She won't know the difference.

Boris: Wendy says food is the body of nature's justice, and when we don't follow the principles of the Order of the Universe, we get sick. Wendy says ...

Daria: OH, WHO CARES!?

Boris *(taking a moment to recover)*: What's the matter with you?

Daria: You don't have to stay here with me, you know. Go on. I don't need you, or anybody else to hold my hand. I'm perfectly capable of being on my own ... BORIS, WAIT! *(beat)* Is there – is there something about me you don't like?

Boris: No, no ...

Daria: Is it something I said? I'll take it back! Is it my hair? You don't like my hair!

Boris: Your hair's fine –

Daria: Is it my nose? I'll cut it off!

Boris: Daria!

Daria: Is it the way I dress?

Boris: It's got nothing to do with you! Why are you always putting yourself down ...?

Daria: Okay, okay, I'm sorry! I promise I won't bother you again as long as I live! Just tell me one thing, okay? What's Wendy What's-her-face got I haven't got?

Boris: Well, for one thing – she's not ... Ukrainian.

Daria: What's that supposed to mean?

Boris: Means I don't feel ... pressured.

Daria: Pressured ...?

Boris: Look, Daria. It's just that ... with you, I can see down the road. I can see round the next corner ... and the corner after that. It's all mapped out for me.

Daria: You mean ... it's all over between us?

Boris: IT NEVER BEGAN!!

Natalka *(enters, holding her head)*: I think I'm getting Daria's headache ...

Boris: Don't you see? I'm too comfortable with you. There's no tension. No excitement. With Wendy, I never know what's going to happen next –

Natalka *(popping aspirin)*: I do. Boris, why didn't you tell us your little Wendy was a linguist?

Boris: Whaddya mean?

Natalka: She just told *Tat* Ukrainian is a dead language.

Boris: OH MY GAWD! *(runs off)*

Natalka *(to **Daria**)*: Some engagement dinner, huh? Right into the old *toilette!* And there's *Tat* playing jovial host – through gritted teeth – while Kenny flashes his "macho" at her. What is it about big boobs that brings out the master in men?

(**Kenny** *enters, struggling with a bottle between his knees.*)

Kenny: I can't pop the top offa Wendy's pop!

Natalka: See what I mean?

Kenny: Do we have a bottle opener!?

Natalka: Coming right up ... (**Kenny** *exits*) ... *master.*

(**Natalka** *starts to follow him off, stops, turns back. A pause.*)

Natalka: Daria, am I doing the right thing here?

Daria: Right thing?

Natalka: It's not just me and Kenny any more. It's his parents, my parents, who's paying, how many guests, which hall – oh, I dunno! Maybe I should travel first. Give it some time. What do you think?

Daria: I've stopped thinking. That's the best solution.

Natalka: Stop thinking. Right. Thanks, Daria. *(exits)*

(A pause. **Daria** *takes another swig of* vishniak.*)*

Daria: This is nice ... very nice ... *(pours herself more)* I think I've found a new friend ...

(Anna *runs in, pursued by* **Boris.***)*

Boris: But Mama, all Wendy said was that she'd rather have a tomato sandwich –

Anna: Boris, I have nothing against this girl –

Boris: On whole wheat, no butter.

Anna: I mean, there is no such animal as a pure this, or a pure that. But *this* girl – Boris! Her father's Jewish, and her mother's what – Spanish?

Boris: Cuban.

Anna: Whatever. And then they split, and her mother marries an Indian –

Boris: Hindu.

Anna: Hindu, schmindu! Boris, this girl is a *mongrel!*

Boris: I don't have to listen to this –

Anna: It doesn't make any sense, Boris! If you were a book-lover, would you marry a girl who couldn't read?

Boris: Who said anything about getting married?

Anna: Think about your year!

Boris: My wha ...?

Anna: Take a year – any year! When you think of Christmas, do you think of December 25th?

Daria: Uh-uh.

Anna: You think of January 7th!

Boris: Wendy doesn't think of Christmas at all! Says it's pagan –

Anna: My point exactly! All the traditional things you do the whole year round are connected with being Ukrainian. That's part of your life, Boris. Part of what you are. And if you live with someone who can't appreciate that, who can't feel what you feel, then ... you're in trouble.

Daria: Absoblooply.

Anna: Tell him, Daria. Maybe he'll listen to someone his own age.

Daria *(tipsily)*: When I was a little girl, I wanted a piano more than anything else in the whole wide world ...

Anna: A piano ...?

Daria: All the Canadian kids at school had one. And I thought if I had one too, maybe *then* they'd ask me to join the Junior Daughters of the Empire. So I asked *Tat* if I could have one for my birthday, and he said, *"Chekay, chekay."* So I *chek-ayed.* I waited and waited, and then finally my birthday came, and this big truck drove up, and delivered this big package – only it wasn't big enough for a piano. But then I thought, well, maybe it's a *baby* piano! And I opened it up, and – you know what was inside?

Anna/Boris: AN ACCORDION!

Daria: And Mama said, "Stop bawling! You want to break your father's heart? Can't you see the apartment's too small for a piano? Besides, an accordion has keys – just *like* a piano!" Took me three years to get past "Lady of Spain I Adore You"! Almost pinched my nipples off ...!

Boris: I think she's bombed ...

Daria: And now I'll never get to join the Junior Daughters of the Empire ...

Anna *(sniffing glass)*: Your father's *vishniak* – lethal!

Daria *(bursts into song)*: Lady of Spain, I adore you ...

Anna: Boris, get your father.

Daria: Lift up your skirt, I'll explore you ...

Boris: *TATO*!!!

Anna: Boris, are you out of your mind? The Crutchkowskis will hear us!

Daria: Whassa matter? Don't they like that song? How 'bout ...

Boris: Should I make some coffee?

Daria: Tam na plaghi na Miami ...!

Anna *(overlapping)*: No, no, let's just get her to bed –

Daria: Pershey raz zustriv yi yi – Get away from me!

Anna: Now, Daria –

Daria: Lemme go! Tam na plaghi na Miami ...

Anna *(overlapping)*: No, no, not that way! The Crutchkowskis will see us!

Daria *(continuing)*: ... Sertse viddala meni – CHA-CHA-CHA!

Natalka *(runs on)*: DON'T MOVE! STAY THERE! I'LL GET A *SCHMATA!*

Kenny *(enters, drenched)*: I don't need a washcloth. I'm already soaked.

Boris: Kenny! What happened?

Kenny: Stop it! Stop mopping at me!

Natalka: I'm sorry, I'm sorry! I didn't mean to spritz you –

Daria *(sniffing)*: Whass'zat smell?

Anna: OH MY GOD –

Boris: *You* tried to spritz *Wendy* ...!?

Anna: MY MUSHROOM SAUCE IS BURNING!

Daria: I think I'm gonna throw up ...

(**Olech** enters, dramatically.)

Olech: *WAIT!* I HAVE SOMETHING IMPORTANT TO TELL YOU!

(Threatening Musical Sting as all freeze. A pause, then **Kenny** *steps out of the freeze, and addresses us as the* **MC**.)

Kenny: What important piece of news has *Pan* Olech for his family?

Olech: THE CRUTCHKOWSKIS ARE LEAVING!

(Big theatrical gasp from everyone onstage.)

Natalka: Does this mean the engagement is off ...!?

(Sting)

Anna: Can Boris find true happiness with a non-Ukrainian, Russian-speaking, half-Jewish girl who refuses to eat Chicken Kiev ...?

(Sting)

Boris: And will Daria ever sober up long enough to get over her yen for me ...?

(Sting goes slightly sour)

Daria *(raising glass in tipsy toast)*: *Die Bozhe ...!*

(And promptly sinks to the floor. Pandemonium and – Curtain)

8. BOY'S NIGHT OUT

We hear **Kenny's Voice** *as the* **MC** *through loudspeaker.*

MC: Ladies and gentlemen, you don't have to be Ukrainian to be a Western Canadian. We're everywhere! And here to prove my point, is the one and only Jerry Bochko, an up and coming country 'n western singer from ... New Jersey!

(Curtain opens for **Country and Western Singer** *with a huge bandura and floppy ten gallon hat.)*

C/W Singer: Thank you, Kenny!
(launches into bilingual version of "My Darling Clementine")
　　　　Oh Natalka! Oh Natalka!
　　　　Hey zoorysia vse alright!

Koopym ford-ah second hand-ah
Tay poyidem for a ride!
(whips off hat, bows exaggeratedly)
Hey, Kenny! I hear you and Natalka are getting married tomorrow!
Take it from me, *boychik* ...
(same tune as above)
If you wed her, if you bed her
You will get no sleep at all!
Wed yourself to liberty, boy
A true Cossack's destiny!

Kenny's Voice: Hey, *Ko-zak!* Phone! It's your wife!

(Hooting, whistling as **C/W Singer** *bolts for the wings.* **Natalka** *runs on, pursued by* **Anna** *and* **Daria**.*)*

Anna: But Natalka, you can't spend the whole night up here! You've got guests!

Natalka: Oh Mama, I can't! I can't go through with it!

Anna/Daria: What?

Natalka *(overlapping)*: Nothing's turning out the way I planned. First Daria deserts me –

Daria: I'm only going to Europe!

Natalka: Then Lesya decides she doesn't like her dress –

Anna: Doesn't like her dress!?

Natalka: And now I've got Kenny's mother mad at me 'cause Aunt Sophronia won't come unless I let her sing at the wedding, and ... oh God! Why did I let you talk me into this three-ring circus in the first place? I mean, nobody has big weddings anymore!

Daria: She's right. Big weddings are passé.

Anna: Daria ...

Daria: And it's not just the Anglos, either.

Anna: Daria ...

Daria: Stefania Zaychik got married in a police station at –

Anna: DARIA! *(beat)* Go make some coffee.

Daria: I'm not thirsty.

Natalka: Why can't I have a simple ceremony? Without all this ritualistic fuss and bother? But no, everybody and their Ukrainian uncle has to get into the act! If I had any guts at all, I'd get Kenny to elope.

Anna: *Elope?* But what about all the food? The band? Your father's already put down the deposit. What do I tell Father Bossy?

Natalka: Oh Mama, I'm not *marrying* Father Bossy!

(**Boris** *and* **Kenny** *burst out, arm in arm, singing tipsily. The women draw back to watch.*)

Boris/Kenny:
>Oh Natalka! Oh Natalka!
>Hey zoorysia vse alright!
>After wedding comes Dorovnia
>We'll be counting loot all night!

Boris: Gentlemen! As chairman of the stag night committee – and best man – it is my happy duty and pleasure to now call upon my father – the father of the bride – to propose a toast to the man of the hour!

(**Olech** *enters to applause and shouted ad-libs of "Hear! Hear!"*)

Olech: *Dyakuyu*, Boris. Before we raise our glasses, I want to tell you a little story.

Boris: Oh, Oh. Here it comes.

Olech: Last Easter, Anna invited some of our neighbours in to sample her Easter bread. After they'd eaten and enjoyed our bread, one of them came to me and asked: "How long do you think you people will keep your traditions alive?" Inside, I was boiling. But I smiled and said, "As long as in *Ukraina*, in my homeland, they don't speak my language. As long as in the cities all the signs on all the buildings are in Russian –"

Boris: Goodbye, Wendy ...

Olech *(threatening gesture)*: *Ya tobie dam* WENDY! Think of it, my friends. If you want to learn Spanish, you go to Madrid. If you want to learn Hungarian –

All: You go to Budapest!

Olech: But where do you go if you want to learn Ukrainian?

Boris/Kenny: Vegreville!

Olech: Yes, yes, make jokes. But without a country, we're nothing. Then I stop and think, well, as long as I have children ... *(looks at Boris) Oy Bozhe! ...* who can pass on to their children some of the traditions of my homeland, some little part of *Ukraina* will survive. With that thought in mind, I propose a toast: To Kenny and Natalka. Long may they live and prosper. Together I know they will keep our heritage alive. To Kenny!

Kenny: To Natalka!

*(All turn to **Natalka**, hold their glasses high.)*

All: To Kenny and Natalka!

*(A pause. **Natalka** looks from the men to the women, and back again. Finally, she lifts her glass. Holds it high. Lights fade)*

9. TRUE CONFESSIONS

*In the dark, we hear the **Church Choir** softly singing.*

Choir:
>Hospody po my luy,
>Hospody po my luy,
>Hospody po my-y-y luy ...

*(Lights up on **Choir** as **Natalka** in her Sunday best crosses in front of them. She genuflects, makes the sign of the cross.)*

Natalka: In the name of the Father, and of the Son, and of the Holy Spirit. Amen. *(She sits down in front of the **Choir**. Lowers her head.)* Have mercy on me O Lord and forgive me all my sins, have mercy on me O Lord, have mercy – *(to us)* O Lord, I *miss* you, Daria! Here I am six months married, and you wanna know something? I think I'd rather be with you, hitchhiking my way around Europe. *(tiny gasp)* What am I saying? We had a *beautiful* honeymoon! Okay, okay so we spent our wedding night trapped at the Airport. But once we caught up with our luggage in Honolulu, Kenny forgot all about suing *Tato*'s travel agency. You haven't lived, Daria, till you've seen Kenny in a grass skirt! Two rum punches and you're out for the night! Or did I mention that in my last letter ...?

Choir:
>Hospody po my luy,
>Hospody po my luy,
>Hospody po my-y-y luy ...

Natalka: Hey, guess what? I finally learned how to make the dough for *varenyky*. My first coupla batches were like cement. But now Kenny says my dough is almost as light as his Mother's! So I must be doing *something* right ... *(small chuckle)* Men. Can you figure them out? If you show them the least little bit of affection, they automatically assume you want to ... do it. *(quickly)* Not that I'm complaining! I'm Mrs. Kenny Crutchkowski now and I've got the ring to prove it! Not to mention the cutest little apartment on Burrows. It's got a dishwasher, and a walk-in closet – it's even got an electric fireplace in the bedroom! Remember how we used to dream about staying up until five in the morning? Without parents breathing down our necks? I can do that now.

Choir:
> Hospody po my luy ...

Natalka: So tell me! Tell me! Who *is* this Brian character you met in Paris?

Choir:
> Hospody po my luy ...

Natalka: Is he French? Is he gorgeous? Has he taken you to dinner at the top of the Eiffel Tower? Details, girl. I want details ...!

Choir:
> Hospody po my-y-y luy ...

Natalka *(beat)*: Oh, did I tell you? Kenny's going to emcee his first concert next week, and I've signed up for a course in creative writing at Red River College, so we're really moving up in the world. Kenny's also thinking of sponsoring his own dance group. I just hope he doesn't dress them up in T-shirts advertising the store – or God, expect me to join. I'm not about to pull out my red boots and start stomping around again. No way! Daria, there just aren't enough hours in the day, what with me trying to keep a house – *and* Kenny going. I'm telling you, Daria. Married life is great! Just great. You oughta try it, sometime. Soon. *(rises to genuflect, crosses herself)* In the name of the Father, and of the Son, and of the Holy Spirit. Amen.

*(She exits as **Boris** comes up the aisle from the back with a collection plate, soliciting donations from the audience.)*

(Lights slowly dim to black. A pause)

10. THE ELEVENTH COMMANDMENT

Spot on **Boris,** *pacing*

Boris: Oh, God. I'm twenty-three years old, for crying out loud! Four years of university behind me! I know what I want. What makes me happy. None of that "who am I, where am I going" garbage for me. I know where I'm going! *(stops)* And it's not to law school!

(to us) So why the hell can't I tell Mama and *Tat* ...!?

(Lights full up. **Olech** *in a bathrobe sits facing* **Anna** *at kitchen table, having breakfast, reading Ukrainian newspaper.)*

Olech: I see in the paper *Pan* Turetski's boy just graduated from dental school.

Boris: I'll call them tomorrow. *(starts to go, stops)* What are you? A man – or a *nunka* ...?

Anna *(falsely casual)*: Why don't we give Boris a call? See how he's doing.

Olech: At eight o'clock in the morning? Have you seen this month's phone bill?

Boris: Okay, okay, I'll write them a letter ...

Olech: He's a grown man, Anna. Let him live his own life.

Boris: I know! I'll get Natalka to call them! No guts, eh? Okay, so what's the worst that could happen? I'll say, "Listen, *Tato*. I've come to a decision, and I want you to be the first to know ..." No, cut the crap. Get to the point. Straight out. Man to man. "Listen, *Tato*. You'll never guess what's happened ..."

Anna: Something's wrong. I can feel it.

Boris: Nothing's wrong ...!

Olech: What could be wrong?

Anna: When I called Boris last night, there was no answer.

Boris: No, no, I don't need money. Everything's fine ...

Anna: And when our phone rang at three o'clock this morning, there was no one there –

Boris: Listen, *Tato* –

Anna: I could tell it was Boris.

Olech: You could?

Anna: I recognized his breathing.

Boris: WILL YOU LISTEN TO ME, *TATO!?*

(Pause. **Olech** *disappears behind newspaper.* **Boris** *swallows hard.)*

Boris: I've won a scholarship. To Banff. Yeah, in Alberta. There's a summer school there. No, no, not for lawyers – for actors. *Acting –* you know, like in the theatre or movies ...?

Anna: Olech, I'm worried.

Boris: No, no, not as a hobby ...

Anna: I don't know what to think.

Boris: Not a part-time job ...

Olech: Anna, please.

Boris: I'm dropping out of law school to take up acting full time. *(sharp intake of breath)* "Czy ty zduriv? Are you crazy?"

Olech *(testily, snapping paper)*: You're driving us *both* crazy.

Boris: "Don't you realize how hard I worked so you could do better?" Yes! Yes, I know you shelled out all that money for me to go away to university, and – I am not throwing anything away! What am I throwing away? If you want my degree so bad, I'll send it to you! I don't want to be a lawyer! I want to be an actor! You're the one who encouraged my singing and dancing! "Oh, that's different. That's preserving our culture. And you can't make a living preserving culture in a country where the *only* culture is hockey!" *(slumps)* Oh, God. It's gonna take me forever to work up enough nerve to call him.

Anna *(beat)*: You want some *chay?*

Olech: No, no tea for me.

Anna: How about some coffee?

Olech: I don't want any coffee.

Boris (*brightening*): Maybe *Mamch*'ll pick up the phone ...!

Olech: Anna, sit down.

Boris: "Boris! How wonderful to hear your voice! How thoughtful of you to call! And if that's what you want, if that's what makes you happy –"

Olech: Where're you going!?

Boris: "I'll help you pack, I'll even drive you out to Banff myself, and –"

Olech: He'll think you're checking up on him!

Boris: Who am I kidding? She'll be bawling her eyes out!

Anna: I don't care! I'm calling Boris! (*exits*)

Boris: And *Tat*'ll grab the phone away from her – "Boris! You're going to be a lawyer! A good lawyer the way we planned! You'll get married. A nice Ukrainian girl. With lots of nice little Ukrainian grandchildren –"

Olech: Anna, put down that phone!

Boris: "Big house in Tuxedo Heights, two cars in the garage –"

Olech: Anna!

Boris: "Mortgaged up to here –"

Olech: Did you hear me!

Boris: NOOOOOOOO!!!

(*Light change. Focus on* **Boris**. *Pause.*)

Boris: No. I can't do that. Those are your dreams. I can't live your dreams. I'm not interested in the money. I don't care about security. I want to go into theatre. It's what I love doing. And I want to give it a try. I've got this scholarship to Banff, and I'm going to take it. It's my life, *Tato*. My life. (*pause*) Hey, that wasn't so hard. Was it? (*pause*) Now all I gotta do is start dialing ...

Olech (*off, shouting*): OKAY, OKAY! PHONE HIM! BUT I WANT TO TALK TO HIM FIRST!

(*Panic on* **Boris**'s *face, and ... Blackout*)

11. SPONSOR'S MESSAGE

In the blackout, we hear a drum roll. **Kenny's Voice** *as the* **MC**.

Kenny's Voice: Ladies and gentlemen, direct from Folklerama, we proudly present the Crutchkowski Cossack Trio! Here to remind us that – Kenny's Paint and Wallpaper Palace always has the solution!

(Lights up on **Kenny** *and a female backup* **Trio**. *All four wearing Cossack hats and T-shirts advertising "Kenny's Paint and Paper.")*

Kenny:
> If you need some paint, wallpaper ...

Trio:
> Varsol, brushes, polyscraper ...

Kenny:
> Come to Kenny's Paint and Paper ...

(with **Trio**)
> You don't pay till one year later!

All:
> Lucho bulo, lucho bulo malyvaty
> Yak vam treba farbu moghna nabraty
> My tut v *Kenny*'s mayemo naylipshi tsiny
> Yak vam treba malyuvaty vashi stsiny!

(Kenny *steps forward to address his unseen wife, Natalka.)*

Kenny: Europe! You wanna go to Europe!? Look Natalka, now that we're married, we gotta start saving for a house. Why? Whaddya mean, why? 'Cause that's what people do when they get married. Besides, I don't want my kids growing up in a shoebox, do you? *(pause)* But I thought you wanted kids ...

(Daria *steps out from* **Trio** *to address her unseen husband, Brian.)*

Daria: No, I don't want to. I'm too tired ...

(Kenny *turns his back to the audience.)*

Daria: I mean it, Brian! I had a hellish day at the office, and I'm dead tired. *(beat)* Well maybe if you helped out around the house more often, I wouldn't be so tired all the time! *(half-beat)* Now look what you've done! You woke up the baby! No, no, don't get up. I'll go ...

Kenny *(turns to face the audience, sings)*:
    For your decorating pleasure ...

Trio:
    You can browse here at your leisure ...

Kenny:
    Milk and cookies for your children ...

Kenny/ Trio
    Have some coffee in our kitchen!

Kenny *(addressing an unseen Natalka)*: Okay, okay, so I forgot about your job interview! Yeah, I know I was supposed to arrange my own ride so you could have the car – what are you saying? That I did it deliberately? To sabotage your chances ...? *(controls himself, with great effort)* Look, Natalka, if you wanna take some two-bit TV gofer job way the hell out in suburbia – whaddya mean I don't take your ambitions seriously?

Daria *(whirls round to face audience.)*: Brian, I mean it!

(Kenny *turns his back to the audience.)*

Daria: Don't you dare turn your back on me! Why is it every time I don't agree with you, *I'm* the one who's emotional? It's my Slavic temperament ...? For your information, Brian, I'm just as Canadian as you are! Do I drag you off to my church? Make you sit through Ukrainian concerts? Force *holoptsi* and *borsch* down your throat? I *know* you like *holoptsi* – that's not the point! *(beat)* The point is, Brian, you're never *here* for me. Yes, yes, your body's here, but I don't want to spend the rest of my life watching you watch television!

(Kenny *turns to face the audience.* **Daria** *stays where she is.)*

Kenny: Okay, okay so I'm not the kinda guy who recites poetry or anything, but we've got a good life here. A nice home. Respect in the community. Three week vacation each summer. What more do you want?

Daria: Attention! I want you to pay some attention to me. Every time I try to talk to you about something's that's bothering me –

Kenny: Career! What career? Your career is *me!*

Daria: Oh for God's sake! What do I have to do to get you to take me seriously? Walk out on you?

Kenny: So, go! Go! Don't let me stop you!

(A pause)

Daria: Mama was right ...

Kenny: I shoulda married a Canadian girl!

Daria: I should've married a Ukrainian guy ...

Kenny: At least then my expectations wouldna been so high ...!

Daria: At least then my expectations wouldn't have been so high ...

Kenny *(softly)*: Natalka ...? Natalka, are you still there ...?

Trio:
> Here at Kenny's you are really a somebody,
> We will try to undercut just everybody,
> Our prices are the lowest and the best,
> We are miles ahead in service from the rest!

(tra-la-la-ing under for:)

Kenny: And wait! Wait till you see our prices! Just twelve ninety-five a gallon for Super Latex House and Trim Paint ...

*(He stops, stares straight ahead. **Trio** continues behind him, then he picks up the thread.)*

Kenny: Just twelve ninety-five. Nobody – but nobody undercuts Kenny's Paint and Wallpaper Palace! Nobody ...

*(Lights change to isolate **Trio**.)*

Trio:
> Nobody, but nobody
> Has better prices than we do ...
> You deserve a break today
> So come to Kenny's, we'll show you ...
> We will always treat you right,
> Compare our prices, we're not jealous
> Eaton's, Simpson's can't compete
> With Kenny's Paint and Paper Palace!

(Spot Out)

12. HOME SWEET HOME

Lights come up on chanting **Pickets**.

Pickets: *Ukrainska mova v schkowy* ... Ukrainian in our schools ... *Ukrainska mova v schkowy* ...

Natalka *enters, speaks to audience as if to TV camera. Behind her,* **Pickets** *circle the stage.*

Natalka: Heritage language rights – the hottest issue on the school scene today. And it's all part of the new consciousness brewing in the Ukrainian-Canadian community – especially among the under 35-year-olds, who may not know Ukrainian themselves, but who want their children to learn.

(**Anna** *steps out from picket line to address the audience.*)

Anna: My grandparents broke the back of this country! Three thousand miles of railway after Thunder Bay!

Natalka: As you can see, our Legislators obviously have their work cut out for them. For S-I-T-Y News Break, this is Natalie Hays at –

Anna: French and English weren't our only founding fathers!

Natalka: Mama, *please. (peers out into audience)* Did you get that on tape ...?

Anna: Don't forget, Natalka. Dinner on Sunday.

(**Anna** *exits with* **Pickets**. *Last* **Picket** *off, stops. Turns back.*)

Daria: Natalka? Natalka, is that you ...? It is! Oh, my God! I don't believe it! Natalka Crutchkowski! It *is* you, isn't it?

Natalka: Daria ...! Last time I saw you – was at Lesya Cebulnik's wedding! Which was what – four years ago?

Daria: Five. But who's counting? *(shared laughter. A pause.)* I heard about you and Kenny.

Natalka: Yeah.

Daria: What happened?

Natalka: Who knows? Maybe we just outgrew each other. What about you and ... Benny?

Daria: Brian. Oh, we split up.

Natalka: I'm sorry, I didn't know.

Daria: You're not the only one. It's been two years, and Mama's family in Ukraine *still* don't know. *(sighs)* Sometimes, I think marrying Brian was a mistake. Like, part of me – the Ukrainian part – I feel like it's been dead and buried for years.

Natalka: And now you've dug it up again to picket the Legislature. Better watch out, Daria. Or you'll turn into one of those professional ethnics!

Daria: Move over, Lesya Cebulnik! *(shared laugh)* Tell you one thing, though. If I could find some nice boring Ukrainian guy, I'd marry him – like that!

Natalka: You shoulda married Kenny.

*(A beat. **Daria** doesn't know what to say.)*

Natalka *(glancing at her watch)*: Listen, I gotta run –

Daria: Will I see you at the Anniversary Concert? I hear Kenny's emceeing. And Lesya's going to dance. It'll be like old times!

Natalka *(half-beat)*: Yeah. Look, why don't we have lunch? My number's in the book.

Daria: Under Crutchkowski or Dutyshyn?

Natalka: Under *Hays*. Natalie Hays. *(defensive little laugh)* Can I help it if those Anglo announcers screw up my name? Nautil-ka! Noodle-ka! You wouldn't believe what they did to my last name!

Daria: And you a big TV star ...

Natalka: Hardly. I leave the star parts up to Boris.

Daria: How is Boris? Is he married?

Natalka: Sorta. He's sleeping with someone, but they keep separate apartments.

Daria: Another Wendy ...?

Natalka: Muffy.

Daria: Why separate apartments? If she's not Ukrainian ...

Anna (*enters, calling back*): It's a phone, Olech. You just pick it up, and dial –

Olech (*off*): I'm not senile, Anna. Just retired!

(**Anna** *bites her lip, hesitates.*)

Natalka: My Dad's still waiting for Boris to come to his senses, and get a *real* job ...

Olech (*off*): And I'm not calling anyone! I'll go to the Concert *alone!*

(**Anna** *makes a dismissive gesture, crosses stage, exits.*)

Natalka: Another Wendy would finish him.

Anna (*off*): *Boris!* What a pleasant surprise ...! (*re-enters with* **Boris**) Olech! Look who's here! It's Boris!

(**Olech** *enters, but keeps his distance.*)

Doesn't he look wonderful?

Olech: Same as yesterday.

Anna: What's this?

Boris: Just a little something I forgot to give you last night.

Anna: A *watch* ...! Oh Boris, you shouldn't have! Look, Olech. Real gold. Isn't it lovely?

Olech: Anna, we'll be late.

Anna: What we need is some *chay.*

Olech: They won't hold the curtain ...

Anna: Milk and sugar for you, Boris?

(**Boris** *nods.* **Anna** *exits.*)

Natalka: Listen, I gotta go. But let's keep in touch, okay?

Daria: Natalka ...?

Natalka (*stops*): Yeah?

Daria (*beat*): Don't you wish we had it back?

Natalka: What?

Boris: Did you say something?

Daria: Nothing.

Olech: I said nothing.

Daria: Never mind.

(**Natalka** *exits. After a moment,* **Daria** *follows her off.*)

Boris: So. Here we are.

Olech: Yes.

Boris: You okay?

Olech: Fine.

Boris: No, 'cause *Mamch* said you had a pretty rough night –

Olech: I'll outlive you all!

(*A pause.* **Boris** *looks around.*)

Boris: So. I see you had the place repainted, eh?

Olech: Same color as last night.

Boris: Uh, yes. Yes, I can see that. Looks nice.

Olech: Glad you like it.

Boris: You should see my place. Took me months to fix it up. I'm looking for a house now. Figure, next place I fix up, it's gonna be my own!

Olech: If you'd been a lawyer, you'd have a house – sooner!

Boris: I'm not starving, *Tato!* I earn a decent living.

Olech: Dressed up like a cucumber!

Boris: Those TV spots pay my bills! Besides, that's not all I do. Next week, I've got a radio play, and the week after that, I start rehearsals for *Death of a Salesman. And,* a director friend of mine has promised me a part in his next film!

Olech: And what *else?*

Boris: What the hell else would be enough for you!? *(pause)* Sorry. Didn't mean to raise my voice.

Olech: Children grow up. They lose respect for their parents.

Boris: Respect? You wanna talk about respect? I *know* how hard you worked all those years to put me through school. My degree that I never used – just listen to me! Everything I do – *every day* – is to get your approval! And you don't *give* me any! That's fine. I'm not even *counting* on that. But I gotta tell you one thing ... I've never ... I've never told you that I love you – and I do! And I know that you love me. I just – once ... would like to hear it. That's all.

(Silence)

Olech: Well ... I ... we ... took it for granted, that it would be understood ...

Boris: What, *Tat? What!?*

Olech *(relief)*: Ah! Here's your Mother at last ...!

Anna *(enters with tea tray)*: We're all out of sugar. I brought honey instead. You don't mind?

Boris: Honey's fine.

(A pause)

Olech: That's – that's a beautiful watch, Anna.

Anna/Boris *(simultaneously)*: Thank you ...!

(They look at each other, and laugh. A pause.)

Anna *(linking arms with both)*: What do you think? Should we have our tea now ... (to **Olech**) ... or after the Concert?

(Curtain)

13. GRAND FINALE

Kenny *as* **MC** *bounces out with great energy.*

MC: Ladies and gentlemen! On behalf of our *Komitet*, I would like to take this opportunity to extend a sincere and profound thank you ...

(House lights up)

... to the many individuals, organizations, and business firms who have made a special contribution to the success of our Anniversary Concert!

(hissing at wings)

Slawko! Slawko! It's not over yet!

War Veteran *(enters from wings)*: Not over!?

MC: The choir, remember?

War Veteran *(low, as he exits)*: *Nay yeeh schlak trafit ...!*

MC *(big smile for audience)*: As I was saying, ladies and gentlemen ...

(House lights go down.)

... their devotion, loyalty, and support enhances Ukrainian culture to the high standard that presently prevails today. And here to demonstrate that high standard with a special *"Dyakuyu"* of their own ... the St. Vladimir and Sophia Church Choir!

(Curtain opens on assembled **Choir**. **MC** *leads them in song.)*

Choir:
>Apple pie, varenyky
>Hot dogs, pizzas, holoptsi!
>Rock 'n' roll, viva Kozaks!
>Fleur de lis, or Union Jacks?

>All our lives we have been taught
>Not for us the melting pot!
>Heaven help us, can't you see?
>Caught between two worlds are we. *(repeat)*

*(***Soloist** *goes into jazzy bilingual version, as the rest of* **Choir** *"be-bops" in background.)*

Soloist:
>Christmas time we so revere
>Celebrate it twice a year!
>Vnas sprava neta sama
>Vnech hot doggy vnas kobassa!

*(***MC** *turns to address audience as* **Soloist** *concludes verse, both voices rising in volume as each fights to be heard.)*

Melting pot tse ne for me,
Tak navchyleh rodychi!
Caught between two worlds are we!
Life is just a co-me-dy! *(repeat)*

MC *(during the above)*: Yes, ladies and gentlemen. Life is just a comedy. And that's the theme of next Saturday's *zabava*-banquet at the U-Know-Who-Hall, where the Ladies' Auxiliary of the Grandsons of Ukraine will be serving *kurka* and Baked Alaska. Tickets are $25 per couple at the door, $20 if purchased in advance. Until then, on behalf of our *Komitet*, I'd like to thank you all for coming here tonight. Please, drive carefully! And remember, life is ... *(pauses dramatically for:)*

Choir: *Chysta Ko-mmedia!*

(**MC** *turns his back on audience to conduct* **Choir** *as they step forward, bringing the song to a rousing climax.)*

Choir:
All our lives we have been taught
Not for us the melting pot!
Caught between two worlds are we
Life ...
(life is just a)
Is ...
(life is just a)
Just
(life is just a)
A ...
(life is just a)
Co-medy!
HEY!

(Curtain)

GLOSSARY

Baba	Grandma
bandura	guitar-like instrument
Banyak	hick, hayseed
borsch	beet soup
blusky	blouses
boychik	little boy (derogatory)
chekay, chekay	wait, wait
Czy vy z durily?	Have you gone crazy?
Darochka	diminutive of Daria
Die Bozhe	God willing
dorovnia	gifts of money to the bride
Dyakuyu	thank you
holera	cholera (a swear word)
holoptsi	cabbage rolls
kasha.	buckwheat porridge
komitet	committee
Kozak	Cossack
kurka	chicken
latrina	outhouse
Mamch, Mamochka	Mom, Mummy
Nay yeeh schlak trafit	May evil befall them
nunka	wimp
Oy Bozhe	Oh God
Pan	Mr.
Raz, dva! Raz, dva!	One, two! One, two!
schmata	washcloth, rag
Stare Baranee	old goats
Tam Na Plaghi Na Miami	There on the beach in Miami
Tat, Tatu, Tatush	Dad, Daddy
Ukraina	Ukraine
varenyky	dumplings
vishniak	homemade liquor
Vse okay	it's okay
Ya tobie dam Wendy	I'll give you Wendy ...!
zabavas	dances, parties
zaraza	pox, pestilence (swear word)

Note: Ukrainian is written in the Cyrillic alphabet. The above is an approximation of these words in the Roman alphabet.

Pronunciation Guide

Baba	Bah-bah
bandura	bun-do-rah
Banyak	Bun-yack
blusky	blue-ski
borsch	bore-ssht
boychik	boy-chick
chay	ch-eye (rhymes with "Hi")
Chekay, chekay	check-eye
Czy vy z durily?	che veh z do-ril-ee?
Darochka.	Dah-roach-kah
Die Bozhe	Die Boh-zeh
Dorovnia	doe-rove-knee-ah
Dyakuyu	Dee-yah-coo-you
Holera	hoe-leh-rah
holoptsi	hoe-lope-tsi
kasha	ka-shah
Kozak	Co-zack
Komitet	co-mee-tet
kurka	coor-ka
latrina	la-tree-nah
Mamch	Mumch
Nay yeeh schlak trafit	Nay-ech sh-lack tra-feet
nunka	knee-yeun-ka
Oy Bozhe	Oi Boh-zhe
Pan	pun
Raz, dva! Raz, dva!	razz, dvah
Stare Baranee	Stah-reh Bah-rah-knee
Tam Na Plaghi Na Miami	Tum nah Pla-zeh nah Miami
Tat, Tatu, Tatush	tut, tatoo, tuh-toosh
Ukraina	Oo-kra-ee-nah
varenyky	vah-wren-neh-key
vishniak	veesh-knee-ak
Vse okay	v-shay okay
Ya tobie dam Wendy	Yah toe-bee-eh dumb Wendy
zabavas	zah-bah-vas
Zaraza	zah-rah-zah

ADDITIONAL GLOSSARY

- honk school: from the word "hunky," a derogatory reference to Ukrainian language school which most students had to attend on Saturdays

- Vegreville: town in Alberta which is home of the world's biggest Ukrainian Easter Egg

- U-Know-Who Hall: a play-on-words, referring to the U.N.O. Hall (Ukrainian National Organization)

- January 7th: Ukrainian Christmas (Julian calendar)

ENGLISH TRANSLATION OF SONGS

Anthem

Choir

Shche ne vmerla Ukraina, ni slava, ni vola,
Shche nam bratia molodii ushmikhnetsia dola
(Ukraine has not died yet, as freedom cannot die!
Be hopeful valiant brothers, our glory will revive!)
Zapanuyem i my bratia,
U svoii storonci!
(The enlightened rule of kin
Our country will regain!)
I pokazhem shcho my bratia,
Kozatskoho rodu!
(And Oh brothers, we'll show them
The path to victory!)

Camping Song *(literal translation)*
Hey! There on the hill a troup of soldiers
Hey! Carrying a maroon-colored banner
Hey, maroons
Our bravely gathered brotherhood,
Hey! Marching one, two, three!

Hey! On the sides, other divisions
Hey! Those guardian warriors,
Hey! Guardians
Our bravely gathered brotherhood,
Hey! Marching one, two, three!

Tam Na Plaghi Na Miami
(Musical Director's Version)   *(Literal Translation)*

There on the beach in Miami	There on the beach in Miami
My true love she had been found	First time I met my true love
There on the beach in Miami	There on the beach in Miami
She was so plump and so round	She gave her heart to me
We went off into the sunset	Thought I'd take a trip to Cuba
Put my hand upon her leg	But I stayed on in Miami
She looked at me and	Blame it on the rhumba
said "Let's Rhumba"	
I said Go suck an egg!	First time that I fell in love
Cha cha cha!	Cha cha cha!

Taps
Znamy boh ...
          (God is with us ...)

Stag Serenade (1)
Oh Natalka! Oh Natalka!
Don't you worry, it's all right
We'll buy us a second-hand Ford
And I'll take you for a ride!

Stag Serenade (2)
Oh Natalka! Oh Natalka!
Don't you worry, it's all right!
After wedding comes the dowry
We'll be counting loot all night!

True Confessions
Hospody po my luy
          (Lord, have mercy on us)

Singing Commercial
(2nd verse is a take-off on a well known Ukrainian song)

All
It's better, so much better to be painting
If you need paint, you can get it here
Here at Kenny's we've got the best prices
If you need to be painting up your walls!

Grand Finale
Christmas time we so revere
Celebrate it twice a year!
With us things are not the same
With them it's hot dogs, with us kobassa!
Melting pot it's not for me
From our parents we've been taught
Caught between two worlds are we!
Life is just a Co-me-dy!

No Man's Land

by RAHUL VARMA

Rahul Varma is a founding member and current artistic director of Teesri Duniya, a multicultural theatre group based in Montreal since 1981.

His first play, written in Hindustani, was *Bhanumati Ka Pitara*, a short comedy about a stereotypical Hindi film from Bombay, the Hollywood of India. This play has been staged in several Canadian cities and was produced by Indian Television. A second play, *Bojha* [The Burden], deals with the evils of dowry.

Varma's first English language play, written in 1987 with co-authors Helen Vlachos and Ian Lloyd-George, was *Job Stealer.* The following year he wrote, with Stephen Orlov, *Isolated Incident.* Both plays, directed by Rahul Varma, won awards in the Quebec Drama Festival. *Isolated Incident* was published by TSAR Publications in *The Geography of Voice*, edited by Diane McGifford. He again collaborated with Helen Vlachos on *Equal Wages*. Rahul Varma's first full length play, written in 1990, was the very successful *Land Where the Trees Talk;* it was produced at Montreal's Centaur Theatre.

Rahul Varma received his B.Sc. from the University of Lucknow, India, and is a research technician at McGill University in Montreal. He originally wrote in Hindustani; English is the language of his adulthood.

ORIGINAL PRODUCTION

No Man's Land was first workshopped and developed in Cahoots Theatre Projects' new play development program, LIFT OFF 93, in Toronto on May 8, 1994. Rahul Varma was the sole author. Dramaturge/Director was Sally Han.

An earlier version, co-written by Rahul Varma and Ken McDonough, was staged by Teesri Duniya in Montreal on October 22, 1992.

ORIGINAL CAST AND PRODUCTION TEAM

Qaiser Quraishi	Ken McDonough
Jeena Quraishi	Raminder Singh
Teja Singh	Andre Martin
Samreen	Dipti Gupta
Martin	Aziz Mulay-Shah
Marie-France	Heidi Imami
Birney	Steve Slawvey
Dr. Khaber	Arvind Jain

Minor roles were played by Sudha Krishnan, Shalini Lal, Andre Deslauriers, Hiram Shmerer.

Director	James Douglas
Set Designer	Lucinda Vandenieuwegiessen
Lighting	Lorin Levine, Blair Lovell, Elliot Smith
Music	Catherine Potter, Ganesh Anandan, Kapil Bawa, Kim Knox

REVIEWS

"The play produces some strong and searing images of immigrant life in our supposedly democratic country." (Montreal *Downtowner*)

"*[No Man's Land]* contains piercing observations and witty lines; ... it's got heart, guts, and an original point of view." (Montreal *Gazette*)

A radio version of *No Man's Land,* titled *Trading Injuries,* was featured on CBC Stereo Drama.

PLAYWRIGHT'S NOTE

Except for the native people, everybody in Canada is either an immigrant or a descendant of an immigrant. Qaiser, Jeena and Samreen are typical new Canadians who have chosen this country as their home. They have gone through certain hardships in settling down in Canada. But there are many families who have gone through the same experience before them, and will do so after them.

PERFORMANCE PERMISSION

For permission to perform *No Man's Land,* please contact **RAHUL VARMA,** 1510 St. Jacques W., #6, Montreal, Quebec H3C 4J4, (514) 938-1854.

Characters

Qaiser Quraishi: A Muslim immigrant from India

Jeena Quraishi: Qaiser's wife

Teja Singh: A Sikh, friend of Qaiser

Samreen: Qaiser and Jeena's daughter, 2nd generation

Martin: Factory worker

Marie-France: Waitress at Teja's Tandoori Dhaba

Birny: Cloth Merchant

Dr. Khaber: Jeena's Doctor

SCENE 1
Buying house; late 1979-80

Sound: car stops, turns off, doors open and close. They inspect the house from outside.

Qaiser: Look at this house. Two stories, balcony, a lawn and a backyard, two car garage and a church within two blocks.... But still the price did not hit the sky. Thank you, God.

Teja: Don't thank God. Thank Mr. Levesque and his sovereignty referendum.

Qaiser: It is a bargain.

Samreen: Baba, whose house was this?

Qaiser: It is going to be ours.

Samreen: I mean, whose house was it before?

Qaiser: I don't know. Jeena, how do you like it?

Jeena: Good.

Qaiser: That's it – just good?

Jeena: It is good.

Qaiser: What is on your mind, Jeena?

Jeena: Has the previous owner left Quebec?

Qaiser: That is not my concern. All that matters to me is that this is what I want. It is a buyer's market out there, Jeena. If I don't buy now, I never will.

Teja: So it's the passion politics.

Sound: (Flashback in Jeena's mind) Mob violence, gunfire, people running, children crying, etc. These sounds gradually increase throughout the next few lines.

Jeena: Thank you, passion politics? It is the passion that drove us out of our home ten years ago ... and half of our family before that from their ancestral home.

Teja: You mean the partition of India.

Jeena: I was only a child and I still have nightmares of that ...

Sound of chaos grows louder

Teja: But nobody is forced to leave Quebec.

Sound comes to an end

Jeena: Yeah, they are made to leave.

Teja: No, they are made to vote. Remember the referendum?

Jeena: Wonderful. Civilization at last.

Qaiser: Jeena, I did not come here to hear about the misfortunes of those who had to leave their homes. I came to show you the house that I want to buy, because now is the time to own our own house. We need this house because we don't have anything here. Nobody to protect us and nobody to guide us. We need this house for Samreen. Okay?

Teja: Like other immigrants – invest in a house, not in the stock market, so that the immigrant children can inherit a secure future.

Samreen: I haven't seen it from inside.

Qaiser: Let's go inside.

SCENE 2
Interior of the house

Qaiser: Look at these large windows, the high ceiling, look at the marble floor, look at the fireplace.

Samreen: Look at the church right from the window. I can hear the church bells right from the bedroom. And wow – two bathrooms!

Teja: Can't afford to be constipated in this house.

Samreen: Baba, I am impressed.

Qaiser: You know what? I am going to give you the best room.

Samreen: Why me?

Qaiser: Because in our old sub-basement apartment, your mother told me every day that Samreen should have the best room.

Samreen: Thanks, ma.

Jeena: I said every girl should have her own room in the house while growing to be an adult.

Samreen: And soon I am going to be a complete adult with complete adult features. (**Samreen** *poses in front of an imaginary mirror with a teenager's innocence.* **Qaiser** *is not pleased.*)

Qaiser: Tut, tut. Think before you open your mouth. Just because you are more Canadian than we are is no reason to act like them.

Samreen: Okay. I love the house and I would love to have my own room.

Qaiser: But remember ... no friends in dirty sneakers.

Samreen: What do you mean? I can't have my friends over?

Qaiser: You won't be allowed to mess up the house, especially my Indian carpets.

Samreen: That's no fun.

Qaiser: We are going to keep it sparkling clean. We are going to show the world we are here and we are here to stay for all our life. Teja, my friend, you met us the first day we came to Canada. And you are with us today when I am buying my first house.

Teja: Typical immigrant. Remember everything they do first in the new country.

Qaiser: That is right, mister. I remember and I want to thank you very much for everything.

Flashback sound: Montreal Street. Canada in the seventies. Winter setting in.

SCENE 3
Montreal Street; flashback

Qaiser: Hey, mister.

Teja: Calling me?

Qaiser: Yes sir.

Teja: Just got off the boat?

Qaiser: Yes please.

Teja: First time in Canada?

Qaiser: Yes.

Teja: It shows. Canada is mighty cold eight months of the year. Wrap your baby in something warmer before the baby catches pneumonia.

Qaiser: Yes sir.

Teja: Don't wait for the snowfall. The national sport here is ice hockey, you know, not field hockey. Come on, let's get you out of the cold before the baby freezes completely. Just around the corner is the YMCA, the shelter for international arrivals. We can sit and talk there.

SCENE 4
YMCA cafeteria; flashback continuing

Teja: By the way, my name is Teja Singh.

Qaiser: I am Qaiser Quraishi. This is my wife Jeena and this is our baby Samreen.

Teja: What a peaceful little baby. Never cries.

Sound: The baby cries.

Teja: Oh, you little cheater. Any trouble at the immigration?

Qaiser: They accepted our refugee status.

Teja: The government won't let you die once you are here. But it is worried. Too many refugees.

Qaiser: From where?

Teja: Mainly from ex-colonies. Some are running from persecution, others "plan" on becoming refugees.

Jeena: Nobody plans on becoming a refugee.

Teja: Oh, the bogus ones do. And they are avid planners. Plan everything, right down to their proof of persecution – an instant snapshot taken in front of their burnt-out shop. Now they spend their days waiting for their refugee hearings. Thank you, Canadian taxpayers.

Jeena: We did not want to be refugees.

Teja: Do you know I am a Sikh from the Pakistan side of the border?

Jeena: You don't look Sikh.

Teja: Just because I am not wearing my turban? Well, with a turban-less head I don't look Sikh. But I had to change my appearance just to escape alive. Ah, well, such were the times and such was the racial hatred. Now I am a weekend Sikh. I put on the turban on the weekends only when I have to go for weekly worship. Ha. Have to keep the culture alive, you know. Rest of the time they take me for a Hindu who prays faithfully to a thousand different Gods. I'd rather not say anything about the Muslims – minimum punishment, death.

Jeena: I wouldn't dare say a word about any one of them.

Teja: They hate each other just the same.

Jeena: Here, too?

Teja: Here too.

Qaiser: In Canada?

Teja: In Canada.

Jeena: Oh, dear God.

Teja: *(laughing)* God does it to them. Can you imagine a Hindu praying five times a day like a true Muslim? Or a Muslim worshipping a phallic symbol like a true Hindu? Or either one of them with a seven yard long turban and a dagger around the shoulder like a true Sikh? Funny! Immigrants become more religious once they come to Canada.

Jeena: So they fight with each other here, too.

Teja: Oh, no. Sometimes they take a break – like when they decide to fight against racism in the Canadian system.

Jeena: Excuse me!

Teja: Canada will teach you some of life's hard realities. Everybody makes it in the end, though. Now, what you need most is a roof over your head, a kitchen to cook in, and a sitting room to watch TV like all other immigrants.

Qaiser: That sounds like a good idea.

Teja: I'll fix things up with the landlord. Nice pot-bellied man. Cheap but not too cheap. I will help you buy a few household things from the co-op.

Jeena: Co-op?

Teja: Co-operation!

Jeena: Co-operation?

Teja: Leftist-minded white folks run it for needy families.

Jeena: Salvation Army?

Teja: Something like that. After all, your countrymen don't believe in co-ops. Na na. First thing they set up is a mosque ... or temple or a *gurdwara*.

Jeena: Please.

Teja: They get an emergency fund set up to import a preacher from India.

Jeena: Didn't we have enough of them already?

Teja: *(sarcastically)* They serve your religious needs.

Jeena: I need pots and pans, Teja.

Teja: Sorry, God doesn't care much for practical needs.

Qaiser: We are lucky we met you. I don't know what we would have done without you.

Teja: The pleasure is all mine. *(laughs)*

Sound of laughter blends into music and brings us to the present.

Jeena: So, will you stand and thank each other or do whatever you have to do next.

Qaiser: We thank the real estate genius and we move in.

SCENE 5
Jeena's Narrative 1 (1980)

Jeena: *(internal)* Moved in we did, into this beautiful duplex. It took us eleven years of hard labour and careful supervision of poverty. And I worked like a dog. Part time, full time, overtime, all the time. Because Qaiser wanted to buy a house. No matter what sacrifices I had to make and no matter what I had to do. I knew it would be hard in the beginning, but did I know the beginning would last forever? And Qaiser, who has been fixated on buying this house, would like me to believe that things will be different for me now! Huh.

SCENE 6
Inside the house

Jeena doing housework

Qaiser: Don't you miss not having that horrible, smelly, sordid rotting sub-basement apartment we lived in for ten years?

Jeena: I do. Because I am so used to clean, scrape, wax and polish. I think I have decorated this house beautifully.

Qaiser: That's for sure.

Jeena: Superb dressmaker, superb factory worker and superb housemaker.

Qaiser: Do I detect sarcasm?

Jeena: When do the facts become sarcasm?

Qaiser: Jeena, I wasn't a fool to have brought a charred brick all the way from India.

Jeena: I know that, Qaiser.

Qaiser: This brick is all the memory I have of my home back home.

Jeena: The memory is well preserved in the middle shelf of the cabinet.

Qaiser: The upstairs tenant has decided to stay on. We can renegotiate the rent once his previous lease expires. But I feel uncomfortable talking to him about money.

Jeena: Then don't talk about money.

Qaiser: There is so much I want to talk to you about, and not about money. There is so much we have been missing ...

Jeena: Have we been missing something?

Qaiser: For too long. Jeena, we have a great bedroom and before we forget all about it ... especially when our teenage daughter is not home.

Jeena: What is it with you, Qaiser?

Qaiser: Remember how we used to meet before we got married?

Jeena: I remember.

Qaiser: You used to hang a green towel on your window to let me know that no one was home. And I used to sneak into your house.

Jeena: I was young then.

Qaiser: Let me care for you the way I used to. Please ... come.

He kisses her.

Jeena: Stop.

Qaiser: Jeena, I am your husband.

Jeena: And so you think you can ask me anything.

Qaiser: I sure can. Take this saree off.

Jeena: Qaiser, we are growing old for that sort of thing.

Qaiser: That is why we should not wait any longer.

Jeena: It is funny the way you display your middleaged hormonal imbalance.

Qaiser: How long is this saree? God, Indian women wear too many clothes.

Jeena: And western women wear too little.

Qaiser: And waste little time.

Jeena: I envy them.

Qaiser: Why? Why after so many years in Canada, you still wear a saree.... Eh ... help me unwind it.

Jeena: NO!!!

Qaiser: What's wrong? Feeling shy with me?

Jeena: I don't want you to see my body. Even I am frightened to see it. It is not the same any more.

Qaiser: Doesn't matter to me.

Jeena: You don't understand.

Qaiser: What?

Jeena: The ugly flab of flesh which waddles around my waist. Veins which are popping up from under the skin of my legs. Looks like the map of the world. That's what I cover under the seven yard long saree.

Qaiser: I can switch off the lights.

Jeena: You don't get it, do you? I can't do it.

Qaiser: I was just seeking some affection.

Jeena: You can't understand that.

SCENE 7
Jeena's Narrative 2

Jeena: *(internal)* How long have I gone on denying that this was coming? How long have I tried to convince myself that this condition is normal because all the women in the factory have swollen legs? God – the more I deny, the more I hate myself, and the more I hate myself, the more I deny. And I don't know why. What will I tell the doctor? That I missed the bus by ten steps because I couldn't walk fast enough? That I was busy setting up the new house? Why have I waited that long to visit my doctor? Fear? Maybe I know what she is going to tell me. She will tell me to stop working. I wish it was as easy for me to do as for her to say that.

SCENE 8
Doctor Khaber's Clinic

Dr. Khaber: I have here your test results, Jeena. And I have some questions.

Jeena: I will try to answer, Dr. Khaber.

Dr. Khaber: Does anybody else in the family have a history of such symptoms?

Jeena: You mean stiffening of the muscles?

Dr. Khaber: And breathing discomfort.

Jeena: No.

Dr. Khaber: No tuberculosis?

Jeena: Not to my knowledge.

Dr. Khaber: Jeena, do you remember having this discomfort before you started working in the sweat shop?

Jeena: I don't remember seeing so much smoke and such noisy machines in my life.

Dr. Khaber: Has any health inspector ever visited your work place?

Jeena: Doctor, I went to the factory to work, not to get involved in politics.

Dr. Khaber: But somebody should care about what is going on.

Jeena: When something goes wrong, they will take care of it.

Dr. Khaber: Like?

Jeena: Like there is this man who comes every month.

Dr. Khaber: With a sandwich in one hand and coffee in the other. And laughs *(mocking)* har har har ...

Jeena: After every line.

Dr. Khaber: That must be the union boss. But I am not worried about general grievances. My concern is your health. Did anybody in your factory ever make you fill out a health questionnaire? If yes, I would like to see it.

Jeena: I don't recall anything of that kind.

Dr. Khaber: Nobody from the government?

Jeena: No.

Dr. Khaber: Now you know who to blame when someone dies in the factory.

Jeena: What?

Dr. Khaber: I am terribly sorry. That was very unprofessional of me. I guess I am frustrated with the lack of action.

Jeena: But what about my treatment?

Dr. Khaber: Oh yeah. I almost forgot. I am ordering some more tests. I will treat you for the medical side of it now and deal with the official side later.

Jeena: Official side?

Dr. Khaber: If this is a work-related thing or a long term disability or anything else. In the meantime, as a precaution maybe you should consider quitting the factory.

Jeena: Doctor, I have to work.

Dr. Khaber: Jeena, you have already bought your house.

Jeena: Now we have to pay off the mortgage. Besides, a second pay cheque is a big help.

Dr. Khaber: I mean, there must be some other kind of work.

Jeena: I did a second job, too. More sewing.

Dr. Khaber: Piecework at home?

Jeena: For this man called Birny.

Dr. Khaber: Another low-salary, no-benefit job.

Jeena: Doctor, we bought a house. Not with the earnings but with the savings and overtime.

Dr. Khaber: I can understand that. My folks are first generation immigrants too.

Jeena: Doctor, the work is what gives me my pride. Besides, I have a daughter to send to university.

Dr. Khaber: I understand. As your doctor, it is good to know your background. Well, here is your prescription, and please make another appointment. I would like to visit your home some time. Is that all right?

Jeena: You are most welcome, any time.

Dr. Khaber: I'd like to meet your husband, too.

Jeena: Then you have to call first. Sometimes he works at night.

Dr. Khaber: Where?

Jeena: Teja's Tandoori Dhaba. It is a restaurant. My husband is part owner.

SCENE 9
Teja's Tandoori Dhaba

Music: popular Indian music playing on tape deck.

Teja: Marie-France.

Marie-France: In the kitchen.

Teja: Factory is out.

Marie-France: I hope they pay their bills.

Teja: Stop serving them on credit. We need paying customers.

Marie-France: I don't know what it is. Bad government or recession, or what?

Teja: Call it resurgence.

Marie-France: What is that?

Teja: Resurgence of shipload of separatists, Captain Jacques Parizeau in control.

Marie-France: Don't they remember the last referendum? The separatists lost their pants.

Teja: You know, there is a saying in India, you can't straighten a dog's tail if you bury it straight in the ground for eight years.

Marie-France: All I want to straighten up is our customers. For goodness' sake – we need money a whole lot more than the strip joints do.

Teja: What do you know about strip joints?

Marie-France: Where do you think I met Martin? I don't want to go back to cha-cha-cha-ing buck-naked for a bunch of toothless old men.... Here comes Martin.

(**Martin** *enters*)

Teja: Martin, we were just talking about you.

Martin: I don't care.

Marie-France: You had a run-in with somebody.

Teja: I will leave you two lovebirds alone.

Marie-France: So, Martin!

Martin: I need official protection.

Marie-France: Is someone after you?

Martin: My living standards are going down the toidy.

Marie-France: What are you going to do to up them?

Martin: Send all the greaseballs back to where they came from.

Marie-France: Martin, shut up.

Martin: Rid the factory of them.

Marie-France: Shhh ...

Martin: And the country.

Marie-France: Did you leave your brain at the assembly line, or what?

Martin: I know your problem.

Marie-France: Enlighten me, Martin.

Martin: You are colour-blind.

Marie-France: Oh, really!

Martin: Look around you. Hordes of coloured women. One baby pulling her saree, another in her arm and one in her belly. Only fun they got is breeding year round. I think the government should do a survey.

Marie-France: Survey?

Martin: Survey of their breeding habits. But instead, what does it give them? Baby bonus! Cash for kids. Do you bring any bonus home?

Marie-France: I am not a breeding factory.

Martin: You are not patriotic. Give them fifty years and we will be the visible minority. Bunch of kids singing the Canadian anthem in Punjabi, with their twisted tongues.

Marie-France: *(clenching teeth)* You better watch your tongue.

Martin: And this manager guy at my factory – Qaiser.

Marie-France: He is my boss too. Part owner of the Dhaba.

Martin: Bloody Paki.

Marie-France: You shut up, Martin. Teja is not too far.

Martin: He is another Paki.

Marie-France: Shh. He might hear you.

Martin: Doesn't he know?

Marie-France: What's your problem, Martin?

Martin: This dwarf Qaiser.

Marie-France: What about him?

Martin: He ain't tall enough.

Marie-France: Is that why you look down on him?

Martin: The guy had to climb on a three inch thick brick to reach the machine. He carried a goddamn brick with him. And look where he is now. Before I could spit, he got a business, sucked up to a manager post and bought himself a house.

Marie-France: Martin, he is coming. You better think before you open your mouth.

Martin: Hell, that's just how I talk. I tell it the way it is.

(**Qaiser** *enters*)

Qaiser: Hello, Marie-France. Martin. *(pause)* What's the matter? No talk? Where is Teja?

Teja: *Assalam-wale-kum*, Qaiser.

Qaiser: *Wale-kum-salam.* So, what will it be for you, Martin? Rum or scotch, or a double draft?

Martin: It's okay.

Qaiser: Martin, I know why you are upset. But I don't think you understand.

Martin: Oh, yeah.

Qaiser: Let me explain.

Martin: *(outburst)* You let go three of my buddies. What are you going to do next? Stop me from taking my union break? Blackmail me by dangling more refugees in front of my face?

Qaiser: Mr. Banks makes the decisions.

Martin: There are rules in this country. Have you heard of rules? R-U-L-E-S.

Qaiser: Look, Martin ...

Martin: Don't order me. I am on my own time. I'll say what I fucking well please.

Qaiser: I don't fire anybody. Mr. Banks orders me and ...

Martin: You order us.

Qaiser: I have to do my job.

Martin: What job? Hire more of your kind?

Qaiser: Your kind don't do the shit jobs that my kind do. You know that.

Martin: Why should they? Why should they work for peanuts?

Qaiser: You know what your problem is? You think you own this country.

Martin: Damn, how long have I been in this country?

Teja: Martin, did you have a bad day?

Marie-France: I think he had a rough day.

Martin: My great-grandfather was born here. My grandfather was born here, my father was born here, my mother was born here. I was born here. My dog was born here. But it's me who lives in the dog house.

Marie-France: Every dog has his day.

Teja: Martin, this man is your boss.

Martin: This man is a job stealer himself.

Qaiser: Martin, you are so stupid, you are so typically stupid, you can't even figure out that if it was so damn easy to steal, I would have stolen something better.

Martin: Oh yeah? How did you become a manager?

Qaiser: I worked hard. If you have a bit of self-respect, work as hard as I do.

Martin: I would rather live on welfare than work for less that what I deserve.

Marie-France: Martin, go home.

Martin: Don't order me around. I will go when I please. *(pause)* Bye.

Marie-France: I am sorry, Qaiser.

Qaiser: It is not your fault.

Marie-France: I can't believe this drivelling idiot is my boyfriend. Trust me, I will have a serious talk with him.

Qaiser: Not on my account, because I am going to give him a chance to see how hard I worked.

Teja: Marie-France, I think you can go home. I will lock up.

Marie-France: Thanks. Bye.

Qaiser: God, I hate it.

Teja: Just ignore it.

Qaiser: How? No matter what, somebody will always make me feel guilty for anything and everything I do. Does he think I enjoyed lining up in front of the factory before sunrise in below twenty cold? Twenty years in this country, and it feels like I just landed.

Qaiser *throws a glass which crashes against the wall. Sound blends into ship hooter, leading us back to 1970 when his family had just arrived.*

SCENE 10
Flashback

Teja: Don't you worry, Mr. and Mrs. Quraishi. They do things to the newcomers that they don't do to their own poor. And while we are at it, have you got any money?

Jeena: Only my gold jewellery.

Teja: Enough to invest? Like, say $250,000?

Jeena: $250,000?

Qaiser: Then you better look for a job. They will ask you, "Have you got any Canadian experience?"

Qaiser: I don't.

Teja: Then they will tell you, "No Canadian experience, no job."

Jeena: How do you know?

Teja: That's my Canadian experience.

Jeena: Then what are we going to do?

Teja: Canada has got tons of factories for you. That's where Mr. Byron Banks comes in.

Jeena: Who?

Teja: A man who knows a good bargain when he sees one. So I will take your husband down to the factory to meet Mr. Banks.

Qaiser: Factory?

Teja: That is right. You can kiss your degrees good-bye. Mr. Banks believes in hard work, not paper work. He would want you to use your hands, not your brain. He would want you to be a family man who would not join the union or go on strike. And he will pay you more than you could ever make in your country.

Qaiser: But I am not in my country any more.

Teja: Then he will remind you about your work visa. There are only two words on the front of that — renewal or deportation. Any questions? Don't bother.

SCENE 11
Jeena's Narrative 3

Jeena: *(internal)* And that's what we have got – a family. What about freedom? I feel that I am caught in a circle going round and round and doing the same thing over and over. First I killed myself to buy this house and now I might die paying it off. I want to scream, yet I don't know if anybody will hear me from the cage I am in. Huh ... the family is like an octopus with a thousand tentacles. You escape from one and another grabs you. That's how it is in my family, I know.

SCENE 12
At home

Qaiser: I pay the bills!

Jeena: They are on the table.

Qaiser: Let's see. Hydro, telephone, TV, gas ...

Jeena: And property tax.

Qaiser: Already.

Jeena: Don't forget insurance and school tax.

Qaiser: Never ends.

Jeena: Lake a master-slave relationship.

Qaiser: Are you calling me the master?

Jeena: Home is our master. Furnish, care, watch, repair, maintain. A task for life.

Qaiser: Here fly in her books, and here comes in Samreen.

Samreen: Hi mom, hi baba.

Qaiser: Where were you? It is quite late.

Samreen: Ma. I want to go to Toronto.

Qaiser: For how long?

Samreen: For the weekend.

Qaiser: Forget it.

Samreen: It is an educational trip.

Qaiser: How much?

Samreen: I already got one hundred working at the gallery.

Qaiser: How much more?

Samreen: Two hundred.

Qaiser: Too much.

Samreen: I will make do with one hundred and fifty.

Jeena: You will have two hundred.

Qaiser: You spoil her.

Jeena: That's how we planned it, dear. Not to have another child so we can give her our best and most.

Jeena: Thanks, mom and dad. You saved me from being jealous.

Door bell.

Qaiser: That must be Teja.

Jeena: Are you going somewhere with him?

Qaiser: To a meeting.

(**Teja** *enters*)

Jeena: *Assalam-wale-kum,* Teja.

Teja: *Sat-sri-kal ji.*

Qaiser: I better get dressed. *(exit)*

Samreen: Uncle Teja, I know why you are dressed in your checkered jacket.

Teja: Why?

Samreen: For the subsidized multicultural dinner.

Teja: Somebody big is coming from Ottawa.

Samreen: A handshake day?

Teja: It is different this time.

Samreen: That's novel. Is it election time already?

Teja: It is constitution talk time.

Samreen: So this "somebody big" from Ottawa is going to pat your shoulders: "Canada is a community of communities."

Teja: You know us ethnics. We have to be assured.

Samreen: By a bureaucrat in a reception hall! And there the East Indian people gather to catch up on the gossip. Whose daughter has run away with whom? Whose son is going out with a white girl? Who had his picture taken with the Minister of Multiculturalism!

Teja: And talk about tax loopholes and mortgage rates.

Samreen: And listen to the priest *(imitating the Mullah)*, "Our women must remain *in purdah.*"

Teja: *(enjoying)* He is protecting women from other men.

Samreen: Women should be protected from him. The asshole says, "Our boys must not get trapped by impure white women. White women are not thoroughbreds. If our boys father a child with a white woman, they are ruining a centuries-old culture." Disgusting bloody old smut.

Jeena: Enough, Samreen.

Samreen: If his culture is so bloody fragile, why did he come here in the first place?

Teja: To save enough to go back to his roots.

Samreen: Bloody hypocrite. If I ever hear him talk like that again, honest to God, I'll puncture his testicles.

Jeena: Samreen.

Teja: Let's be honest, Samreen. He gets hundreds of people for his weekly lectures.

Samreen: Which people, and what lecture? Five hundred East Indian people telling another five hundred East Indian people what it is like to be East Indian in the western context?

Teja: *(jokingly)* I think you will understand that when baba finds a suitable match for you from India.

Samreen: No thank you, I am not interest in training an apprentice in integration.

Jeena: Enough, Samreen.

Car horn

Teja: Who is that?

Samreen: No one.

Teja: Where are you going?

Samreen: Library. *(exit)*

Teja: She means Talat.

Jeena: Yeah, I remember the look.

Teja: Samreen is a smart girl.

Jeena: It's the boy I'm worried bout.

Teja: Talat is a good boy. And the family is good, too.

Jeena: You never know these half-Indian, half-Canadians. They want the best of both worlds. I have seen so many immigrant sons do the same thing.

Teja: You mean return back to their roots and marry a certified virgin?

(**Qaiser** *enters*)

Qaiser: Where did Samreen go?

Teja: Library.

Qaiser: Let us go. There are plenty of our people in this country. We should build contacts for our Dhaba.

Jeena: Qaiser, the doctor is coming today.

Qaiser: What?

Jeena: You want me to repeat?

Qaiser: Why do you invite people who ...

Jeena: Who do what?

Qaiser: Never mind.

Jeena: I did not call her. She was driving by this way and wanted to drop by. She thinks the work is killing me and I must stop. She wants to talk to you, too. What was I supposed to say? Please don't come?

Qaiser: You don't need a doctor to convince me. If you want to stop, you don't need my permission. But there is talk of a strike in my factory.

Jeena: Strikes are happening all over these days.

Qaiser: People are losing jobs all over, too. In case you forget, we have a mortgage to pay.

Teja: Big deal; you have a Dhaba to fall back on.

Jeena: Go and build contacts in the multicultural conference. I will explain to the doctor.

SCENE 13
Jeena's Narrative 4

Jeena: *(internal)* Lately the separatists are gearing up to do their thing again. *(sarcastically)* "Le Québec aux Québecois." I remember such slogans back in India the year we lost everything. If it wasn't for them, we wouldn't have fled our home in the first place. And I wouldn't have been killing myself to make a home because we had a home back home. I want to grab hold of one of those separatists and shake him up: "Do you know what you are doing? Look at me. This is what fleeing home has done to me. It is for people like you that a man has to run away with a brick in his hand." Companies are closing all over since the separatists got active again. Then there is this strike that is dragging on in Qaiser's factory. Just the thought that I may be uprooted a second time in my life frightens me to death.

SCENE 14
Teja's Tandoori Dhaba (across from the factory)

Sound: pro- and anti- separatist slogans (Vive le Québec libre, Quebec yes, Canada no ...)

Martin: Marie-France, it is all over.

Marie-France: The strike?

Martin: The company slammed the door on us after six weeks.

Marie-France: What do you mean?

Martin: Declared bankruptcy. Just like that. You know, there are lots of guys who have poured blood, sweat and tears into the factory. And, just like that, all gone, not even a good-bye.

(**Qaiser** *arrives, throws his briefcase on the counter.*)

Qaiser: Are you happy now, Martin?

Martin: Some of us didn't want to live in shit and feel great about it.

Qaiser: It is stupid to go on strike when the economy is in a mess.

Martin: When is a good time to go on strike? When the economy is booming? Striking is all we had left for our pride.

Qaiser: What pride are we going to experience lining up in front of the U.I. office?

Marie-France: Makes you sick, doesn't it.

Martin: Do the politicians know about it?

Marie-France: Do they care? I mean, they have been locked up somewhere talking about the constitution, they don't even remember there is a recession. One day one of them will need a screwdriver and get lost looking for Pascal's.

Teja: This English-French thing is so stupid, you don't know which one will sell the other out before selling you out.

Martin: I bet our trouble started with this separatist thing.

Marie-France: What more do the separatists want?

Martin: I think they want to separate.

Teja: Good answer.

Martin: They want to bring Québecois babies into the world from the old-stock Québecois.

Marie-France: Everything of their own, right down to the dirty movies. And all for them and them alone. So that Celine Dion wouldn't have to go to L.A.

Martin: But what am I going to do? Move out west? Or live on $250 a week U.I. and six weeks of job retraining?

Qaiser: What retraining? Who will hire a fifty year old man? I will be turned down wherever I go. It's so depressing.

Teja: Don't worry, you will get used to it.

Qaiser: What? Being depressed?

Teja: No, being turned down.

Qaiser: You are so depressing.

Teja: Qaiser, let's face it. You were manager in a third-rate factory which hired cheap labour to work their 1970-model machines. But I guess you heard words like modernization, high tech, cost cutting and computer. My friend, your best bet is the Dhaba.

Qaiser: Where will we get customers? Factory is closed. Dhaba will have to be folded too.

Teja: If we fold up now, we may not have customers waiting when things get better.

Qaiser: We may not have to fold up, if we had customers now.

Teja: That is another Catch-22. That is why I say it is time to move to a new location. Re-invest a hundred or couple of hundred thousand dollars ...

Qaiser: Where will we get the money?

Teja: Borrow! Use your house as collateral.

Qaiser: Are you crazy? We still have a mortgage to pay off.

Teja: That is why I am saying don't condemn your lifelong struggle to futility. I am not begging for alms. I am making a business proposition.

SCENE 15
Jeena's Narrative 5

Jeena: *(internal)* Survival at all costs. Even Qaiser doesn't think about it – he believes in it. But I am running out of excuses. Excuses like, "So what? If it is not the disease, the age will stop me."

Or, "What will Samreen do?" as if she is helpless without me. And the recent one – "The way factories are closing these days, it would be stupid to quit while they are still in business, especially now that Qaiser's company has gone bankrupt."

Too long I have convinced myself that all success stories are similar: all struggles are struggles in different ways. Not any more. Now I have begun to question. He wants to save his house at any cost. But how will I save my lungs and legs?

And there is this Doctor Khaber! She keeps coming with new ways. Now she has begun to talk about suing the factory.

Door bell

Qaiser: I have to go out for a while.

Jeena: Qaiser, stay. She wants to talk to you.

Qaiser: Nobody told me.

Samreen: You didn't tell anybody that you had to go out.

Qaiser: Is that how you talk to me?

Jeena: Qaiser, Doctor Khaber is going to stay until you come back. So please open the door.

Sound. **Qaiser** *opens the door.* **Khaber** *enters.*

Dr. Khaber: Hello, Mr. Quraishi. I am glad I found you home.

Qaiser: Where could a jobless person go?

Dr. Khaber: Mr. Quraishi, I wanted to talk with you both. About Jeena. I have got some of the test results and I'm afraid the news isn't good.

Samreen: Oh no.

Jeena: I didn't think it would be.

Qaiser: Yes, Jeena has been complaining for some time.

Dr. Khaber: Well, she hasn't quit yet, but I have been complaining for a long time.

Samreen: I have been begging her to quit.

Qaiser: Samreen.

Dr. Khaber: She is showing signs of acute vascular clotting in her lower extremities, and the X-ray suggests deposition of fibrous agents, probably due to inhalation, which might cause irreversible pulmonary damage.

Qaiser: I only speak English and Urdu, doctor.

Dr. Khaber: I am recommending that she rests.

Samreen: It is about time.

Qaiser: What?

Samreen: There is no "what" about it, baba. Working in thirty degree heat with buzzing machines is no job for my sick mother.

Jeena: But it is better than *no job* at all.

Dr. Khaber: Jeena, I am ordering you to rest. NO WORK.

Qaiser: That is fine, but you are scaring her.

Dr. Khaber: No, Mr. Quraishi, I am doing my job. I am taking care of my patient.

Samreen: Thank you very much, Khaber.

Dr. Khaber: Jeena, now I have strong evidence that your injuries are related to your work. So with my letter you can stop work without loss of your income for some months. In the meantime, a few other doctors, social workers and lawyers will take legal action against the company on behalf of the victims.

Jeena: Victims?

Samreen: That includes you, ma.

Dr. Khaber: Mind you, most of them are immigrant women.

Jeena: What does it mean, Doctor?

Dr. Khaber: It means, if we win, and that is still a big if, you might collect some compensation.

Jeena: What will it compensate?

Dr. Khaber: Permanent injuries that the sweat factory gave you.

Qaiser: Could it be substantial?

Dr. Khaber: My main concern is her health.

Qaiser: Yes. Of course. Thank you very much, Doctor.

Dr. Khaber: But I want you to do some work for me, Mr. Quraishi. I want you to find this character Birny.

Qaiser: Why?

Dr. Khaber: Because, like Jeena, some other women did piecework for him besides working in the factory.

Samreen: And you figure that the factory will try to establish that the piecework is responsible for the illness.

Dr. Khaber: A number of these women are from the same neighbourhood and like Jeena they all worked at home.

Samreen: Implying that the conditions at home were hazardous?

Dr. Khaber: Yes, and implying that the women brought illness upon themselves.

Samreen: Disgusting.

Dr. Khaber: So, Jeena, are you ready?

Jeena: Ready for what?

Dr. Khaber: To sue the ...

Samreen: ... bastard factory owner.

Qaiser: Samreen!

Jeena: Compensation is a silly word.

Dr. Khaber: Yes, it is. It is a silly word. Nothing could compensate you for the injuries to your legs and lungs. But I had asked you to stop. Did you? Now I am asking you again. Compensation does sound silly, but it is your right. I am leaving these papers. Read them, think about it, sign and call me. I promised to visit two more women. Bye now. *(exit)*

Samreen: Bye, Khaber.

Jeena: Bye, Doctor.

Qaiser: Thank you very much, Doctor.

Jeena: *(softly)* Sure.

Samreen: I will find Birny. I will go to my old neighbourhood.

Qaiser: Teja will know. He brought him to us.

Jeena: *(sarcastically)* Didn't waste any time. I had not written a letter back home and he was on my door with his sewing machine and rags.

Qaiser: He has to be in the city. Because he left his machine downstairs ... just in case.

Jeena: *(sarcastically)* As a souvenir. Every time I pass by, it buzzes in my ears ... What a bargain Teja had brought for me....

Sound: flashback. Sewing machine resonates, blending into flashback music taking us into the past, a little after the family arrived in Canada.

SCENE 16
Flashback in old apartment

Birny: *(annoying voice)* Hi. Are you Jeena? I know you are. Hi, I am Birny. I better slam down the machine on this table before I wreck my waist.

(**Birny** *slams down the sewing machine on the table.*)

Jeena: I don't think I know you.

Birny: That just proves you are new in the neighbourhood.

Teja: Birny, tell her about the bargain.

Birny: *(to Jeena)* You run my machine. I will lease it to you. I bring the rag, you sew the label. I deliver, I pick up and I pay you cash ... no tax. And if you don't mind my saying, you will be sitting pretty with a deal like this, because the more you work the more you get. You can build your future stacking up labels right here in the comfort of your home. *(pause)* What's the matter? Don't you talk? Do you understand English? Eh? Speak French, or what? *Parlez-vous français?*

Jeena: No, Mr. Birny, my country was colonized by the English.

Birny: Whatever that means. I don't care whether you speak English or French. I would prefer it if you spoke neither.

Jeena: I prefer to go out and look for a job.

Teja: But Jeena, where will you leave your one-year-old?

Birny: Listen lady, there is no shortage of your kind in Canada.

Jeena: *(to Teja)* What does he mean by that?

Teja: You know ... the runaways, the boat people, the aliens, the refugees ... you know.

Birny: And their women work for less.

Teja: *(patronizing, to Jeena)* Shit, I don't know why these refugees jump the boat and bring down the wages of senior refugees. I mean, if they stayed home ...

Birny: What would I do? Har har har ... just kidding. Look, madam, if you have something else lined up, I will take my mobile business back. I haven't got all day.

Teja: Jeena, he hasn't got all day.

Birny: Look, lady. I know why Teja and your hubby came to me. If a man wants to put jewellery and furs around his wife's neck, send his children to private school, own a Pontiac, a station wagon and a boat and live in a brick house, he has got to work like a dog, and make his wife work like a dog. So be a good girl, okay? I am going to show you how this machine works. Like this ... pedal back and forth.

Sound of machine blending into music brings us to the present.

SCENE 17
In the house, same day

Qaiser: Jeena, Samreen has gone to look out for Birny. She should be back soon.

Jeena: I know she has gone to look out for him.

Qaiser: The factory should be sued for every single penny for doing this to you.

Jeena: The factory, Qaiser?

Qaiser: Didn't you hear the doctor? She sounds very confident that you will win.

Jeena: And also pay off your house.

Qaiser: Our house.

Jeena: I just don't understand, what is in this house that I have abused myself so much. For what? The walls, the ceilings, the window, what? What about me?

Qaiser: This is about you. Besides, we can pay off the mortgage.

Jeena: Is that what I am worth? I don't want to live here any more.

Qaiser: Jeena, I understand you are upset. I am upset too. But if you sign ...

Jeena: How long have I been in this country?

Qaiser: About twenty years.

Jeena: Not about twenty years. More than twenty years. And now I must depend on whether or not I find a man called Birny.

Qaiser: No Jeena, you must trust your doctor. Sign these.

Jeena: Compensation. What does she think I am? What do you think I am? Stuff of trade? Is that what I have to do? Trade my injuries to save this house? Answer me, Qaiser.

Qaiser: Don't scream.

Jeena: Answer ...

Qaiser: Jeena, if you think any wrong has been done to you for the house, the compensation is going to make up for it.

Jeena: Will it? Look at me. What will it make up for me? I don't even remember how I looked when I was younger. Am I the same? Is this me? *(She pulls her stiff and twisted fingers)* Is this my face, my hair? *(She scratches her face, pulls her hair)* Look at my belly.

(Jeena *beats herself.)*

Qaiser: *(screams)* Stop it. Stop it.

Jeena: No, this is not me.

Qaiser: You want proof. Look into that mirror. That is you. Feel your face between my hands? That is your face. I am only trying to make the best out of the situation. So stop acting mad. Sign the form and I will take it to the doctor when I come back from the Dhaba. *(exit)*

Jeena: *(sarcastically)* Please sign the form and I will take it to the doctor.

(Samreen *enters.)*

Samreen: Ma, what is wrong with baba? He was so uptight. Says the woman doesn't understand anything.

Jeena: Woman meaning me?

Samreen: *(noticing her face)* Ma, is everything okay? Are you all right, ma?

Jeena: I am all right.

Samreen: You don't look okay.

Jeena: I don't know what to look like.

Samreen: Okay. Ma, I am sorry, I didn't find Birny.

Jeena: I didn't want you to.

Samreen: The women say they haven't seen him for some time, but they suspect he is still in town.

Jeena: I didn't want you to go looking for him.

Samreen: Ma, it is not a small claims court settlement.

Jeena: I don't want it.

Samreen: You what?

Jeena: Didn't you hear?

Samreen: Ma, you still make less than I do at my summer job.

Jeena: I have made up my mind.

Samreen: You are sure you don't want to think it over? Least you could do for yourself is get paid for the damages.

Jeena: No. Funny – now everybody is calling it damages. Earlier it was called building the future. I want to tell you something, Samreen.

Samreen: Let me get your medicine.

Jeena: No, let me tell you.

Samreen: You can tell me while I apply medicine on your leg. Okay.

Jeena: Can you believe it happened for a brick?

Samreen: How many times I told you to stop, but you didn't.

Jeena: Let me tell you. I want you to hear it carefully. You had just started going to kindergarten. Which gave me hope that I will start my career as a teacher. But I couldn't stop the realities of the life

cycle. Whether I wanted to or not I had to make certain choices –
for you, for your father and an authentic brick that meant
everything to him. For him, a man once dispossessed of his home
would remain a man without an identity unless he gets one....

Samreen: That's all you have done. Made sacrifices.

Jeena: That's the story, and it goes on.

Samreen: And, stupid me, I never wondered why it is the same
people who go on working in the factories.

Jeena: I still don't believe I worked twenty years in a factory that
crippled me. And it happened for a brick.

Samreen: If it wasn't for the doctor you wouldn't stop.

Jeena: Samreen, I am scared. I was scared like this only once
before in my life. Back in India during the riots when masked men
attacked me. And now when I am going crippled. I am beginning
to hate myself for letting this happen to me.

Samreen: Why didn't you stop?

Jeena: That is the million dollar question. But I knew I had to look
after you.

Samreen: Look at you, ma. You could not look after yourself. How
do you think you were looking after me?

Jeena: That's how you will behave with me?

Samreen: Do you think I will enjoy the future you built for me on
your injuries?

Jeena: I know I am not going to trade my injuries to build any
future.

Samreen: You are sure you don't want to think it over one more
time?

Jeena: Whatever is left of my life, I want to live the way I want to.

Samreen: Now you say that, ma. Ma, I have inherited lots of things
from you. But silence is not one of them. I think somebody will
have an earful from me. Bye, ma. *(exit)*

SCENE 18
Flashback; Jeena recalls when Samreen was five

Jeena: Where are you going?

Samreen: To play.

Jeena: At Silvie's house?

Samreen: Why do you ask when you already know where I am going?

Jeena: Why don't you tell me before you make your plans?

Samreen: Who would I tell? You weren't home.

Jeena: Why didn't you tell your father?

Samreen: He is never home.

Qaiser: When I come back from work, I want to see you home.

Jeena: And I want to see you eat my curry.

Samreen: When I come back from school nobody is home. When I go to play, both of you wait for me at home.

Qaiser: This is what Canada does to children. If I talked to my father like that, he would have knocked some sense into my head.

Jeena: And if I insulted the curry like she does, my mother would have shoved some chicken curry down my throat.

Samreen: I don't like chicken.

Jeena: I cooked it fresh for you, and it smells so good.

Samreen: It smells of curry.

Qaiser: See how she insults the curry that made us world famous.

Jeena: There is a sandwich on the table.

Samreen: I don't want it. It has cheese.

Jeena: What's wrong with the cheese?

Samreen: It has holes in it.

Jeena: *(frustrated)* Eat the cheese and leave the holes. Okay?

Samreen: Mama, Mrs. Thomson said you must come to the parent-teacher meeting.

Qaiser: You eat your food.

Samreen: Mama, did you hear what I said?

Jeena: Yes, I did.

Samreen: Why don't you answer, then?

Jeena: What don't I answer?

Samreen: I am saying come to meet my teacher and you are telling me to eat curry.

Qaiser: Eat and go to your room.

Samreen: Why do you stop me from going to Silvie's, then you send me to my room?

Jeena: Because you are better off in your own home than at Silvie's.

Samreen: Then why can't I stay with both of you?

Jeena: You are staying with both of us.

Samreen: But baba said to go to my room.

Qaiser: Because children should leave their parents alone sometimes.

Samreen: Is that why parents have children, so they can leave them alone?

Qaiser: Jeena, make her eat before she goes to play.

Jeena: But I can't quarrel with her to feed her.

Samreen: Mama, what is a quarrel?

Jeena: When you fight with someone without a weapon.

Samreen: A weapon?

Jeena: A weapon is what you fight with.

Samreen: Is daddy a weapon?

Qaiser: What?

Samreen: You always quarrel for money to buy a house.

Jeena: Little chatterbox. She won't inherit my silence.

SCENE 19
Home; same day, the present

Qaiser: Okay, Jeena, on my way from the Dhaba, which is doing very bad, I stopped over at the bank to rearrange the mortgage payments. Because even with the rent coming from the tenants upstairs, the installments are getting harder to pay.

Jeena: Qaiser, why do you bring out your violin now?

Qaiser: I asked for an emergency loan, and there are none even for an emergency. But the bank man did some calculations for me. Even if we sold our house at the going price, after the usual deductions we will lose about seven thousand dollars.

Jeena: Sacrifices are always a loss.

Qaiser: There is a way to cut the losses.

Jeena: Has the bank man told you how?

Qaiser: We can stop paying the installments and let the bank take it over.

Jeena: I don't want to know.

Qaiser: So, I am saying what I am saying, not because it makes me happy, but with the thought that we can save our house if ... Well, the doctor needs your signature in five days. She has a deadline.

Jeena: Another one of those things?

Qaiser: Another what?

Jeena: Blackmail.

Qaiser: What is blackmail about it? This house is all we have worked for.

Jeena: What about me?

Qaiser: God, you are so aggravating. What about me, what about me, what about me? Is that all you care about?

Jeena: Really. *(laughs)*

SCENE 20

Flashback; time, five years after their arrival in Canada

Qaiser: *(laughing)* I met the real estate genius today.

Teja: Jeena, do you want to help your husband buy a house?

Jeena: Oh, my apologies, Teja, that I am not convincing enough. But I guess that's all I have been doing – helping him.

Teja: I have some advice for you.

Jeena: Why not? When it comes to advice you are only next to God. You gave Qaiser one advice and he ended up with Mr. Banks. Gave me another advice and I got Uncle Birny. There must be some better advice somewhere.

Teja: That's the next advice I was going to give you.

Jeena: I am waiting.

Teja: I have a real job lined up for you.

Jeena: So I can say bye bye to the piecework?

Teja: You shouldn't. Since women are paid only half the wages, you should do two jobs.

Jeena: And may I ask what is this job?

Teja: A friend of mine has connections in the factory.

Jeena: That's what Canada has become to us – a big factory.

Teja: I know you want to be a teacher. But let me tell you what you are up against. When you apply for a teaching job, only two things could happen. You want to know what? Either they will reject you flatly or recommend you to an evaluation committee. If it is rejection, well, the case is closed. But if it is the evaluation committee, only two things could happen. Either the evaluation committee will sit on your application or forward it to a higher committee. If they sit on your application, well, good luck. But if it is the higher committee, only two things can happen. Either they will send it back to the first committee or send it to the next committee. If it is the first committee, well, let's start all over again.

But if it is the next committee, only two things could happen. Either they will ask you to take a proficiency exam or call for an interview. If it is the interview, watch your accent. But if it is the proficiency exam, only two things could happen. Either you pass or fail. If you fail, well, chapter closed. But if you pass, only two things will happen. Either they will ask you to present the original transcript, which you can't present because it is burnt to ashes, or you will be put on a waiting list until the facts are established some other way, so that you could become a substitute teacher in some elementary school. And then you are going to say you could have helped your husband better by working in a factory than being on the waiting list. Now, if you still want to try something new, remember, you will have to start from scratch and only two things could happen. You want me to go on?

Jeena: This is blackmail.

Teja: But there is a certain logic to it.

Jeena: There sure is. *(sarcastic laugh)*

End of flashback; the present

Jeena: So, what's your logic now?

Qaiser: No blackmail, but the deadline is in five days. That's why I have to find Birny for you, because if I don't find him, the doctor's struggle will be futile and you might not win. And if you don't win, the factory will not re-hire you when you get well. So while I go on trying to search for Birny, you have five days to sign the papers.

Jeena: And you said no blackmail.

Qaiser: I said I want to save the house.

SCENE 21
Five days later at the Quraishi home

Samreen: Ma, are you all right?

Jeena: *(startled)* You gave me a fright.

Samreen: Ma, you are very quiet.

Jeena: I have been doing some thinking on my own.

(**Qaiser** *walks in.*)

Qaiser: Jeena, I am heading out to the doctor's office.

Samreen: Baba, she has already said she is not signing.

Qaiser: Samreen, I am not talking to you.

Samreen: But you are talking about my mother.

Qaiser: And you are talking in my house.

Samreen: Baba, why don't you listen to anyone for once? Sell this stupid house. Move to an apartment which we can afford, without trading her injuries.

Qaiser: Where do you get the idea that Jeena will be better off in an apartment than in a house?

Samreen: Baba, I think you don't listen. Ma has made up her mind.

Qaiser: Listen, young lady. I don't need some twenty-one year old to tell me what to do.

Samreen: She is my mother.

Qaiser: She is my wife.

Jeena: My mother, my wife, your mother, your wife, does anybody want to talk to Jeena? I came here to live and all I have done is work, work, and work. And now the doctor is blaming me for my own injuries. I will be a prisoner of my own faults for the rest of my life.

Qaiser: What faults?

Jeena: Qaiser, we didn't come here to get rich. We came here because the fanatics chased us out as traitors. Since then we have been trying to build our house in this country. And that's all we have done. Build, build and build. We were so busy building the house that I did not even have time to live in it. I am going crippled. Soon I will be locked in some rest home for the rest of my life. Who will shed tears for me? And now you want me to trade my injuries so that you can save your house.

Qaiser: That's what you think of me? Hah.

Samreen: Baba, ma is trying to communicate something to you.

Qaiser: You listen to me, young lady. From the very day I set my foot in this country, they called me a runaway, an alien, boat people, and – the latest one – an allophone. Do you think it has been easy for me? I also have scars on my back. That's what I had to do for this house. Do you think I will let it go just because Jeena will not sign a piece of paper?

Samreen: What are you going to do?

Qaiser: I could do it all over again.

Jeena: What are you going to trade, Qaiser?

Qaiser: You watch and see.

Samreen: Baba, where are you going?

Qaiser: Out. *(exit)*

Jeena: Samreen, bring those papers the doctor left for me to sign.

Samreen: But you said you are not signing.

Jeena: But I didn't say I am.

Samreen: Are you playing games, ma?

Jeena: Bring the papers.

Samreen: I think everybody is going bonkers.

SCENE 22
Dhaba

Qaiser: Teja, where are you?

Teja: You look angry, brick man.

Qaiser: Don't you call me brick man.

Teja: Sorry, brick man.

Qaiser: *(loud, angry)* I said, don't call me brick man.

Teja: What's the matter? The wife giving trouble?

Qaiser: Teja, what is the name of this Dhaba?

Teja: What's wrong with you today?

Qaiser: How come it is Teja's Tandoori Dhaba? How come it is not Qaiser and Teja's Tandoori Dhaba?

Teja: Are you drunk? I am scrambling to get customers and you are crying about your name.

Qaiser: I won't have to, because I want to pull out from the business.

Teja: You are what?

Qaiser: You heard me.

Teja: Without consulting me?

Qaiser: When did you consult me?

Teja: I made you a fifty-fifty partner when you needed credit, confidence and contacts.

Qaiser: You needed my savings to invest in the Dhaba.

Teja: So you can use the Dhaba as collateral to get the mortgage. And I let you do your regular job while I minded the Dhaba. I helped you when you needed help. Now you are leaving me when things aren't going good.

Qaiser: You talk like you are my wife. My decision is strictly business.

Teja: Qaiser, the partnership is based on trust.

Qaiser: So?

Teja: You are betraying it.

Qaiser: I am only human.

Teja: So our entire investment goes to waste. just like that.

Qaiser: That sums up the fate of an immigrant business. You told me Canada will teach me some of life's hard realities. Well, I have to prove some realities to my family.

SCENE 22
Back at home

Qaiser: *(calling loudly)* Jeena. Jeena. Where are you?

Samreen: Welcome to the museum of mama's sacrifices.

Qaiser: Don't talk nonsense. Where is she?

Samreen: When I saw her last she was sitting with your favourite brick. Then she said she was going for a walk.

Qaiser: Now what is she waiting for? A grand entrance? You go get her. Right away. *(pause)* Why aren't you saying anything?

Samreen: *(shattered)* Baba, she is not coming back to this house.

Qaiser: What? I am up to my neck with her irrationality. Where is she?

Samreen: Baba ...

Qaiser: *(loudly, ordering)* Where is she?

Samreen: *(choking)* Baba, she has signed the papers as you wanted her to.

Qaiser: I don't need her signature – not for me, not for my house. I know how to make sacrifices too. I just sold my share in the Dhaba. Where is she? I want to tell her that.

Samreen: She left a letter for you. *(starts sobbing)*

Qaiser: Letter? What for?

Samreen: It is under the brick. Baba, ma has left. She is not coming back.

Qaiser: *(gradually becoming frantic)* Where has she gone? Which corner has she chosen to brood this time?

(frantic) Where is your mother? Where is her letter?

Samreen *points at the letter which Jeena had left for Qaiser.* **Qaiser** *reads the letter.*

Jeena: *(reads letter)* Dear Qaiser: There was this family of birds ... and there was me, you and baby bird. But she was too small to remember. And this family of birds lost its nest. How? Well, even though they had shared the same home for thousands of years, some birds felt that only blackbirds should live in one part of the forest, and only sparrows in the other. How loudly they squawked! And if you did not squawk as loudly as they did, they called you traitor. So one after another, more voices joined the chorus until their strength was unstoppable. Soon all the birds in the forest began carving up the woods. Then the forest was blackened by fire: the ground was littered with bodies fallen from the sky; baby birds were stolen from their nests. I was afraid for my baby bird. Where would she nest? Qaiser? I was afraid for my daughter. The family flew to another wood and they started building all over again. They worked and worked and put pebbles in a pitcher and the baby bird grew big and the mama was so busy building the nest that there was no time left for her to live in it. Until one day it became unlivable for mama bird. She did all she could to build the nest, until there was no more she could do to keep the family of birds together.

Qaiser, there is the nest.

Qaiser *tales the brick and gives it to* **Samreen** *and leaves.* **Samreen** *stands frozen.*

Blackout

Glossary

Assalam-wale-kum	greeting in Urdu
Sat-sri-kal ji	greeting in Punjabi
Wale-kum-salam	response to greeting
gurdwara	temple
in purdah	wearing the veil

Tandoori Dhaba: An East Indian restaurant that prepares a particular kind of barbecue chicken dish using a special oven called *tandoor.*

Going Down the River

by KEVIN LONGFIELD

Kevin Longfield grew up in a family of six children in Winnipeg. He earned a degree in mechanical engineering and worked as an engineer in Winnipeg and Ottawa before his love of writing took over his life. *Going Down the River* grew out of a playwriting class he took under Dennis Noble at the University of Winnipeg.

Since then he has earned a degree in theatre and written two other plays, *You Were Expecting Maybe Robin Hood?* and *Playing by the Rules*. *You Were Expecting Maybe Robin Hood?* was commissioned by the Manitoba Association of Playwrights and performed at their Short Shots festival. It has since appeared in the anthology *Short Circuits*. Kevin Longfield received a Manitoba Arts Council grant to write *Playing by the Rules,* which was a finalist in the Ferndale Repertory Theatre's New Works Competition.

Besides writing plays, Kevin is the Winnipeg correspondent for *Theatrum,* Canada's national theatre magazine, and Managing Editor of *STREET,* a Winnipeg-based arts magazine. He is also the author of *Dream for a Winter's Night,* a poetry chapbook published by Southwestern Ontario Poetry.

He has been active in the writing community, serving as National Vice President of the Canadian Authors Association, and as a local representative for ACTRA and Freedom to Read Week.

Kevin Longfield lives in Winnipeg with his wife and three children. His two older children are members of Bent Forks, a comedy troupe.

ORIGINAL PRODUCTION

Going Down the River was first produced at the University of Winnipeg in 1989. Non-traditional casting was used because of a lack of black students on campus who were interested in acting.

ORIGINAL CAST AND PRODUCTION TEAM

Lettie	Jolie Lesperence
Father	Glenn Krushel
Nigel	Kent Suss
Paula	Kelly Daniels
Director	B. Pat Burns
Lighting Designer	Randolph Wall
Stage Manager	Jacqueline Easton
Assistant Stage Manager	Jana Rubin

REVIEWS AND COMMENTS

"*Going Down the River* manages to evoke an entire set of social and historic problems through one pivotal incident." *(Globe and Mail)*

Kenneth Dyba, adjudicator, Ottawa Little Theatre Competition: "This is a beautiful script ... right from the strong and effective title ... to the first rate characterizations, terrific dialogue, strong story and genuine stage sense.... It is a feat to juggle the two plots, then and now [past and present] and have them mesh so effectively, each illuminating the other and seemingly so effortlessly; ... the sense of theatre is exquisite."

Awards: 1990 Dorothy White Prize, Ottawa Little Theatre competition; Lucy Bertzinger Prize, University of Winnipeg; Honourable Mention, *Writer's Digest* Script Competition.

PLAYWRIGHT'S NOTE

I started writing this play first because I wondered how anyone could see *The Adventures of Huckleberry Finn* as racist, and second because I wondered how those who believed otherwise could allow themselves to give in to pressure. Then I noticed that this is what *Huck Finn* is really all about: making tough decisions. I have always believed that most of the evil in the world is caused not by one person making a bad decision, but by many people not making the right decision: the decision to follow their consciences instead of the herd.

PERFORMANCE PERMISSION

For permission to perform *Going Down the River,* please contact **KEVIN LONGFIELD,** 646 Beaverbrook Street, Winnipeg, Manitoba R3N 1N6, Fax (204) 489-2782; phone (204) 489-2236.

CAST

Lettie Thomas: About 40 years old, black. Principal of a large city high school. An intelligent, sensitive woman, she has risen to her position through merit and political savvy. Being both politically correct and at peace with herself is getting harder.

Father: He is over 60 during the play, but he appears to be forty. In Freudian terms, he is Lettie's super ego. Lettie has subconsciously conjured his image to make sure that this time she follows her conscience rather than the expedient path.

Nigel Brownstone: Mid-twenties, white. He approaches teaching with the same zeal his father approaches making money. He unfortunately has a tin ear when it comes to dialects.

Paula Morgan: Mid-to-late thirties, black. Mother to a "problem" child.

Playing time 45 to 50 minutes.

The action takes place in the principal's office of a large high school. Flashbacks take place in a working class living room circa 1960. A few items of furniture can suggest this locale. Lighting cues suggest how Lettie's subconscious (her father) gradually intrudes into the action.

Scene: the office, approximately 4:05 p.m. On one wall is a portrait of an aged black man. Lettie's desk and chair are about centre stage. A few file folders lie on her tidy desk.

Lettie *enters, but stops at the doorway. Her dress is tasteful but conservative. In the childhood flashbacks she has a southern U.S. accent, but she has lost it as an adult. She has a recently-opened letter in her hand. She turns to speak to Elsa, her secretary, who is off-stage.*

Lettie: See you tomorrow, Elsa. *(waves letter)* This? Nothing to get excited about yet. *(pause)* Well, there's a big difference between getting an interview and getting a promotion. Oh! Nigel's performance appraisal will be on your desk when you get in tomorrow. Could you make sure it goes out first thing? Thanks.

She returns to her desk and resumes work on the appraisal. She speaks into a dictaphone.

Lettie: Suitability for future assignments: Nigel Brownstone shows exceptional promise. He deserves a permanent assignment as soon as possible.

She leaves the office to put the tape on Elsa's desk, returns, and tidies up. She is about to put the letter in her briefcase, but on impulse re-reads it. She walks over to the portrait, touches the frame, and freezes. The lights go down on her and come up on the living room area.

Father *appears in living room. The lights go down slowly on the office. The father looks around to see where Lettie is. He is about forty, but looks older. He is dressed circa 1960, with white shirt and narrow dark tie. He carries a bag of take-out food.*

Father: Lettie, where are you, child? I brought dinner.

Lettie: Coming, Daddy. *(she enters living room)*

Father: *(looks around)* Why, you've got the place looking just grand, Lettie! A stranger would think we've lived here all our lives. How did you put everything away so quick?

Lettie: I put most of the boxes in the bedrooms. We'll have to unpack in there anyways, so it will save steps.

Father: Well, aren't you the smart one? Honey, tomorrow you'll be able to put those brains to work when you start your new school. That reminds me – did you iron the new dress we picked up for your first day?

Lettie: Yes.

Father: What's the matter, child? Aren't you excited about your new school?

Lettie: I just don't understand why we had to move.

Father: I told you before. Up here you can talk to white folks without looking at the ground. Maybe you don't understand it now, but up here your future has a chance. You're going to make something of yourself, honey, be someone important, somebody folks look up to.

Lettie: But isn't leaving quitting? Aren't we just deserting our people?

Father: We are NOT quitting – understand? Quitting is licking someone's boots so they won't spit on you. Quitting is being satisfied with the scraps someone leaves you, instead of making your own decisions. Meridian is an immoral place, and when you live in an immoral place, you leave, just like when Lot left Sodom in the Bible. *(living room lights begin to fade)* You leave, and you don't ever look back.

(office phone rings)

Lettie: Hello, Letitia Thomas speaking. Yes, Mrs. Morgan, how are you? *(pause)* But that's impossible. Mr. Brownstone is a very good teacher. I've watched him teach – in your son's class as a matter of fact. *(pause)* Did your son say why he's quitting school? *(pause)* Mrs. Morgan, Nigel Brownstone is not a racist. He's a talented young man. He is inexperienced, and maybe not as sensitive to the problems in teaching *Huckleberry Finn* in today's world, but – *(a longer pause)* Mrs. Morgan, please don't do that. At least give me a chance to talk to Nigel – Mr. Brownstone – first. I'm sure it's all a misunderstanding. *(pause)* Of course you're welcome to attend.

(pause) Yes, well it so happens I have a conference with Mr. Brownstone in ... ten minutes. *(pause)* I understand. How long will it take you to get here from work? *(pause)* Okay, five o'clock then. Good bye.

She picks up Nigel's file, puts it down and paces. She goes to bookshelf and picks up a well-thumbed copy of Huckleberry Finn.

Lettie: Why does it have to be this book. *(She sits at her desk, thumbs pages and begins reading silently at a selected passage.)*

(lights come up slowly on **Father***)*

Father: *(reads aloud)* "... as they went by I see they had the king and the duke astraddle of a rail – that is, I knowed it was the king and the duke although they was all over tar and feathers, and didn't look like anything in the world that was human. Human beings can be awful cruel to each other sometimes.

Lettie *gets up and goes to living room, sits on arm of chair with one arm around father's neck.*

Father: "So we poked along back home and I warn't feeling so brash as before, but kind of ornery and humble and to blame, somehow – though *I* hadn't done nothing. But it's always the way. It don't make no difference whether you do right or wrong, a person's conscience ain't got no sense, and just goes for him *anyway.* If I had a yaller dog that didn't know no more than a person's conscience does I'd p'ison him."

Lettie: What does that mean, Daddy, "a person's conscience doesn't have any sense"?

Father: It means that sometimes what your head tells you is right is wrong, and you have to listen to your heart instead. Your head will tell you what the world thinks is right, but your heart always tells you what you know is right – if you listen to it.

Lettie: But how do you know when your head is wrong?

Father: Your heart will always find a way of telling you.

Father *freezes.* **Lettie** *walks back towards her desk. The lights fade on the living room and come up on the office.* **Lettie** *sits at her desk and resumes the pose she had before the memory sequence.*

Nigel *knocks.*

Lettie: Come in.

Nigel: Hello, Lettie. You wanted me for something?

Nigel *is twenty-five, casually but expensively dressed, and carrying a gym bag. He is well-groomed. He leans on the doorway.*

Lettie: Yes, thanks for coming 'round. I hope I'm not keeping you from anything important?

Nigel: Nope, I've got nothing pressing from now until nine tomorrow morning. Oh, except for picking up my wife at the airport at seven tonight. *(enters, notices portrait)*

Lettie: Well, I won't keep you that long.

Nigel: When did you get that?

Lettie: Actually, I've had it for years. I just put it up here this week, though. I got tired of that 1954 portrait of Queen Elizabeth.

Nigel: It's signed "L. Thomas." You?

Lettie: No, my father. It's a self-portrait. *(pause)* As you know, Board policy requires me to submit a written performance report on all supply teachers ...

Nigel: And you missed mine last month.

Lettie: I know. You wouldn't believe how upset they get if one piece of paper is late.

Nigel: *(moves into office)* They're important. Good assessments are the only way people in my position get long-term assignments.

Lettie: I know. I'm sorry you were missed, but it was a horrendous month. Parent-teacher interviews, the roof leaked, and four teachers were off with the 'flu. Anyway, if there were any serious problems, I'd have let you know.

Nigel: But I need documentation of my performance to get a permanent assignment.

Lettie: I realize that, and I'm sorry. Actually, though, the policy says that assessments are only needed if the teacher has worked for two weeks in the school, and you were only here for eight and a half working days. In any event, this month's is due. Here's my handwritten copy. I don't think you'll find too much to complain about.

(**Nigel** *begins reading the assessment.* **Lettie** *looks at her father's portrait. They both freeze. The lights go down on the office and come up on the living room.* **Lettie**'s *father enters. It is the day after the previous memory sequence.*)

Father: Lettie ... Where are you, child?

Lettie: *(enters the living room)* Here, daddy.

Father: How was your first day at school?

Lettie: Oh, just fine, Daddy. It was just like you said. No segregated washrooms, everyone uses the same drinking fountain, and the teachers and other kids treated me just fine. How was your day?

Father: Not as good as yours, I'm afraid. The Association of Professional Engineers won't recognize my engineering degree.

Lettie: What does that mean?

Father: It means I can't be an engineer here.

Lettie: But that's not fair. Did you tell them you graduated fourth in your class?

Father: That doesn't make any difference. They don't know anything about Mississippi Carver University, so they don't know if its program meets their standards.

Lettie: Isn't there anything you can do?

Father: I could write an exam, but it costs a lot of money, and I'm not sure I could pass it right now. College was a long time ago.

Lettie: You took me away from my friends and Aunt Etta, and you didn't even know if you could get a job here?

Father: I wish I'd had more time to check things out, but that cross on the lawn in Meridian changed priorities. I didn't have any choice any more.

Lettie: You left because you were scared. You ran away.

Father: I suppose a lot of people would think that, and in a way it's true, but not the way you think.

Lettie: I don't understand. You always talk in riddles.

Father: Lettie, sometimes a choice isn't between good and bad. Sometimes you get to choose between good and better. Other times, you have to choose between bad and worse. I'll never forget the looks on the faces of some of our friends as we drove out of town, but staying would have been worse.

Lettie: How could it be worse? We've got no friends, no job ...

Father: It was the only decision I could live with. I'd heard some of our people spewing the same venom that bigoted whites use, I'd seen young men get bitter and hostile – there's hard times coming back there, Lettie, bloody times, and I don't want you to have any part of it. Coming here is a chance for you to avoid all that, and I couldn't have called myself your father if I denied you that chance.

Lettie: So what do we do now?

Father: Same thing I always planned on doin' – look for a job.

Lettie: But what kind of a job? Pumping gas like back to home?

Father: If I have to, yes.

Lettie: Then we'll be no better off than we were in Meridian. It's just as unfair here. Things aren't going to be any different.

Father: Oh, yes they are, Lettie. *You* are going to make it different. We came here so you would have a chance. You're a smart little girl, and you would have worked waitressing, or in the fields back to home. Up here, you have a chance to become whatever you want to become. It doesn't matter what happens to me, because you are going to make something of yourself, you hear?

Lettie: If I do, I won't be so unfair to people.

Father: I'm sure you won't, Lettie. I'm sure you won't.

(Both freeze. The lights fade on the living room, and come back up on the office. **Lettie** *moves back to her location at beginning of memory sequence.)*

Nigel: This is better than I'd hoped. Thanks.

Lettie: You've earned it. Not every supply teacher treats his temporary classroom as his or her own. Not every substitute can establish an atmosphere of respect with twenty teenagers who know the sub will be gone sooner or later.

Nigel: I've always thought that if you are interesting, class control wouldn't be a problem.

Lettie: Right. It certainly was a lively discussion ... Many beginning teachers are afraid to give a class free rein, and they therefore direct the discussion rather than steer it – particularly with a potentially difficult book like *Huckleberry Finn*. (*pause*) Before I forget, I have to ask you something.

Nigel: Yes?

Lettie: Do you memorize everything you "read" to the class? I noticed that when you read the passage about where Huck tries to make Jim think he'd dreamed about them being separated in the storm, you never turned the page.

Nigel: (*his accent is a poor approximation*) "Jim looked at the trash, and then he looked at me, and then he looked back at the trash again. He had got the dream fixed so strong in his head that he couldn't seem to shake it loose and get the facts back into its place right away. But when he did get the thing straightened around he looked at me steady without ever smiling and says: 'What do they stan' fo? I'se gwine tell you. When I ...'"

Lettie: I believe you.

Nigel: "'... got all wore out wid work, en wid de callin' for you, en went to sleep my heart wuz mos' broke becuz you wuz los' en I didn' k'yer no mo' what became of me en de raf.' En when I wake up en fine you back agin, all safe and soun,' de tears come en I could a got down on my knees en kiss yo' foot, I's so thankful. En all you wuz thinkin' 'bout wuz how you could make a fool uv ole Jim wid a lie.'"

(*A follow spot comes up on* **Father**. *He is sitting in the living room chair, reading from* Huckleberry Finn. *He recites the rest of the passage in unison with* **Nigel**. **Lettie**'s *attention is diverted to the father.*)

Nigel and Father: "'Dat truck deah is trash; an' trash is wut people is dat put dirt on de head er day frien's en makes 'em ashamed.'"

(*follow spot goes down on* **Father**)

Nigel: "Then he got up slowly and walked to the wigwam and went in there without saying anything but that. It was fifteen minutes before I could work myself up to go humble myself to a nigger; but I done it, and warn't sorry for it afterward, neither."

Lettie: That's very unusual. Why do you do it?

Nigel: It's something I read in Mark Twain's autobiography. He always memorized his readings, and it occurred to me that I could do a better job of observing the class' reaction if I weren't always forced to look at the text. It has other benefits, too. I can see who is really caught up in the story and use them to open the discussion.

Lettie: That's something we've talked about before. I didn't mention it in your review, because I knew I'd have a chance to mention it off the record. Remember that you are teaching the whole class, not just the animated ones. Sometimes the quiet kids have something profound to say, but they are too shy to speak up.

Nigel: I don't think I neglect anyone ... *(freezes)*

Lettie: Winston Morgan, for instance.

Follow spot comes up on **Father**, *sitting in the living room chair, looking at* **Lettie**. *He disapproves of this ambush.* **Lettie** *glances at him briefly before pressing on. Follow spot fades.*

(**Nigel** *unfreezes*)

Lettie: He never said a word. He's the only black in your class. He could have had some interesting perspectives to offer.

Nigel: Don't forget, you've only seen two classes. I give everyone an equal chance to speak out, if they want it. Winston doesn't seem to want it. He doesn't seem to be interested in anything, as far as I can see. I have tried to draw him out, for the obvious reasons you just pointed out. He just isn't interested. Some kids aren't.

Lettie: Nigel, this is serious. As I was saying, don't write any student off. It's part of your job to reach everyone. Besides, the uninterested students often have very interested parents who will accuse you of ignoring their child, or worse, when the child does poorly.

Nigel *freezes.*

Follow spot comes up on **Father**. **Lettie** *glances at him briefly before pressing on. Follow spot fades.* **Nigel** *unfreezes.*

Nigel: I know that. I'll keep at it. Like you say, I have the gift. *(examines portrait more closely)* Is your father a professional?

Lettie: In a manner of speaking. He worked in an auto body shop, painting cars. Painting was his hobby – he never pursued it seriously.

Nigel: He looks like a man with a lot of character. I suppose you learned a lot from him. Tell your father he has a lot of talent. I'd love to see more of his paintings.

Lettie: I'd love to be able to tell him that. He died a year ago.

Nigel: Oh –

Lettie: At any rate, we're not here to discuss my father and his unique talents. As I was saying, while there is some room for improvement – which is to be expected from someone with your limited experience – your work has been excellent. I would love to have someone like you on my staff. Unfortunately, one rarely gets to do what one would like to in a bureaucracy. Mr. Phaneuf, the man you are replacing, has had another stroke, and we've been advised that he will not be returning to work. In the best of all possible worlds, I would be able to offer you his job, and that would be that. But ...

Nigel: But school board regulations say ...

Lettie: The regs aren't the villains this time, Nigel. Your collective agreement provides for open competition for all vacancies. With jobs as scarce as they are in the division right now, I can't say I blame them. You of course are welcome to apply, and naturally I will give you every consideration. But I can't make any promises. And to be fair, I have to tell you that because of the weight given to years of service, it will be very hard to appoint you without bucking a pile of grievances as high as the Rocky Mountains.

Nigel *freezes. Follow spot comes up on* **Father** *again.* **Lettie** *has more trouble than the last time ignoring him. Follow spot fades.*

Nigel *unfreezes*

Nigel: So that's it. I bust my butt for six weeks, and in gratitude I get tossed back on the slush pile. Then some broken-down clock-puncher with seniority gets the job because his school was closed down.

Lettie: Calm down. It's not as bad as all that. Look, I can probably get away with leaving the job open for the rest of the school year. I'm naturally not going to replace you until the permanent position is filled. By then you will have more points, and even if you don't get this job, you will be better placed for others.

Nigel: That's not exactly something I can take to the bank.

Can't you pull any strings? *(freezes)*

Lettie: Look, I've done as much as I can do without creating ... problems.

Follow spot comes up on **Father** *again. It remains up, even after* **Lettie** *turns her attention to* **Nigel**.

Father: Problems for whom?

Nigel *unfreezes*

Lettie: It's better than advertising the job right now, which I could do. And if your performance continues at its high level, and if you work on your problem area, I can give you the kind of recommendation that will practically assure you of a permanent position somewhere next fall.

Nigel: Particularly if you get one of the Assistant Superintendent's jobs that's open. Been offered one yet? Or is that why you're fudging? Afraid of rocking the boat? *(freezes)*

Father *moves near imaginary boundary between the living room and the office.*

Father: He's on to your game, Lettie.

Nigel *unfreezes*

Lettie: *(to Nigel)* As I said, keep up the good work, and positive things should happen. Now. There's one more thing we have to take care of, and time is short. I mentioned earlier that you have to pay attention to the uninterested students, because they sometimes have very interested parents. Winston Morgan is such a student.

Nigel: So?

Lettie: I had a call from his mother today. She was very upset, and accused you of deliberately poking fun at blacks. She said that Winston feels humiliated in your class, and you go out of your way to make blacks look stupid.

Nigel: That's a lie!

Lettie: We have an explosive situation on our hands.

Nigel: He's just using me as an excuse for his poor grades. It's not just my class, you know. He's failing nearly everything.

Lettie: Be that as it may, Paula Morgan is a force to be reckoned with. She says Winston gets laughed at in school. The kids taunt him in the accent you use when you recite Jim's lines.

Nigel: There are a couple of beauties in that class. I'll straighten them out.

Lettie: They're not the ones who are upset. Mrs. Morgan says the book makes blacks look stupid.

Nigel: But that's not fair! Jim talks the way he does to be true to the way slaves talked over a century ago. I am just giving a faithful reproduction ...

Lettie: Look, Nigel, I admire your dedication, but the only people who talk like that wear blackface in minstrel shows.

Nigel: Come on, it's not that bad.

Lettie: Winston thinks you do it on purpose. His mother believes him.

Nigel: You don't think ...

Lettie: I happen to think she is wrong, but the reasons why are not as important in this case as dealing with the situation which has resulted. She wanted to go to the School Board to lodge a formal complaint. As you know, race relations are very "big" right now. Neither of us needs the embarrassment of going before the Race Relations Committee.

Nigel: Look, we both know she's way off base. We tell her it's all a misunderstanding, calm her down, and send her home. What's the problem?

Lettie: You don't get it. She's an angry person. She's been dealt a pretty rotten hand, so I suppose it's natural to be bitter. Winston's father was white.

Nigel: Oh?

Lettie: Her parents disapproved of the relationship, so she ran away with this guy. She gets pregnant, he leaves. There's lots of prejudice in Canada, and every time she sees it, it confirms what she thinks she already knows: the white establishment is out to get her.

Nigel: But I'm not against her. I became a teacher to help people like her son –

Lettie: Nigel, you don't have any idea what life is like for her. You've never had to worry about anything in your life.

Nigel: Hey, wait a minute –

Lettie: Try and imagine coming to a strange country, a single parent, with no job, very little money, and two strikes against you because of your colour. The only thing in the world she has is her son. How would you feel if you thought your only son was threatened?

Nigel: But you just said ...

Lettie: And, to a certain extent, she's right. For a borderline student like Winston, colour could be the factor that tips the scales. She has all the emotional factors on her side, and all we have is the facts. The only way I could keep her from going over our heads was by promising her a face-to-face meeting at five.

Nigel: That's in ten minutes! *(freezes)*

Father: That was a dirty trick, girl. He means well. You know that. Why don't you stick up for him?

Lettie: *(to Father)* It's not that simple. I've got my career to think of, remember?

Nigel *unfreezes*

Nigel: We don't have much time. How are we going to handle this?

Lettie: Well. If you follow my lead, I think we can diffuse the situation. She can be pretty provocative, but try to keep a rein on yourself. If you butt in at the wrong time you could ruin everything for both of us. And the last thing we want is a confrontation.

Nigel: But if we are in the right, why should we knuckle under? The book has nothing to do with him wanting to quit. She'd believe me if you backed me up.

Lettie: You and my father would have gotten along famously. Trust me on this one. We can't win a confrontation. She gets what she wants, or she goes public – and we get tried in the papers. It could get out of control.

Nigel *freezes.* **Lettie** *glances back and forth between* **Nigel** *and* **Father.**

Father: This isn't just one more touchy situation you can smooth over with no fuss. You know that, don't you?

When **Lettie** *makes eye contact with* **Nigel,** *he unfreezes.*

Nigel: It wouldn't go that far, would it? *(freezes)*

Lettie: *(to Father)* Sometimes you have to be flexible. If you bend a little bit, like the reed, you don't come crashing down, like the oak.

Father: But even the reed kept its roots in the ground.

Nigel: *(unfreezes)* I said, it wouldn't go as far as the papers, would it?

Lettie: *(to Nigel)* Pardon? Oh, yes, yes it could. You don't know her like I do.

Nigel: So, what is "our" approach?

Lettie: We give Mrs. Morgan a sympathetic hearing, agree with as much of what she says as dignity permits ...

Nigel: What?

Lettie: And promise to take care in the future. I know you will find this difficult, but it's best to play safe.

Nigel: But I haven't done anything wrong – if I could explain my teaching philosophy to her, I'm sure she'd understand that. Look,

I've been more than fair with her son, and I could prove it to her if I went over some of his assignments. She'd be welcome to sit in on one of my classes – I bet it would blow her away.

Lettie: I admire your confidence, but that just won't do. First of all, she works in a sewing factory. I very much doubt she could get any time off. Secondly, we can't safely predict her reaction – especially with the accent you use.

Nigel: Yes, but ...

Lettie: You don't mean any harm, I know that, but she has an axe to grind. She will see what she wants to see: an upper-class snob making fun of her race.

Nigel: I'm not an upper-class snob. Just because my father owns ...

Lettie: How many blacks have management jobs in your father's company, Nigel?

Nigel: Leave that old – leave him out of it. I'm nothing like him. I wouldn't be here if I were.

Lettie: Paula doesn't think that, and neither will the people who read the papers.

Nigel: That's not fair. If I could just show her –

Lettie: And finally, if she sits in on one of your classes and there's a confrontation, it could be impossible to diffuse, as well as being highly embarrassing.

Nigel: How could she possibly be offended by my interpretation? We both know the book is anti-racist, and that's the way I teach it – we're all on the same side. You said yourself a few minutes ago that I'm a gifted teacher. How could she possibly misunderstand?

Lettie: You have a lot to learn. She's viewing the situation from the eyes of a parent who is defending her son against what she sees as a hostile world. Sure, it's possible we could convince her that her son is making excuses for his own shortcomings, but the odds are against it. There's too much at stake to take that chance.

Nigel: We could do it if we tried.

Lettie: What if we don't? What if she decides the book is at fault, and starts a movement to have it banned? Neither of us needs that kind of ... complication in our careers. I repeat, the easiest ... ah, the safest course is a quiet solution, even if it means swallowing some pride. I don't like it either, but that's the way it is.

Nigel *freezes*

Father: Why don't you just once do what you know is right, instead of what you think others expect of you?

Lettie: *(To Father)* It's their game, and their rules. I'm just a player.

Father: Is that the way you were brought up? What are you ... a sheep?

Nigel *unfreezes*

Nigel: You'd do anything to get into the superintendent's office, wouldn't you?

Lettie: *(to Nigel)* I don't think that's fair. I was merely advising the safest course for both of us. I could quite easily have promised to send you packing, and you'd never have known the reason why. Instead I've promised to help you with your career. If we can get through the next half hour without incident ...

Father: You'll spend the rest of your life on your knees. Is that what you want? Is that what we came here for?

Nigel: Be a good boy, and mommy will give you a cookie, right? That woman is pushing us around – and you're letting her. You know, up until now, I really admired you. I figured you were the only person in this school who knows what teaching is all about. And then the first time I see you in a tight spot, you cave in.

Lettie: Look, I can be just as tough as anybody else when the chips are really down. But this is a very minor incident! One of the things you have to learn is that life is full of compromises. You have to compromise on the small things if you want to get the big ones.

Nigel: Like a permanent appointment?

Lettie: Like a permanent appointment. You don't get anywhere being combative.

Father: How would you know? When the going gets tough, Lettie caves in. "Yes, massah, right away massah."

Nigel: And I'm supposed to allow myself to stand accused of being a racist, apologize for it, in fact, so that I can be guaranteed a permanent position? Is that what you call a small compromise?

Lettie: I never promised you a permanent position ...

Nigel: Boy, you're really something. I always defended you in the staff room, said their criticisms of you were unfair.... I figured they were just jealous of your success, and maybe just a bit racist. Boy, was I ever naive.

Lettie: What criticisms?

Nigel: That you're a consummate political operator, that you'd stab your grandmother in the back if it meant getting your next promotion.

Lettie: *(to Nigel)* That's a lie!

Lights come up on entire stage

Father: See what happens when you don't keep your roots planted?

Nigel: I'm just repeating what I've heard. *(pause)* I, uh, suppose I should dig out Winston's student records? *(Goes over to filing cabinet. Freezes)*

Lettie: *(to Father)* You never told me it was going to be like this.

Father: I never said it was going to be easy, either. You just remember what you want to.

(Lights fade on office area. The phone rings in the living room. It is 1967. Lettie is 19.)

Lettie: I'll get it, Daddy!

(Lettie just beats her father to the phone. She is flushed and excited.)

Lettie: Hello? *(disappointed)* Oh, hi, Ronnie. Yes, I got the message. I've just been too busy studying. Saturday? Oh, I'm sorry, Ronnie, I know I promised we could go out, but my mid-terms are just a week and a half away. I really can't afford the time. Maybe the week after, okay? Yes, I know, but I can't disappoint my father with bad marks. Maybe I'll see you in church Sunday. Bye.

Father: I don't mind you having fun once in a while, Letitia. You make me sound like an overseer.

Lettie: I know, Daddy, but I needed a good excuse. He can be so persistent.

Father: It's because he's fond of you. He's a nice boy. You shouldn't keep putting him off like that.

Lettie: I know, but ... well, I just don't see a future with him. He never even finished high school.

Father: Then why keep him hanging on? Wouldn't it be fairer to end it? Other young girls might not be as particular as you. They might even think a hard working young man with good character is a good catch. And that medical student I heard you mooning over the phone about yesterday might never call.

Lettie: Daddy, Ronnie will never be anything but a construction worker.

Father: And a person who cared enough about his brothers and sisters to quit school so he could support them. A person like him – with integrity and ambition – could make something of himself one day. But if you're too high and mighty for him, why do you bother with him? Why not be honest?

Lettie: Okay, you're right. Maybe after the Grad Dance.... *(She looks at her father)* You're right. I'll tell him on Sunday.

Father: The right thing to do isn't always the easy thing, but it's always the right thing to do.

*(**Lettie** moves towards office.)*

Lettie: If I see him, that is. He might not be there ...

*(Lights come up on office as **Lettie** returns to where she was at the beginning of the memory sequence)*

Nigel *finds Winston's file and stands up.* **Paula** *knocks on office door.*

Lettie *and* **Nigel** *scramble to take their places.*

Paula *knocks again.*

Lettie: Come in, please.

Paula *enters. She is about same age as Lettie.*

Lettie: *(stands, offers her her hand)* Hello, Mrs. Morgan. Please sit down.

Nigel: Hello, I'm Nigel Brownstone.

Paula *glares at him.*

Father: This is the person you are so afraid of? Just do what's right, girl.

Lettie: Nigel Brownstone is the teacher we ... spoke about earlier today. As I said then, I am very distressed that your son, ah ...

Paula: Winston.

Lettie: Yes, Winston, feels he is being discriminated against. I have discussed this matter at some length with Mr. Brownstone and I am sure this matter can be resolved to everybody's satisfaction. Your son is a clever young man, and both Mr. Brownstone and I would like to see him achieve his potential, as I am sure you would.

Father: Why don't you get out a shovel.

Lettie: Now, in trying to bring *Huckleberry Finn* to life, Mr. Brownstone may have unwittingly exposed Winston to ridicule, but I assure you that no malice was intended. The important thing is that the three of us establish a relationship where we can work together to help Winston achieve, as I said before, his academic potential.

Paula: But this man is responsible for my son wanting to quit school. Winston doesn't want to go to school no more because the other kids make fun of him. That ... person is exposing my son to ridicule. He is either doing it deliberately, or he is incompetent, and I demand to know what you are going to do about it.

Nigel: That's ridic- ...

Paula: *(to Nigel)* What kind of a chance will my son have without an education?

Father:) *(overlapping with next speech)* It seems you're the only one here without convictions, Lettie.

Nigel:) *(overlapping with next and previous speech)* What?

Paula:) *(overlapping with previous speech)* He doesn't have a rich Daddy paying his way like you do.

Nigel: Could we leave my family background out of this?

Lettie: I don't think you are being fair, Mrs. Morgan. And we won't get anywhere by hurling accusations. Mr. Brownstone is very sorry for any anguish he caused your son, as he will tell you if you let him. He is not incompetent, and if you will give him a chance, I am sure he will show you he can be very helpful to your son. I have sat in on his classes, as I do with all my staff, and I can assure you ...

Nigel: You see, Mrs. Morgan, what Winston probably doesn't understand is that Jim, although ignorant in the classic sense of the word, is nonetheless a noble, and indeed, a wise man. Have you read the book?

Paula: I have.

Nigel: All of it? Not just selected passages?

Paula: What do you think I am? Some ignorant nigger like Jim? We have schools in Trinidad, too, you know. I can read. And I know when my son is being persecuted by some rich snob who ...

Lettie: Paula, please. Please calm down. He didn't mean to imply that you are ignorant. He was merely trying to establish a basis for discussing his teaching methods. They are unusual, but ...

(Nigel *is about to speak;* **Lettie** *puts her hand up to stop him)*

... they can in no way be called discriminatory. In fact, he is highly respected by most of the students he teaches – even some black kids in other classes. The first inkling of trouble I had was your call today. In retrospect I can see that ...

Father: It's safer to dump Nigel than it is to stand up to Paula.

Lettie: Don't you see how dangerous she could be?

Nigel: You see, I recite pivotal passages of *Huck Finn* to make them real to the class ...

Lettie: Nigel –

Nigel:) ... to make them see the socio-political context they were written to illuminate.

Father:) *(overlapping)* Why don't you stop this?

Nigel:) Twain was a master practitioner of irony.

Father:) *(overlapping)* Show Paula that Nigel means well.

Nigel:) His intent is not always evident on a perfunctory reading.

Lettie:) *(overlapping, to Father)* How would it look?

Nigel:) Now, some of my readings deliberately illustrate Jim's ignorance, or more accurately, his lack of worldly sophistication.

Lettie:) *(overlapping, to Father)* A black woman siding with a white man against her own people.

Nigel:) A prime example is the passage where Huck has played a trick on him.

Father:) *(overlapping)* Her own people? Child, who cares about appearances?

Nigel:) Upon discovering the ruse, he upbraids Huck.

Father:) *(overlapping)* Do you want to be on the side of right or the right side?

Nigel:) His integrity, his natural dignity, are such that, in what was at that time a cultural taboo, Huck feels compelled "to humble himself to a nigger."

Lettie:) *(overlapping, to Father)* If you want to progress in the system, you have to work within it.

Nigel:) That passage is a climactic one.

Lettie:) *(overlapping, to Father)* I can't be a success if I have to work by the old-fashioned ideas you used to spout at me all the time.

Nigel:) It shows how far the runaway boy has progressed towards true morality.

Father:) *(overlapping)* Is that what you call success?

Nigel:) Now, naturally, to make Jim believable in the historical context of the book, I have to give him the accent and syntax Twain uses.

Father:) *(overlapping, to Lettie)* Being in a position of authority so you can let people push you around?

Lettie:) *(overlapping, to Father)* It's not that simple! everything's always so simple to you.

Father:) *(overlapping)* It's simple, alright. It's just not easy.

Nigel: That doesn't mean I personally ...

Paula: Winston says everyone laughs at him in class. Why do you do that? What did he ever do to you?

Lettie: *(to Paula)* I think you've missed the point Nigel was ...

Nigel: Look. I have absolutely no hard feelings towards your son. None. I'm sure he's a good person ... and I'm sorry if his feelings have been hurt in any way. I really am. If he thinks I was poking fun at him, it's because he is over-sensitive, that's all. I never intended to embarrass him, and if he had even once expressed his feelings, I would've put his fears to rest.

Father: Are you going to step in before Nigel hangs himself?

Lettie: *(to Father)* Why do you do this? Why do you complicate everything I do?

Nigel: Do you know that he has not once, in the six weeks I have been here, volunteered one word to class discussions? And the twice I asked for his input, he just shrugged.

Father: *(in Lettie's ear)* Don't let her scare you.

Paula:) Why should he say anything to you in class? He says you have it in for him.

Father:) *(overlapping, to* **Lettie**) You can handle her if you try.

Paula:) And now he says he's quitting school – and if he does, it will be your fault.

Father:) *(overlapping)* Just stand up straight, look her in the eye, and tell her the truth.

Paula:) I don't work ten hours a day doing piece work so my son can turn out to be a no-good drifter like his father.

Father:) *(overlapping)* She's made a mistake, and you're not going to be influenced by her anger.

Lettie: Mrs. Morgan, I assure you ...

Nigel: That's nonsense. I've even talked to other teachers about him.

Father:) *(overlapping)* You'd better show some backbone, or you're going to lose control of this.

Nigel:) *(overlapping)* Now, he's your son, so naturally you accept what he says without question.

Lettie:) *(overlapping, to Father)* Stop it!

Nigel:) But I ask you: ...

Lettie:) *(overlapping, to Father)* I can't concentrate!

Nigel:) ... is it possible that he may be accusing me as a smoke screen?

Father:) *(overlapping)* Make up your mind, girl.

Nigel: He wouldn't be the first student to say "the teacher hates me," as an excuse for poor marks.

Paula: Are you calling my son a liar?

Lettie: Paula –

Nigel: Of course not. But sometimes it is easier for someone to find fault with someone else than it is to affix the blame on one's self. I have heard that Winston is a bright boy. Apparently he does very well in shop. That indicates good mechanical reasoning ability.

Father: Here it comes ...

Lettie: Nigel ...

Nigel: Quite often people who are skilled mechanically are poor in other areas. Perhaps an academic program isn't the best for him ...

Paula: So! Blacks are good with their hands, but they're intellectually inferior, right?

Father: Home run! You're off the fence now, Lettie!

Nigel: I never said ...

Paula: Racist pig! I knew it! *(to Lettie)* See? See what you have on your staff? And you said I was over-reacting! *(to Nigel)* I'll sue your pretty pants off. You snake. You ...

Nigel: I am not ...

Lettie:) Please! Please! This isn't getting us anywhere.

Father:) *(overlapping)* If you had just listened ...

Paula:) You are a menace!

Lettie:) *(overlapping, to Father)* Please, let me do my job without interference.

Paula: Why don't you go back to South Africa?

Nigel:) What? Who's a racist now? For your information, I was born here.

Father:) *(overlapping)* Even if it means doing something you'll never forgive yourself for?

Paula: And I wasn't, so I have no rights, is that it?

Nigel: You know what? You're crazy – that's what you are. Absolutely nuts.

Paula: You can't talk to me like that. You –

Lettie: *(aloud, without realizing it)* Stop it! Stop it! Stop it! Why can't you leave me alone? I can't take this any more. Just let me get on with my life ... *(pause)*

*(**Paula** and **Nigel** quiet down)*

Lettie: I had hoped we could have a reasonable discussion. Please calm down, Paula. Shouting won't accomplish anything.

Paula: But he –

Lettie: Paula, calm down. You have misinterpreted what he has said. Do you seriously think I, of all people, would have a racist on my staff, even as a substitute?

Father: That's more like it!

Nigel: I told you –

Lettie: Nigel, shut up.

Lettie: Now, I am sure Mr. Brownstone is willing to apologize for any offense, however unintentional, he might have caused.

Nigel: Of course I didn't mean to offend anyone ...

Paula: Humph. You're just on his side because you want to protect your ass. You can't push me around that easily. He deliberately tried to get my son to quit school.

Nigel: I didn't.

Paula: You're just sorry you were caught, that's all.

Nigel: What? That's nonsense – please, just tell her how completely out of touch she is.

Paula:) You're not fooled by his act, are you, Lettie?

Father:) *(overlapping)* Don't cave in, Lettie.

Paula:) You're one of us.

Lettie:) *(overlapping, to Father)* I knew it would come to this.

Nigel:) There's no "us" and "them" here.

Father:) *(overlapping)* Nigel is in over his head. He needs you.

Paula: You know what ...

Nigel:) Yes. There's just a spoiled kid trying to blame someone for his own shortcomings.

Father:) *(overlapping)* Don't let him down.

Nigel:) Lettie knows that, don't you Lettie?

Lettie:) *(overlapping, to Father)* I don't want to let him down... I just want a peaceful solution. *(pause)*

Nigel: Lettie?

Paula: Lettie!

Lettie: *(raises voice)* Regardless of anyone's intentions, however, feelings have obviously been hurt. And the last thing either Mr. Brownstone or I want is for Winston to quit school. The safest way to prevent a recurrence of the problems your son has experienced is to alter the teaching methods.

Nigel: What?

Lettie: In future, I, uh, suggest that readings from the text be done by Winston, or by one of the other students. Now, Paula, that should prevent your son from being the butt of any jokes. Mr. Brownstone has apologized to you for any feelings he might have hurt, and ... I'm sure he would do the same in class. Does that sound reasonable to you?

Nigel: If you think I am going to stand in front of a bunch of young people who respect me and tell that I've been unfair when I haven't, you don't know me very well.

Paula: How can you even suggest letting him speak to a class again?

Nigel: And what's this business about not letting me read to my own class? Am I a teacher, or aren't I? *(to Paula)* The last thing I would ever do is deliberately cause any hurt to any of my students. They are all important to me. All of them. If Winston had just once opened his mouth in class or afterwards, this meeting would never have taken place. Instead, he went running to his mother like a five-year-old.

Paula: That's it! *(Starts packing her things to leave.)*

Nigel: I'm sorry you're upset by what has happened, and I understand your concern, but it wasn't my fault. *(to Lettie)* And I absolutely refuse to alter my teaching methods to suit an immature whiner and an over-sensitive parent. And if you won't back me up, I'm sure the teacher's association will.

Paula *stops preparing to leave, and turns to confront* **Nigel.**

Lettie: Look – You are both over-reacting. I'm sure if we discuss this rationally, we can come to a reasonable compromise.

Father: There is no "reasonable compromise" this time. You know that, don't you?

Paula: And if you can't control your staff, I'll go over your head until I can find someone who will. This man is a menace.

Nigel: *(to Paula)* You are an hysterical, raving lunatic. I would like nothing better than to face you in a full hearing. The truth, as Martin Luther King said, will set you free. Do your worst, woman. I shall be ready for you. *(gets up)*

Lettie: Nigel, please sit down!

Nigel: *(to Lettie)* I'll see you first thing in the morning.

Paula *applauds his exit.*

Lettie: Nigel! Come back here ... please?

Paula: Well?

Lettie: He's young. And hot-headed. And a fool. But he means no harm – really.

Paula:) So what are you going to do about him? I told you before, If you don't do something, I'll find someone who will.

Lettie:) *(overlapping, to Father)* See? You can't reason with her.

Paula:) I don't want to go over your head, but I'll do anything to keep Winston in school.

Father:) *(overlapping)* Don't let her push you ... talk to her.

Lettie:) *(to Paula)* First of all, in spite of what you think, Nigel Brownstone is not a bigot. Stubborn, inexperienced, infuriating sometimes, but not a bigot.

Father:) *(overlapping)* That's it! You can do it.

Paula: But ...

Lettie: And even if he were, we'd have a devil of a time proving it. It would be messy, and would expose your Winston to even more hurt.

Paula:) More hurt than leaving school? More hurt than never, ever being able to earn a decent living for his family? Don't talk to me about hurt, lady. I been there.

Lettie:) *(overlapping, to Father)* You see? If she says that to the Board, I'm sunk.

Paula:) *(pause)* Well? Whose side are you on, lady, our side or that white jerk's? It's us or them, Lettie Thomas.

Father:) *(overlapping)* No, Lettie. She's wrong. You know it. Tell her.

Lettie: Mrs. Morgan, I ... *(She accidentally knocks Nigel's file off her desk.)*

Paula: *(picks it up)* Performance Appraisal on Nigel Brownstone ...

Lettie: Mrs. Morgan, that is an internal School Division document ...

Paula: Nigel Brownstone shows exceptional promise?

Lettie: Give it back!

Paula: You were going to promote him?

Lettie: Mrs. Morgan, I can explain ...

Paula: Oh, so it's Mrs. Morgan, now, is it? Am I to call you Miss Thomas? That's just like you. Anything to get ahead, right?

Lettie:) Mrs. Morgan – Paula – I wrote that this morning – before I knew ...

Father:) *(overlapping)* Nothing's changed, Lettie.

Lettie: *(to Father)* Everything's changed, Daddy. My future is on the line.

Father: You're right about that.

Paula: Before you knew what?

Father: What future is it going to be? The simple one or the easy one?

Paula: Before you knew what, Lettie?

Lettie: Before I knew about Winston's troubles.

Paula: You were in his class before. You must have known. You're just covering up, aren't you? As soon as I leave this office the whole thing is forgotten, isn't it?

Father: You promised Nigel you'd help him. You know he didn't mean any harm.

Lettie: No, really Mrs. Morgan – Paula – I ...

Paula: You're just like all the rest. See you later, Whitey. *(rises to leave)*

Lettie: No, don't.

Father: Tell her she's wrong.

Lettie: Please, Paula, sit down.

Paula: You're not going to sweet-talk me, Lettie Thomas.

Lettie: Please? Let me explain.

Father: Play straight with her.

Lettie: *(to Father)* Let me handle this.

Father: Play straight with her.

Paula: Well?

Lettie: *(to Father)* I ... can't. I'm sorry, Daddy.

Lettie: *(to Paula)* With your co-operation, I think we can still achieve our ends, without any mess.

Father: Why are you letting her push you around like this? Stand up and be counted!

Paula: I'm listening.

Lettie: *(puts her head in her hands for a few seconds) (to Father)* Please, Daddy, just let me get this over with, please? *(raises her head) (to Paula)* As you know, Paula, Nigel Brownstone is only a temporary replacement for Mr. Phaneuf. I just learned today that Mr. Phaneuf will not be returning to the classroom.

Paula: So?

Lettie: So I have to find a replacement. Ordinarily I would keep him on till the end of the year, in the interests of continuity.

Lettie: But as you have so capably shown me, that has clearly become an impossibility. So what I propose is that I expedite the paperwork – I can get most of it done tonight after you leave – to hire a permanent replacement. Naturally he will not be considered. Does ... does that solve your problem?

Father: No!

Paula: How long will that take?

Father: Traitor.

Lettie: *(to Father)* I'll make sure he's posted somewhere else. If I can just get rid of her ...

Paula: Well?

Lettie: Normally two to three weeks, but if I put some heat on, I can probably get a replacement in a week.

Father: Weakling. You're not my daughter.

Lettie: Please stop it, please? I don't have any choice, and you're just making it harder on me.

Father: There's always choices. Some are just tougher than others.

Paula: And in the meantime, he's still teaching his lies in front of my Winston. I want him out!

Lettie: Paula, you are wrong about him.

Paula: How would you know? You don't look up from the bottom, like I do. Sure, he's as nice as pie with you. You have power over him. Winston and I are just "dumb niggers" to him.

Lettie: It's not like that. Please believe me. Mr. Brownstone will only be here one week more. Why can't you be flexible?

Paula: You can't be flexible where injustice is involved. You have to stand up for what is right!

Lettie: Oh, come on. Your son will only see him two or three times, less if Winston comes down with ... a cold or something.

Father: Is that where your roots are planted?

Paula: Yes ... but that snake gets to slide away to some other place and start over again. You've got to put a stop to this.

Father: Don't let her do this to you.

Lettie: You don't have to worry about that. *(pause) (to Father)* See? She's not going to change. *(to Paula)* Look – Mr. Brownstone is a substitute. He doesn't have a permanent certificate. Any future assignments he might have will be heavily dependent on the appraisal I give him, which by the way is due at the school board offices tomorrow afternoon.

Paula: How do I know you're not just trying to get rid of me?

Lettie: Please. You have to trust me.

Paula: I don't trust you to sneeze if you sniff pepper.

Lettie: What would it take to convince you?

Paula: Sit down right now and we'll rewrite that appraisal. I'll drop it off myself tomorrow morning.

Lettie: I can't do that. If anyone saw us ...

Paula: It's now or never.

Father: Who are you, Lettie? Do you still know?

Lettie *hesitates.*

Paula *starts to leave.*

Lettie: Stop! Please wait. I'll write it after you go. Come and see me tomorrow at seven. I'll give you the appraisal in an unsealed envelope. You can check it before you deliver it.

Paula: I see. Thank you, Lettie.

Lettie: Thank you, Mrs. Morgan. I hope you are as satisfied as I am over this.

Paula: You're not the one with your future at stake. Goodbye. *(exits)*

Father: *(crosses imaginary boundary into office space)* So now what are you going to do?

Lettie: This is all your fault! If you hadn't interfered ...

Father: It would have been simple, right?

Lettie: I had to do that. You don't want Winston to quit school, do you?

Father: What about Nigel?

Lettie: He'll be all right. He can work for his father.

Father: Is that what he wants? Is that what you'll tell him tomorrow? Tell me, how are you going to look him in the eye tomorrow? How are you going to look anyone in the eye again?

Lettie: I didn't have any choice! Leave me alone!

Father: The devil made you do it. Is that it? Is it all Paula's fault? Don't blame her. She's just trying to help her son.

Lettie: Nigel wouldn't stand a chance in a public hearing. You saw him. If I'd supported him, I would have gone down the river with him. And I'd be known as the black who backed a racist. Is that what you wanted when you left your whole world behind? A daughter in a white sheet?

Father: So what do you do if it's a black person next time? Desert him, too? Is that what we came here for?

Lettie: Other people can get on with their lives – they can do what they have to to get ahead, and never give it a second thought. But not me. I would have been happy to stay in the classroom, but what would Daddy think if his pride and joy were just a teacher? So now I have to play the power game, and every time I have to make a move, there's this little voice that says, "Daddy wouldn't like it." Do you have any idea what you are doing to me?

Father: So go ahead – rewrite the appraisal. I'm not stopping you – I never have.

Lettie: All right. I will. You've interfered for the last time. *(picks up dictaphone) (turns to Father)*

Father: *(recites)* "I about made up my mind to pray, and see if I could stop being the kind of boy I was and be better. But the words wouldn't come. Why wouldn't they? I knowed very well why they wouldn't come ... I was trying to make my mouth say I would write to that nigger's owner and say where he was. But deep down I knew it was a lie – and you can't pray a lie – I found that out."

Lettie: Stop it!

Father: It's the truth, isn't it?

Lettie: Go away.

Father: That's why you're finding this so hard, isn't it?

Lettie: Go away! I can't finish this with you here. I'm going to lose my mind if this goes on any longer.

Father: So you've finally figured out why you brought me here.

Lettie: I brought you here? The only reason I'd want you here was if I didn't know what to do. And I know what I have to do – you just won't let me. Why can't you rest in peace, and let me live in peace? I can't stand it any more. I can't stand it. Please leave me alone.

Father: Of course you want to live in peace, child. Why else would I be here?

Lettie: Look. The only way I'll be able to live is peace is if you leave me alone! Why can't you understand that?

Father: Why can't you? I said it before. You brought me here.

Lettie: *(sits at desk and puts head in hands. A beat)* This isn't going to be easy.

Father: *(moves behind her. Places hands on her shoulders as she raises dictaphone and clicks it on.)* You can do it.

Lettie: *(picks up dictaphone)* Elsa? This is Lettie. I'm going to try to catch Nigel on the phone tonight, but in case I don't, tell him not to do anything rash until I talk to him. And please type up the following memo. Dear Mr. Rubin: After some reflection, I have decided to withdraw from the assistant superintendent's competition mentioned in your letter yesterday. I feel I can make a greater contribution to the students who need me in my present position. Thank you for the confidence you have shown in me. Sincerely, etc.

Father *kisses top of her head.*

Lettie: *(picks up phone and dials)* Hello, Winston? *(pause)* It's Miss Thomas calling. Is your mother home yet? *(pause)*

(Throughout the rest of this speech, **Father** *disappears. He takes a few slow steps backwards, then turns and leaves through the living room.)*

Lettie: Could you turn that down please? *(pause)* Thank you. When your mother gets home, tell her there's been a change in plans. I'm coming over right now to discuss your future with both of you, and if you care for your mother at all, you'll be there, and in a mood to listen. *(pause)* I'll see you in a few minutes, then. Goodbye. *(She hangs up, puts on coat, and starts to leave. She stops in front of the portrait, and touches the frame)* Goodnight, Daddy.

(exits)

End

Questions

Path With No Moccasins
by Shirley Cheechoo

1. Discuss the following images and how they reflect the play as whole: Star Blanket; The Moon; Water Spirits; the title, *Path With No Moccasins*.

2. Loss permeates Shirley's life: loss of identity, dignity, and self-esteem; loss of her grandmother, grandfather, and father. How does she finally heal herself?

3. What is the significance of Shirley's dreams and visions: the "operation" dream; the "steel blade" dream; the "wall of stone" dream; the "I see myself being born" vision?

4. The residential school attempted to impose a process of assimilation of the native children into white society. There was generally no compassion for the children's feelings, nor understanding of their needs. Cite examples of hard-heartedness toward the children in this play. How do you account for the cruelty inflicted by some of the instructors?

5. In her monologue, Shirley speaks to Us (the reader/audience); to the Moon; to the Water Spirits; to her father. What circumstances prompt her to select whom she addresses?

6. How does Shirley find some solace in her early years at the school?

7. The character resorts to alcohol in a self-destructive attempt to escape the memories of the past and the brutal present. How does she regain the ability to pursue a career and secure a family?

8. The residential school forbade the Cree children to speak their native language. What effect did this decree have on them?

9. Research the following topics:
   History of the Cree
   Manitoulin Island
   Department of Indian Affairs

The Tale of a Mask
by Terry Watada

1. Why does America hold such a fascination for Masato? Describe life in Japan.

2. Trace Aiko's mental state throughout the play. Compare her state in Japan to her state in Canada. Discuss the causes of her breakdown.

3. What are Masato's attitudes toward marriage and family?

4. How does the playwright use *karaoke?*

5. What are the reservations Aiko has about Canada? Describe life for immigrant women in Canada.

6. Account for the attitude Japanese Canadians have toward mental illness.

7. What is the purpose of the mask? How does it reflect Japanese attitudes toward mental illness?

8. In his conversations with Mrs. Harrison and Ms. Henry, Masato obviously doesn't see what they do in his family situation. Why doesn't he believe his wife is in trouble?

9. How does the playwright employ myth in the play? What are the effects?

10. Imagine living in a foreign country where you cannot speak the language. Describe how you would deal with living there.

11. How do the Noh elements of the staging contribute to the action of the play?

Dance Like a Butterfly
by Aviva Ravel

1. Tillie, a Jewish immigrant from Rumania who arrived in the 1930s, appears to have adjusted easily to life in Canada. Why?

2. How important is Tillie's past in relation to her present situation?

3. Many Biblical passages refer to old age, such as:
   Thou shalt rise up for the aged, and honour the elderly (Lev. 19:32).
   Do not cast me out in my old age, and when my strength fails me, do not forsake me (Psalms 71:9).
   Analyze each passage as it may pertain to Tillie.

4. Identify some of the problems Tillie faces in the geriatric ward. How does she cope?

5. Why is Tillie "nice to everybody except to the nieces"? Rachel, after all, visits her regularly and looks after her interests.

6. The frail elderly, totally dependent on doctors, nurses and family members, have lost their autonomy. How can they retain their dignity in such circumstances?

7. Tillie's hired companion performs an important function in her life. What are the qualifications for an ideal companion?

8. Tillie is obliged to choose a new home when she leaves the hospital. How does she arrive at her choice?

9. What does the play have to say to young people?

10. In your opinion, what are the prerequisites for quality care in a home for the elderly?

Just a Kommedia
by Nika Rylski

1. These characters grew up during the sixties. Are the issues of cultural duality – of being caught between two cultures – the same for the children of immigrants growing up today?

2. In *Just A Kommedia*, Daria's Teacher makes fun of her name, a form of oppression which partially reflects attitudes towards new immigrants that still exist in this culture. If someone had made fun of *your* name, how would you have handled the situation?

3. Should heritage languages be taught in the public/private school system? Discuss the pros and cons.

4. Do you think that Boris would have been so passionately attracted to non-Ukrainian girlfriends like Wendy Waggonheimer had his parents approved of the relationship? Does forbidden fruit taste twice as sweet? If so, why?

5. Role-play: In twos, as parent and offspring, use the following first and second lines:
   Parent: I forbid you to go out with that girl/boy!
   Offspring: But why?

6. Is Olech's reaction to Boris's choice of career unreasonable? Sound off about it from *your* viewpoint: First line:
   "Listen to me for a minute, will you?"
   Or change the scenario: "If I were my own parent, I'd ..."
   Now put the case forward from an opposite point of view to your own.

7. Do you think ethnic minorities in Canada should be encouraged to hold on to their language, culture and traditions, or should they be encouraged to blend into the mainstream?

8. Boris, Natalka, Daria and Kenny each respond to the problem of being caught between two cultures in a different way. Which way do you think is the most successful? Why?

9. Are there issues in this play that are not resolved? How would you resolve them?

No Man's Land
by Rahul Varma

1. Do you think all immigrants to Canada are treated equally? Why?

2. How do immigrants enrich the cultural fabric of Canada?

3. Immigrant communities have lived in Canada for several generations. Do you think it would be better if they stopped thinking of themselves as immigrants and started treating themselves as citizens of Canada?

4. What would you say to a person who tells someone, "Go back to where you came from"?

5. What are some of the things we could do to make things easier for new immigrants?

6. Jeena wanted to be a teacher, but ended up in a sweat factory. Do you think she had any other choice? Why? Why do you think she sacrificed her health and her well-being?

7. What does Jeena's story tell you about working conditions in sweat factories? Do you think Dr. Khaber will succeed in improving conditions in the factory?

8. Why was Qaiser so obsessed with buying a house?

9. In what ways is Samreen different from her mother? Do you think Samreen considers herself a Canadian, an East Indian, or an Indo-Canadian? Discuss the so-called "hyphenated" designations, such as "Indo-Canadian" or "Black-American." Do you approve of the use of such terms?

10. Does the story of the Quraishi family encourage you to learn more about the countries of their origin? Do you think this will help you understand their problems better?

11. Is there something special about this family, or do you think that the experiences of all cultures are fairly similar?

Going Down the River
by Kevin Longfield

1. What two distinct functions does the Father perform in this play?

2. This dispute arises out of an incident in the classroom which we as an audience never see. Why do you think the playwright chose not to portray that incident? What difference do you think it would make to the play if we were to see it?

3. In this play the same person plays Lettie at three different ages. Why do you think the playwright did this? Could three different actors play Lettie without changing the play? Why?

4. What does the playwright tell us about Nigel? What can we guess? If you were to play Nigel, how would you interpret his character? Why is he so desperate to succeed at teaching?

5. A play with a traditional structure has a protagonist (hero) and antagonist (villain). Who plays these roles in this play?

6. The protagonist has a main conflict to resolve (an action) in a traditional play. What is the protagonist's action in this play? What forces act against the protagonist? What forces act in the protagonist's favour?

7. If you rewrote this play with a different protagonist, who would it be? What difference would it make to the action?

8. This play has a relatively small cast (four). If you were to add characters, who would you add? How would they change the play?

9. In non-traditional casting, actors are in roles that their physical attributes do not specifically call for: having a woman play Hamlet, for instance, or having an Asian play Willy Loman. In this play, three of the four roles call for black actors. In the first production, at the University of Winnipeg, no black actors auditioned. Non-traditional casting thus had to be used. If you were the director, how would you handle this? What conventions would you use so that the audience would know which actors were black and which were white?

10. The action in this play shifts quickly from the two locations, the principal's office and a living room. How would you design the set so that the action could proceed smoothly without confusing the audience? (Include a sketch if you wish.)